FIRST 50 BLUEGRASS SOLOS

YOU SHOULD PLAY ON GUITAR

Arranged by Fred Sokolow

Editorial assistance by Ronny S. Schiff

ISBN 978-1-5400-5879-9

Visit Hal Leonard Online at
www.halleonard.com

Contact us:
Hal Leonard
7777 West Bluemound Road
Milwaukee, WI 53213
Email: info@halleonard.com

In Europe, contact:
Hal Leonard Europe Limited
42 Wigmore Street
Marylebone, London, W1U 2RN
Email: info@halleonardeurope.com

In Australia, contact:
Hal Leonard Australia Pty. Ltd.
4 Lentara Court
Cheltenham, Victoria, 3192 Australia
Email: info@halleonard.com.au

CONTENTS

INTRODUCTION

You're looking at a collection of essential repertoire for the bluegrass guitarist. These songs have been performed and recorded by countless bluegrass bands and you will be expected to know them at bluegrass jam sessions. The solos in this book are arranged at an intermediate level and present typical ways to play in several keys using just the first four or five frets. Each solo closely follows the tune's melody with a few embellishments, traditional bluegrass runs, and tag endings.

A note about keys: There are several popular fiddle tunes presented here. Fiddle tunes are almost always played in the keys of A or D (the easiest soloing keys for fiddle). For example, everyone plays "Soldier's Joy" in D, so guitarists need to play it in that key. To play a fiddle tune or song in the key of D, simply capo at the second fret and use the C position. Most bluegrass guitarists prefer to play in the keys of C or G (the easiest soloing keys for bluegrass guitar) and will use a capo to play in other keys. To play in the key of A, just capo at the second fret and use the G position. These capo instructions are included in the arrangements that follow. Keep in mind that when using a capo, the fret at which it is placed becomes the new "0" in the tab, 1 fret above the capo is the new "1" in the tab; and so on. Nevertheless, you'll also find several tunes in this book in D, A, or E position because it's good to know how to solo in those keys as well.

Songs, on the other hand, can be played in any key that suits the singer's voice. For example, if you go to YouTube and look for different versions of "Blue Ridge Mountain Blues," you'll find it's played in various keys by different bands.

In some songs the verse and chorus are musically identical, though the lyrics differ. For these types of songs, this book includes two solos (one in a higher register than the other) to show that there are a variety of ways to approach a solo. Other songs contain choruses that are completely different from their verses. In these cases, you'll find solos written out for both the verse and the chorus, even though a bluegrass instrumental solo is usually played over just the verse. Studying examples of both will give you more soloing options, techniques, standard licks, and embellishments.

Most of the songs in this collection are from the "golden age of bluegrass"—the 1950s—and were performed by bands like Bill Monroe and His Bluegrass Boys, Flatt and Scruggs and the Foggy Mountain Boys, the Stanley Brothers and the Clinch Mountain Boys, Reno and Smiley, and many more. The tunes have stood the test of time and are still heard at bluegrass festivals and concerts all over the world. Learning how to solo over them will help build the repertoire you need if you want to play bluegrass with other pickers. Hopefully, in the process of learning these arrangements you'll also learn the licks, styles, and techniques that will enable you to make up your own bluegrass-style guitar solos.

Good luck and good picking!

Fred Sokolow

Fred Sokolow

P.S. The lyrics written in between the notation and tab are there simply to help you correlate the solos to the songs (you don't normally sing while playing solos.) Additional lyrics are also presented in case you ever want to perform these songs in their entirety.

Arkansas Traveler

Southern American Folksong

Many lyrics have been written to this 150-year-old fiddle tune (perhaps most notably a children's song about a baby bumblebee). In the days of medicine shows, an entire comedic skit was performed with the tune involving a farmer and a traveling salesman. Bluegrass bands play it as an instrumental.

Like most fiddle tunes, it's always played in a certain key (in this case the key of D) and has two sections (an A part and a B part). You play each part twice, and once you've played "AABB," you've gone around the tune once. Every fiddle tune in this book follows this format. In this arrangement of "Arkansas Traveler," you play through the tune once and then play it a second time in a higher register.

Key of D

A
D
G
D
A
D
G
D
G
1.
A
D
2.
A
D
B
D
A
D
A
D
A
D
A
D
A
D
A
D
G
1.
A
D
2.
A
D

Ballad of Jed Clampett

from the Television Series THE BEVERLY HILLBILLIES

Words and Music by Paul Henning

Written as a theme song for the television series *The Beverly Hillbillies* (1962–1971), "Ballad of Jed Clampett" tells the story on which the show was based. The Flatt and Scruggs recording of the song was played at the beginning and end of the show, and they appeared in several episodes playing themselves. On the TV show it was sung at a leisurely country tempo, but Flatt and Scruggs kicked it up to a fast bluegrass cut-time tempo when performing it instrumentally. Both tempos are represented in the following arrangement.

Key of G

Verse

Moderately

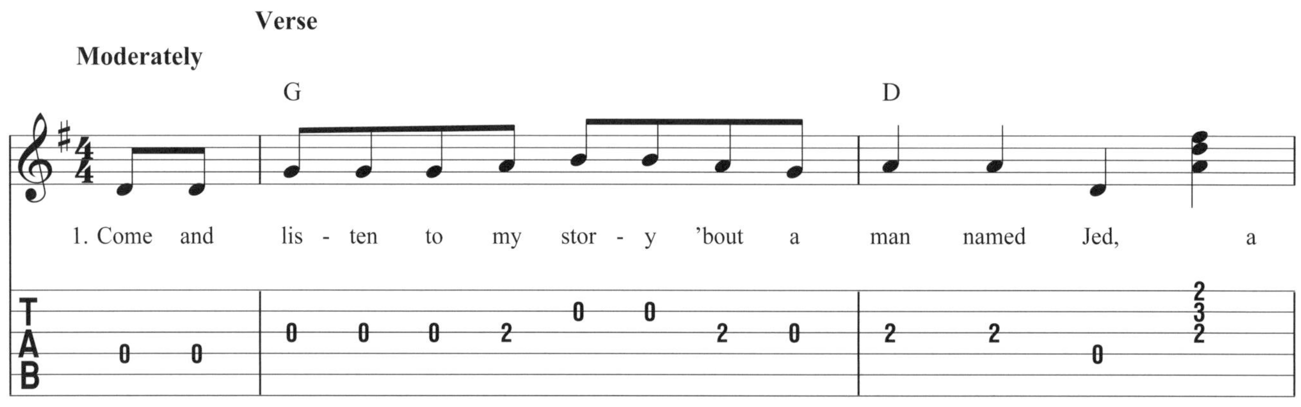

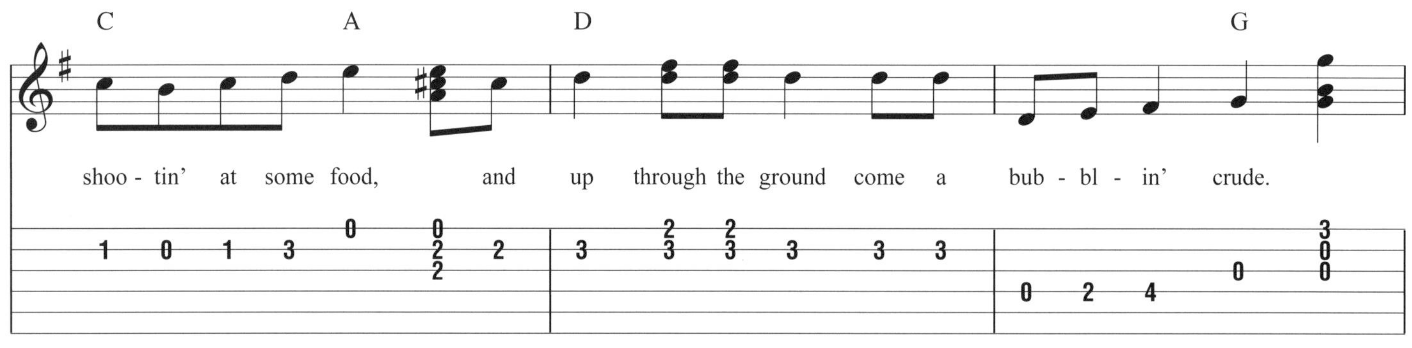

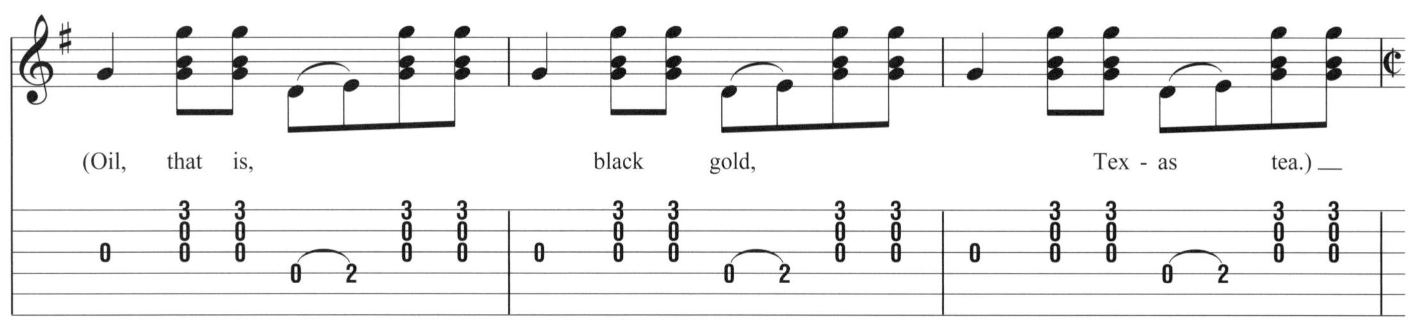

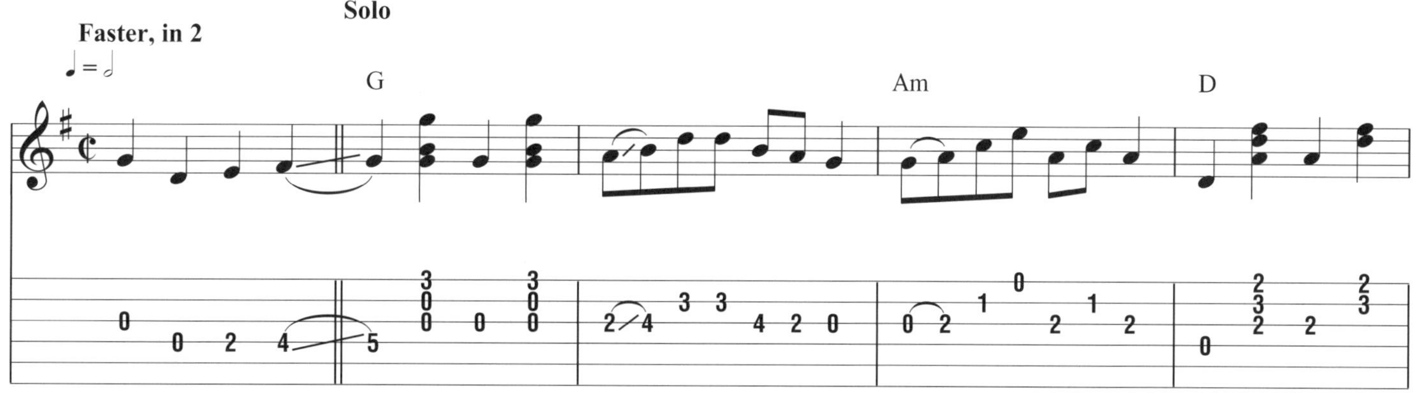

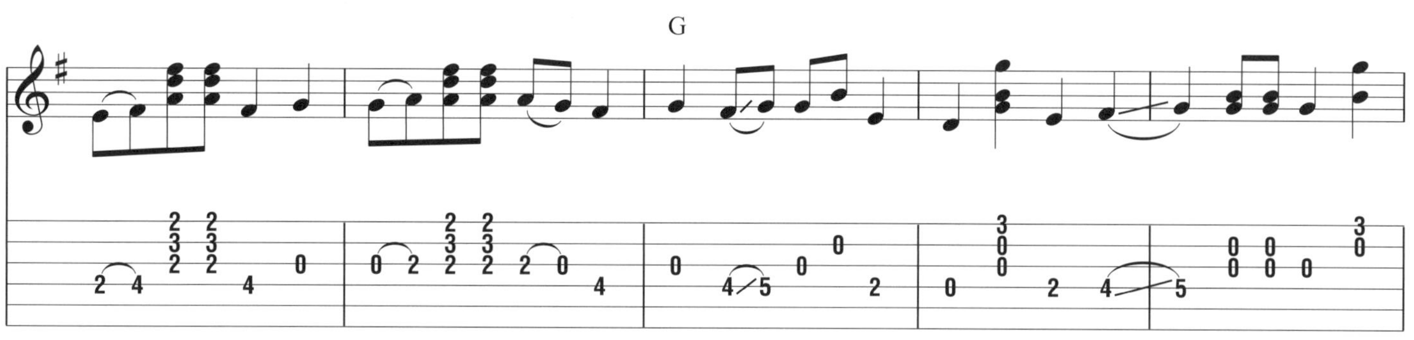

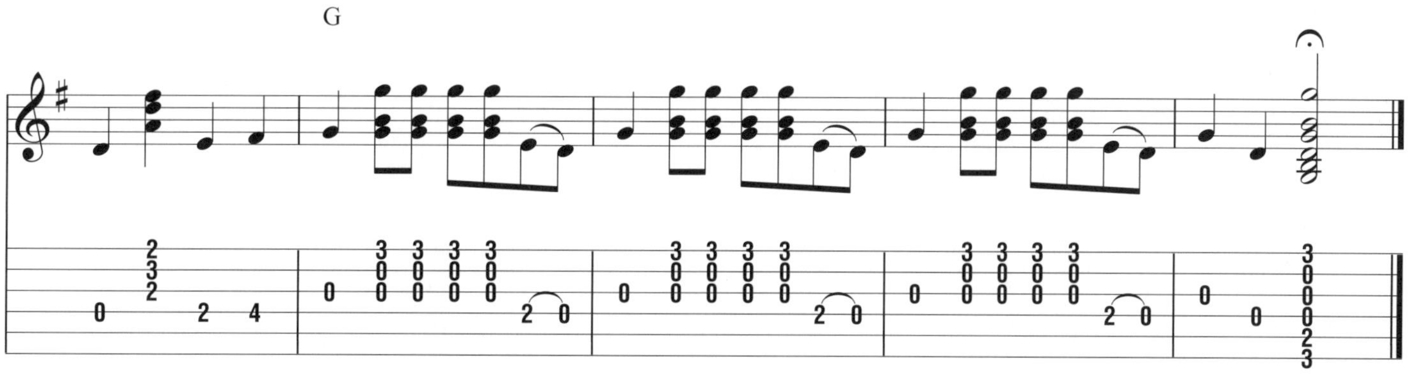

Additional Verses

2. First thing you know, old Jed's a millionaire.
   Kin folks said, "Jed, move away from there."
   Said, "Californi is the place you ought to be,"
   So they loaded up the truck and they moved to Beverly.
   (Hills, that is, swimming pools, movie stars.)

3. Well, now it's time to say goodbye to Jed and all his kin.
   They would like to thank you folks for kindly dropping in.
   You're all invited back again to this locality,
   To have a heaping helping of their hospitality.
   (Beverly Hillbillies, that's what they call 'em now.
   Nice folks. Y'all come back now, hear?)

Banks of the Ohio

19th Century Western American

This nineteenth century song predates bluegrass but has become a bluegrass standard. It's one of the more well-known tunes in the "murder ballad" genre–several of which involve a perpetrator named Willie. The verses use the same melody and chord progression as the chorus. In the following arrangement, the verses are presented in a higher register than the chorus.

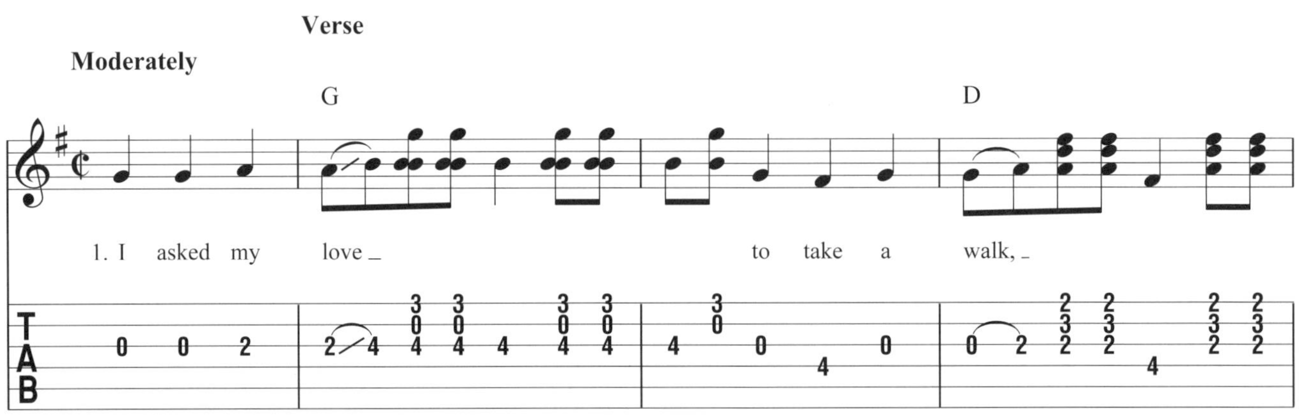

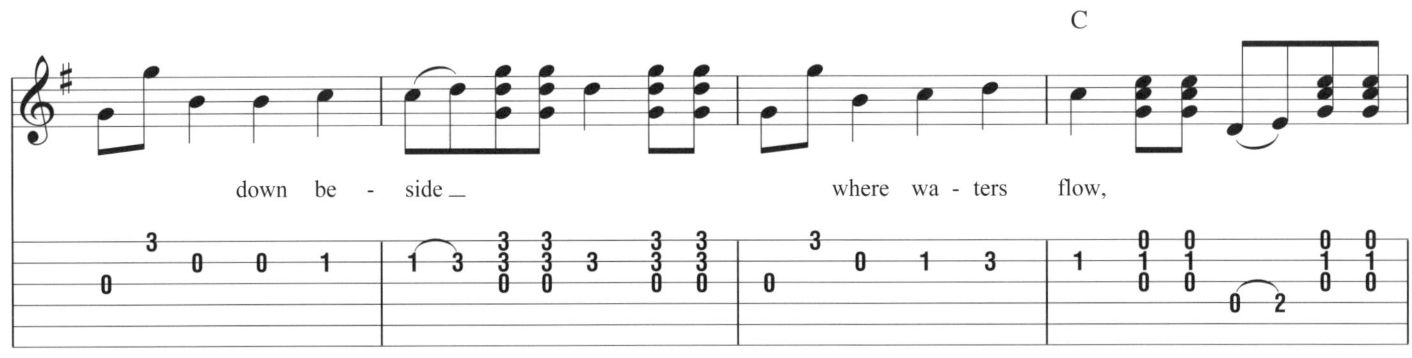

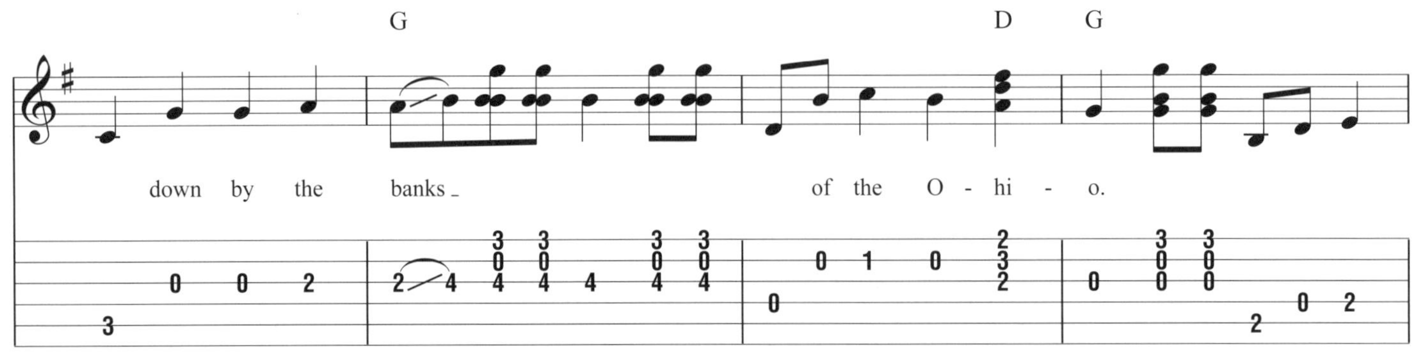

Additional Verses

2. I took her by her lily-white hand and led her down where the waters stand.
   There I pushed her in to drown, and I watched her as she floated down.

3. I started home 'tween twelve and one, I cried "My God, what have I done?
   I killed the only woman I loved, because she would not marry me."

Bill Cheatham

Traditional

"Bill Cheatham" is a fiddle tune in the key of A. Going back to the late 1800s, it has been played by countless string bands and bluegrass groups. It uses the usual AABB format, but the second time around it's arranged in a lower register.

Key of G (Capo II for Key of A)

1.
2.
A
D G D G G
C G
1.
2.
B
C D G D G G C
D G D G C
1.
2.
D G C D G D G

Blackberry Blossom

Traditional

It may have been written in Ireland, but in the 1930s American fiddler Arthur Smith brought this fiddle tune to the attention of country and old-time music fans in the U.S. In the early 1960s Bill Keith's banjo version made it a bluegrass standard. The tune's pretty melody is a good showcase for Keith's innovative "melodic picking" style. "Blackberry Blossom" has become an essential bluegrass instrumental.

1.
2.
A
D G D G G D C G
C G A D G D C G
1.
2.
B
C G D G D G Em
B7 Em
1.
2.
G C D G D G

Blue Moon of Kentucky

Words and Music by Bill Monroe

Bill Monroe wrote and recorded "Blue Moon of Kentucky" as a waltz in 1946. When he heard Elvis Presley's 1954 boogie-woogie version, he instructed the Stanley Brothers to record it "the way that Elvis kid did it." They started it as a waltz and segued into a cut-time, up-tempo version—and that's how the song has usually been performed ever since. This arrangement follows the meter and tempo of the original waltz version.

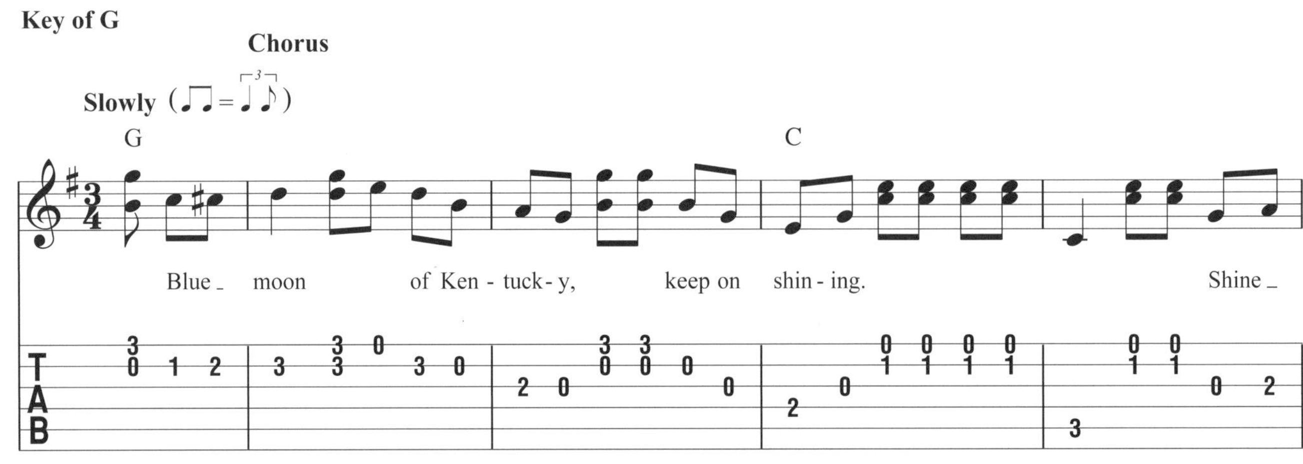

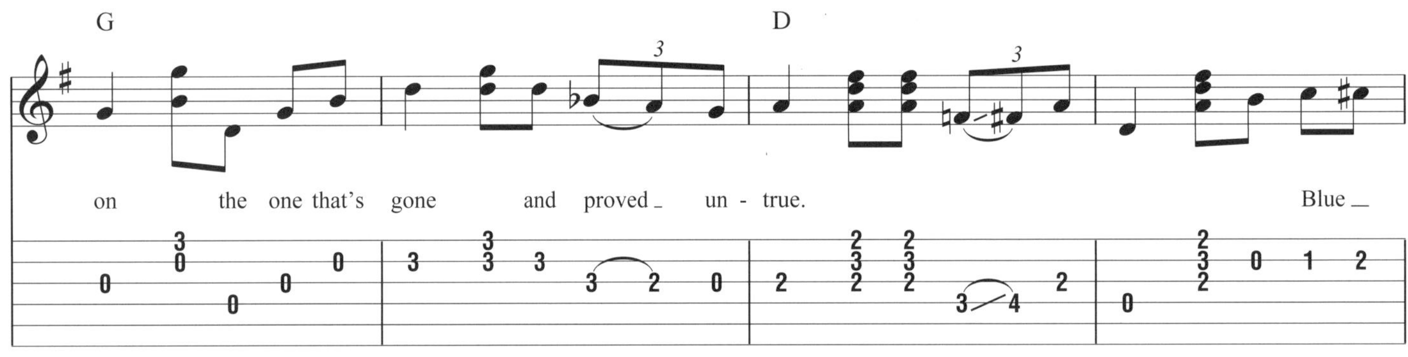

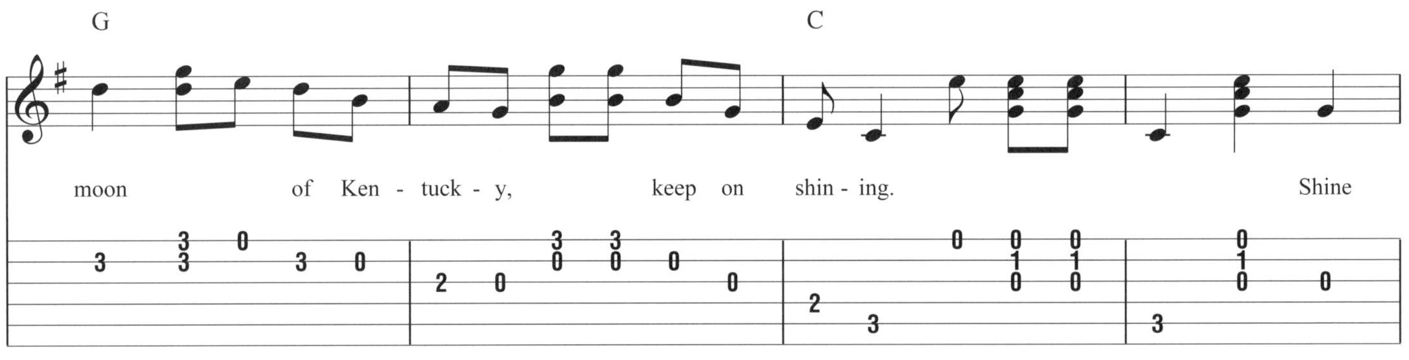

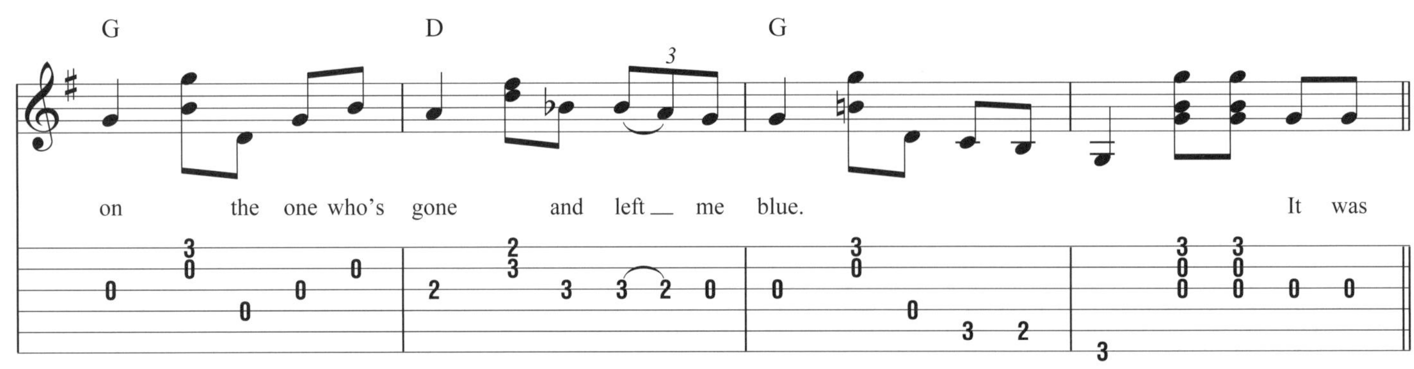

Bridge

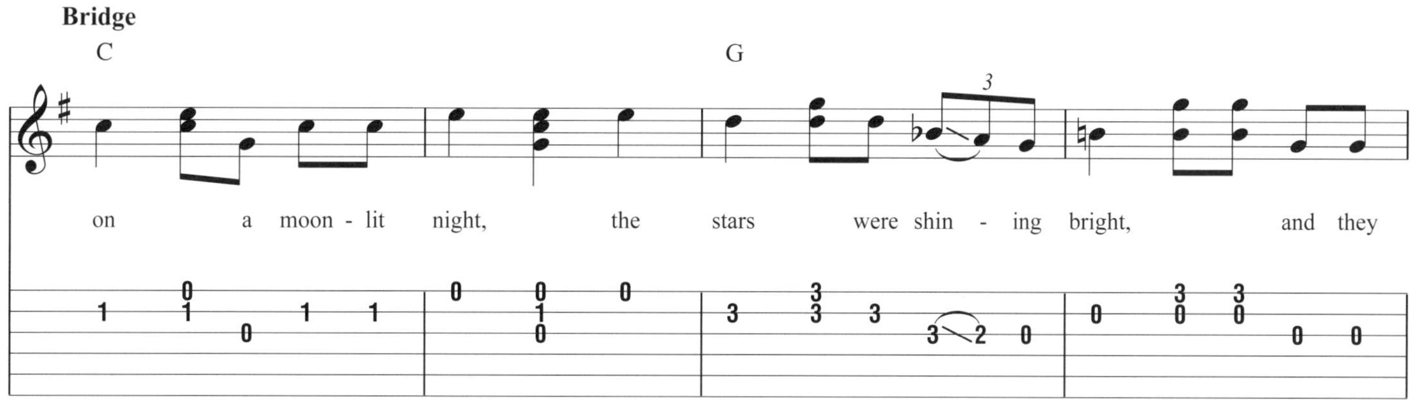

Chorus

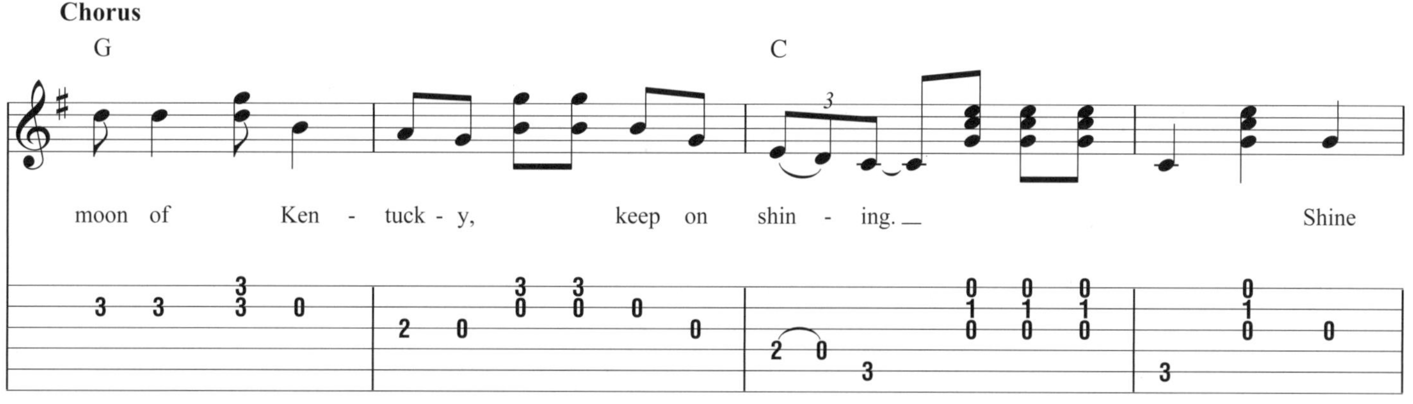

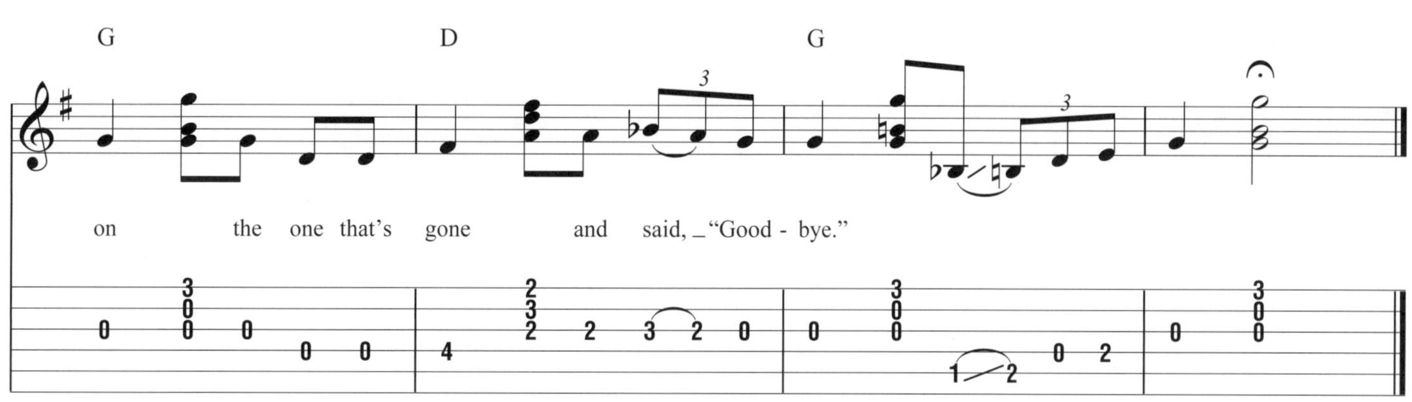

Blue Ridge Mountain Blues

By Bill Monroe

The Blue Ridge Mountains—part of the Appalachian mountain range—are the subject of many a bluegrass song, including this Bill Monroe standard. The tune is unusual in that it features a different set of lyrics for each chorus. Though sometimes credited to Bill Monroe, the song was probably written in 1924 by a Tin Pan Alley composer and pianist named Cliff Hess. Many versions were recorded by string bands during the 1920s and 30s, including The Hill Billies (1926) and Riley Puckett (1935).

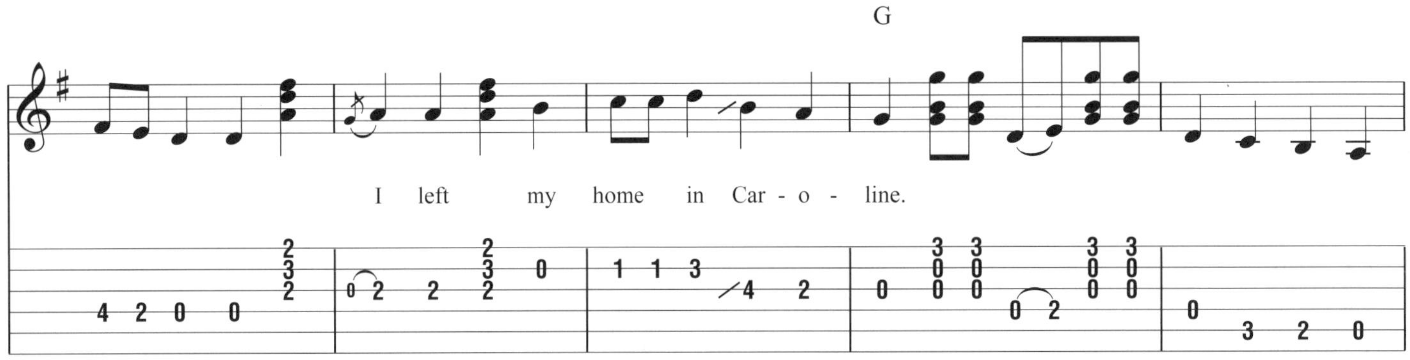

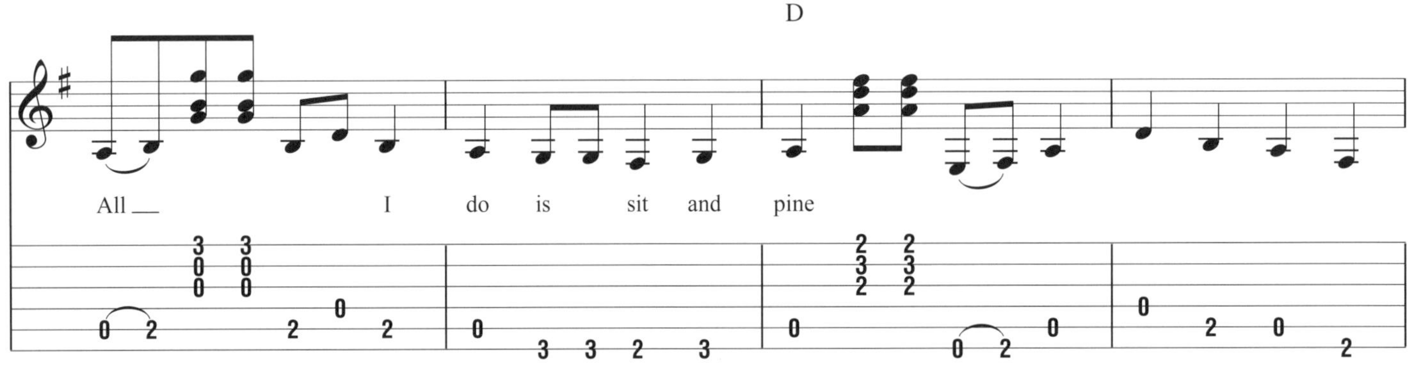

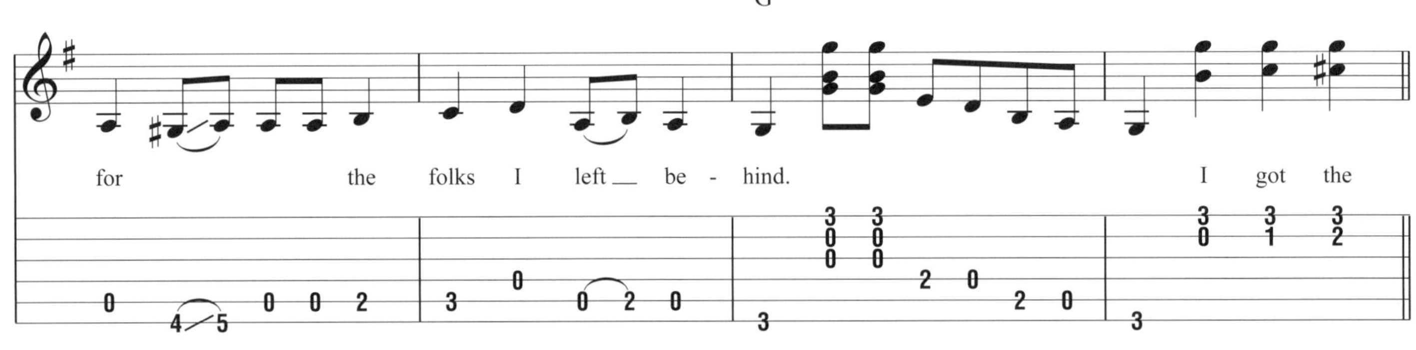

Chorus

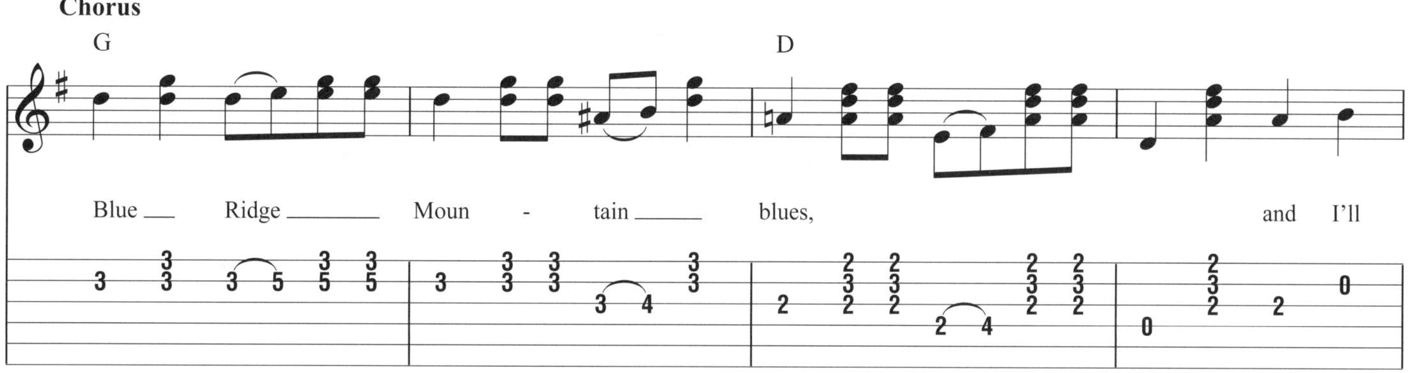

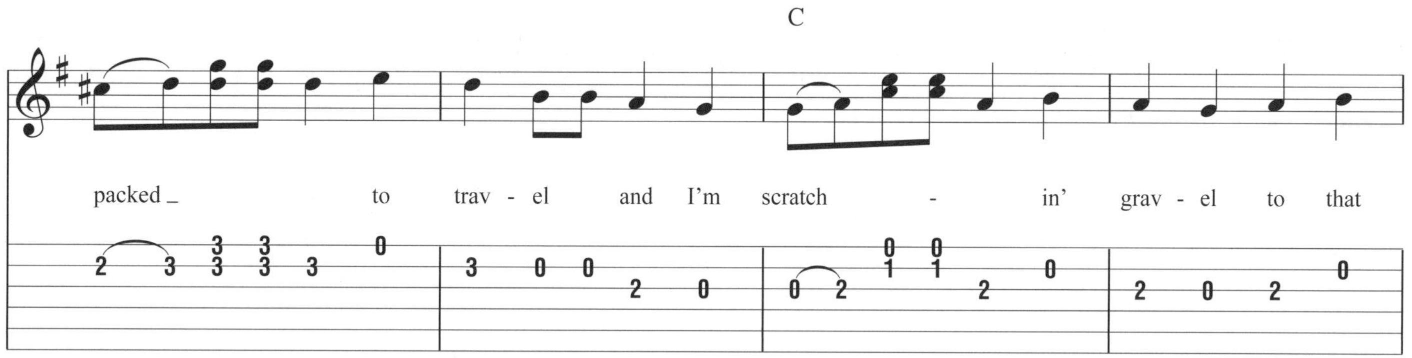

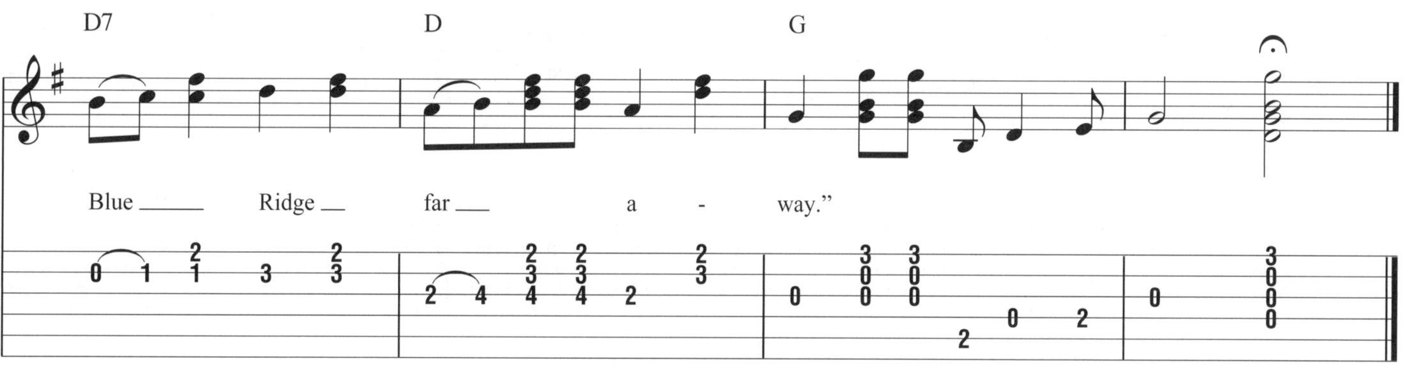

Additional Verses

2. I see a window with a light, I see two heads of snowy white.
   I seem to hear them both recite: "Where is my wandering boy tonight?"
   I've got the Blue Ridge Mountain blues, gonna see my old dog Tray.
   Gonna hunt the 'possum where the corn tops blossom, on that Blue Ridge far away.

3. I'm gonna do right by my pa, I'm gonna stay right by my ma.
   I'll hang around the cabin door, no work or worry anymore.
   I've got the Blue Ridge Mountain blues, and I'll stand right here and say:
   "Every day I'm counting 'til I find that mountain on the Blue Ridge far away."

Bury Me Beneath the Willow

Traditional

The Carter Family recorded this old folk song in 1927 at the famous Bristol Sessions where they and Jimmie Rodgers were discovered. The tune was archived by a music professor in 1906 but is probably much older than that. The verse and chorus share the same melody.

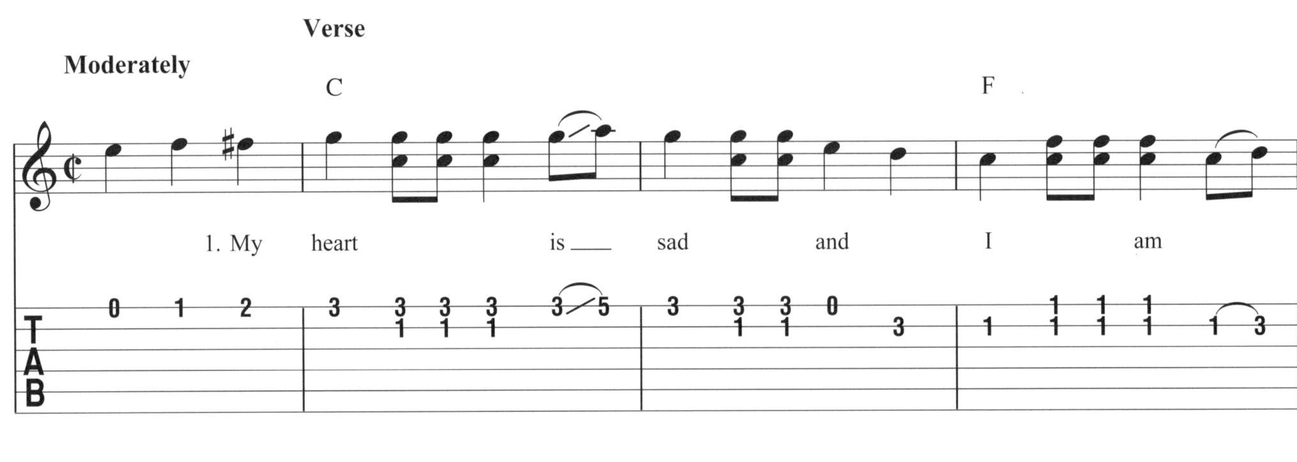

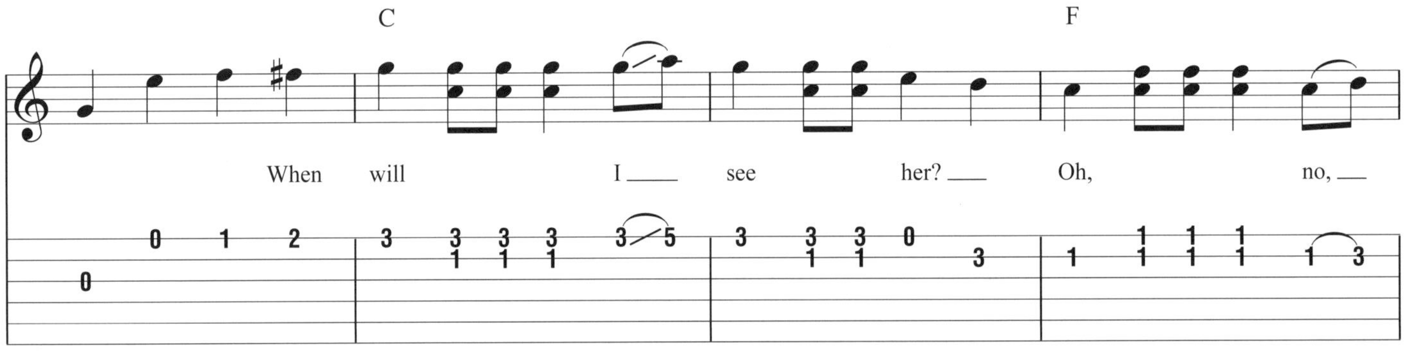

Chorus

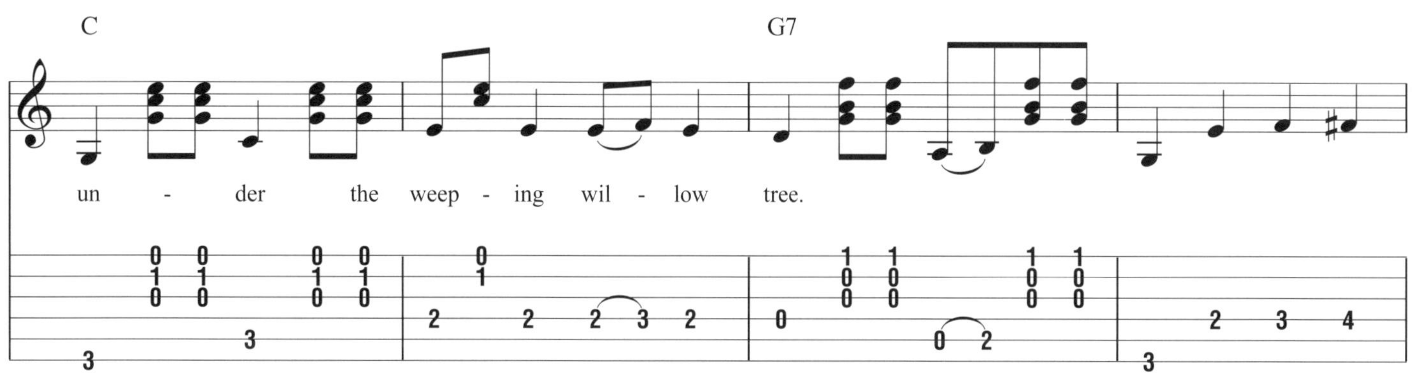

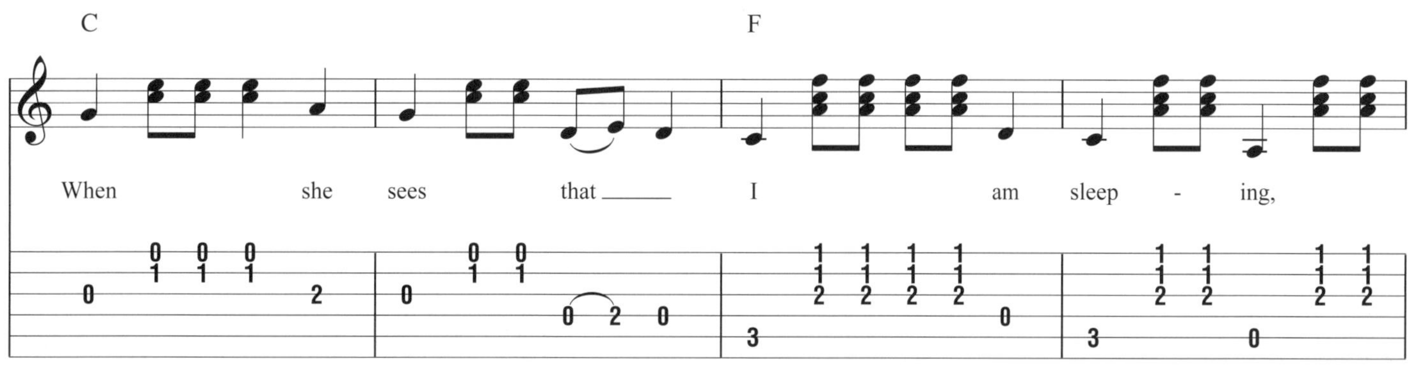

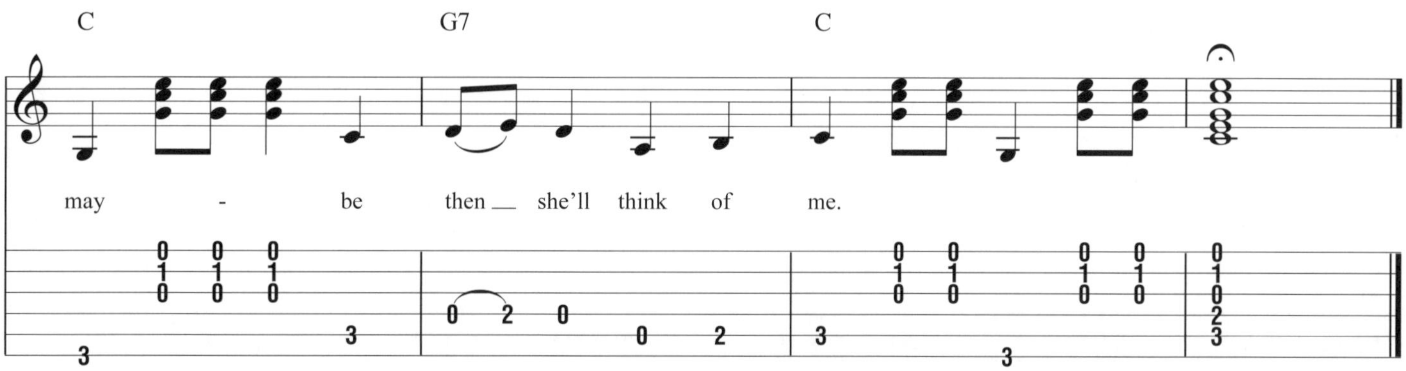

Additional Verses

2. They told me that she did not love me, I could not believe it's true,
   Until an angel softly whispered, "She no longer cares for you."

3. Tomorrow was to be our our wedding. Lord, oh Lord, where can she be?
   She's gone, she's gone to find another. She no longer cares for me.

Can't You Hear Me Callin'

Words and Music by Bill Monroe

This bluesy, tortured love song is one of many Bill Monroe tunes inspired by Bessie Lee Mauldin, a singer and bass player who toured with the Bluegrass Boys for many years.

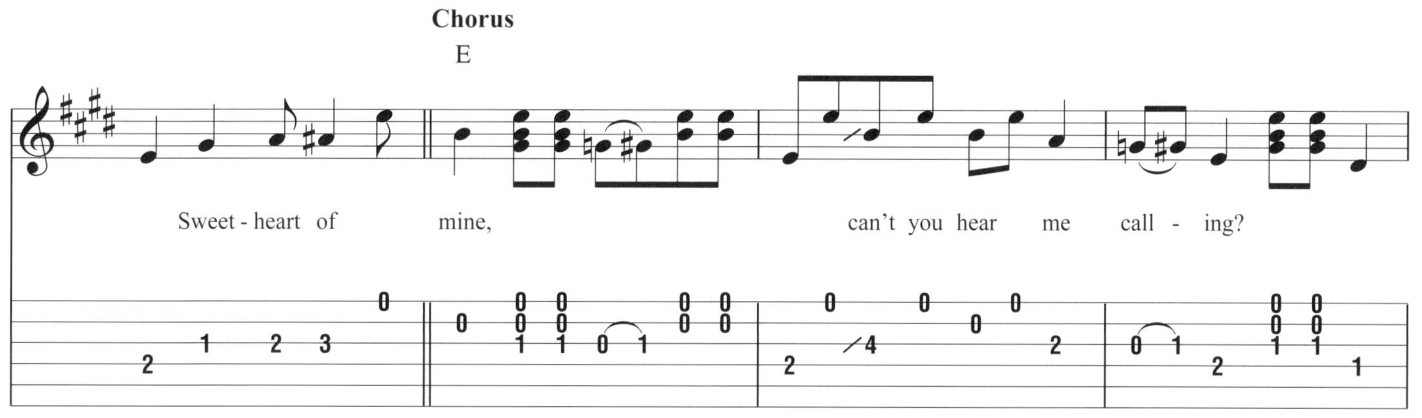

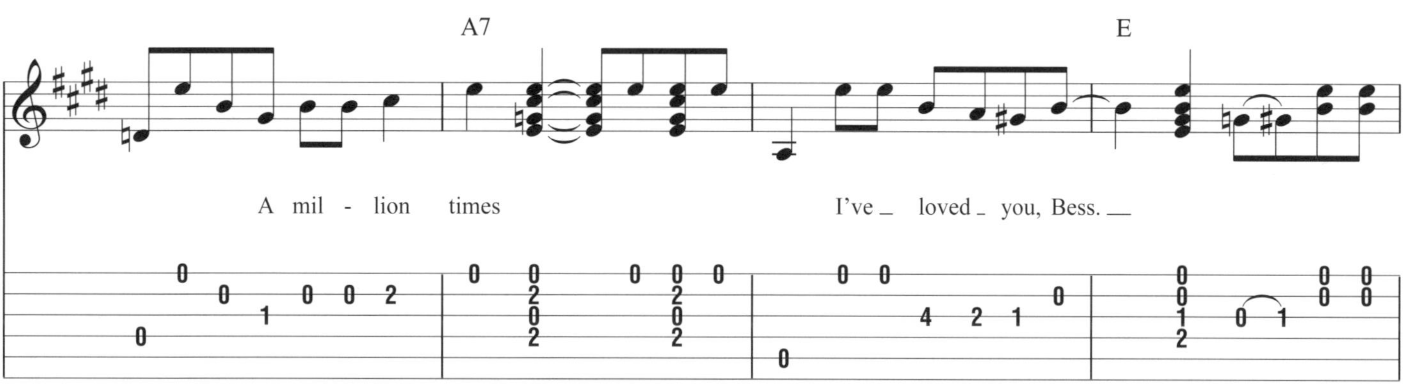

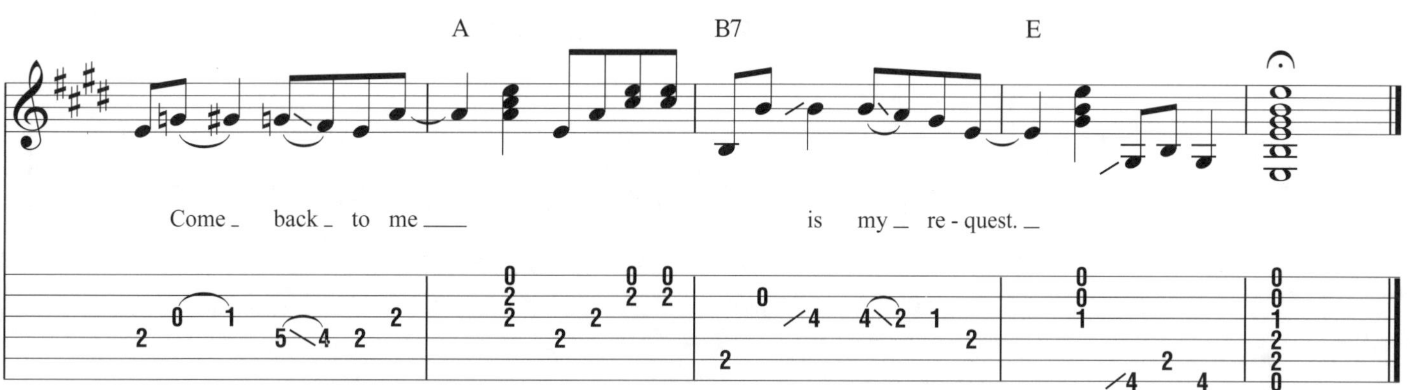

Additional Verses

2. I remember now the night we parted. A big mistake had caused it all.
   If you return, sunshine will follow. To stay away would be my fall.

3. The days are dark, my little darling. Oh, how I need your sweet embrace.
   When I awoke, the sun was shining. When I looked up, I saw your face.

Clinch Mountain Backstep

Words and Music by Ralph Stanley and Carter Stanley

This instrumental was composed by Ralph Stanley, the banjo player and singer for one of the first bluegrass groups, the Stanley Brothers and the Clinch Mountain Boys. He developed it by re-working an old fiddle tune by John Morgan Salyer called "Lonesome John." The Stanleys began their career in 1946, and after Ralph's brother (Carter) died in 1966, Ralph carried on with his own group and became one of the most renowned bluegrass singers of all time. The tune is based on a bluesy scale that includes flatted thirds and sevenths (no major thirds!), and the B part features a bar of 3/2 time (two extra beats).

Key of G (Capo II for Key of A)

A

Brightly

G5 D

G5 D 1. G5

2. G5 B G5

D G5 D

1.
2.
A
G5
G5
G5
D
G5
1.
2.
B
D
G5
G5
G5
D
G5
1.
2.
D
G5
G5

Cripple Creek

American Fiddle Tune

There's a Cripple Creek in Virginia and one in Colorado, and this key-of-A fiddle tune could refer to either one. The melody is well over a century old and words were put to it in the early 1900s, but bluegrassers play it as an instrumental. Popularized by Earl Scruggs, it's one of the first solos most bluegrass banjoists learn.

Key of G (Capo II for Key of A)

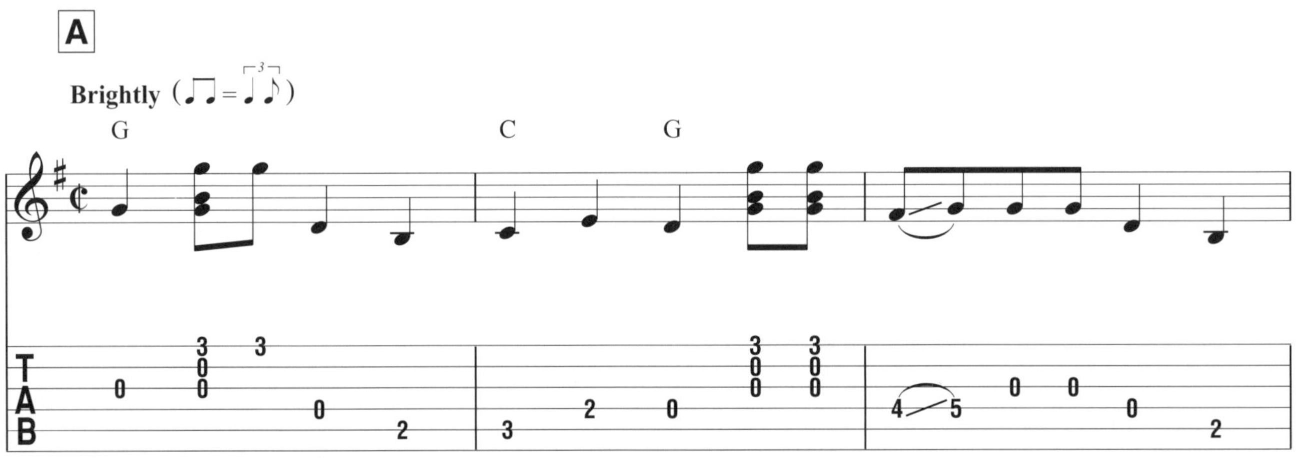

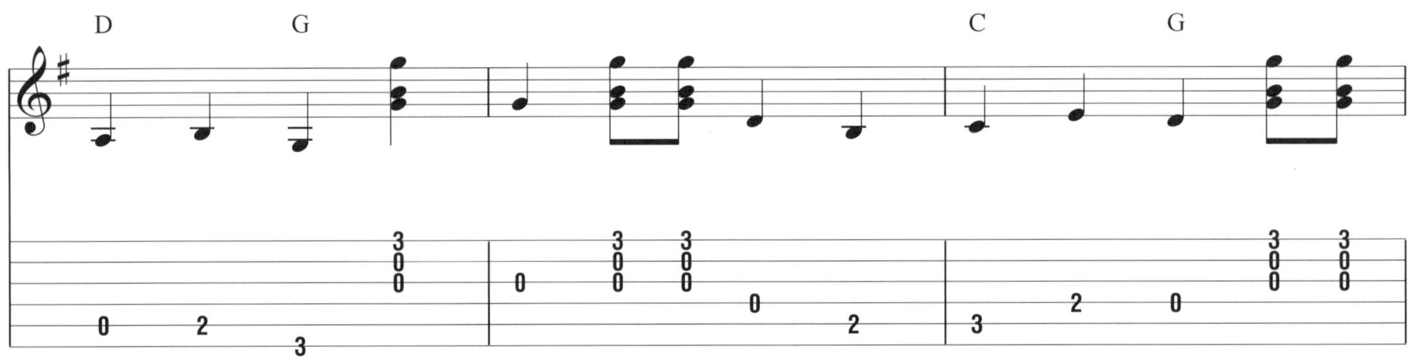

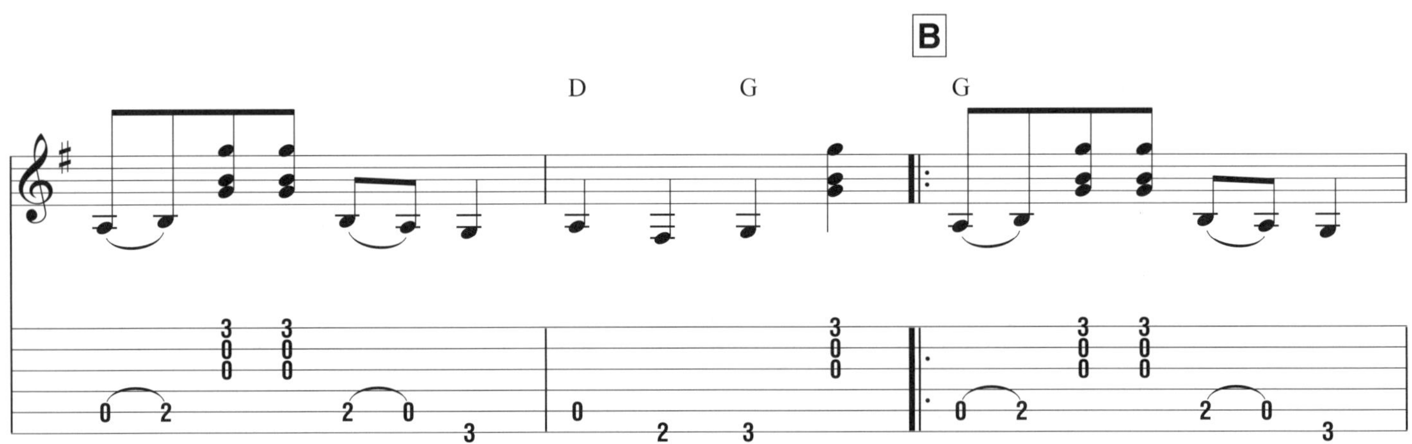

D G
A
G C G
D G C G
B
D G G
1. 2.
D G D G

Dark Hollow

Traditional

Before the Grateful Dead began playing this song in the early 1970s, "Dark Hollow" had already been a bluegrass standard for over a decade due to recordings by Mac Wiseman and others.

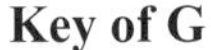

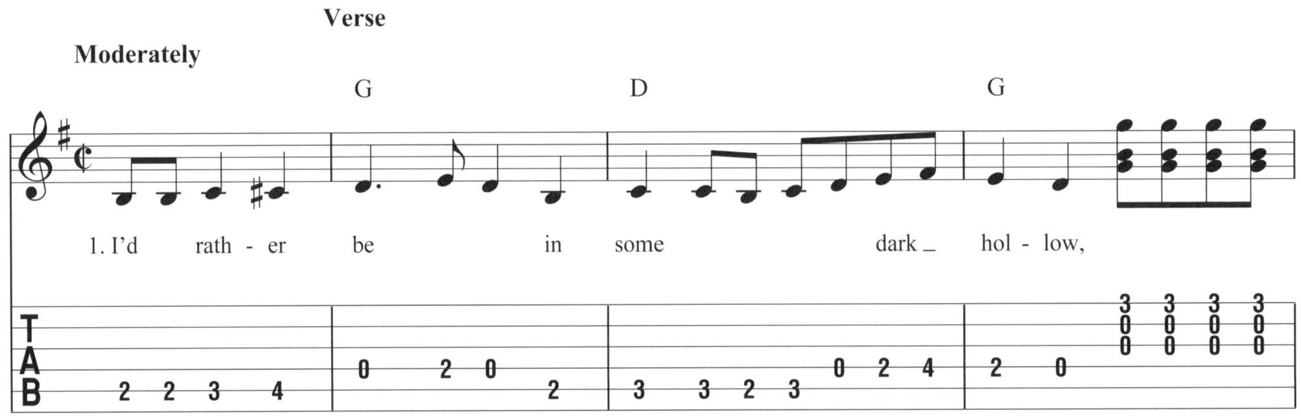

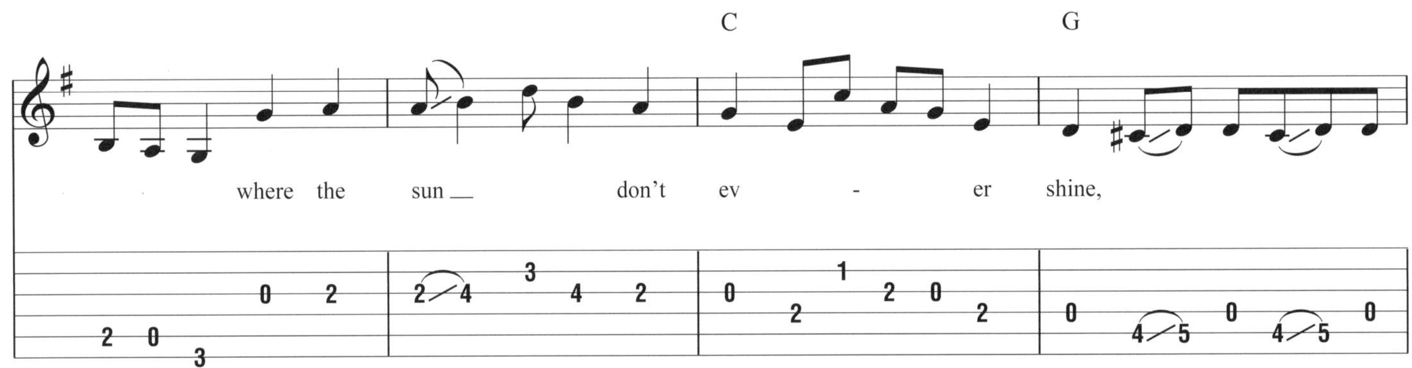

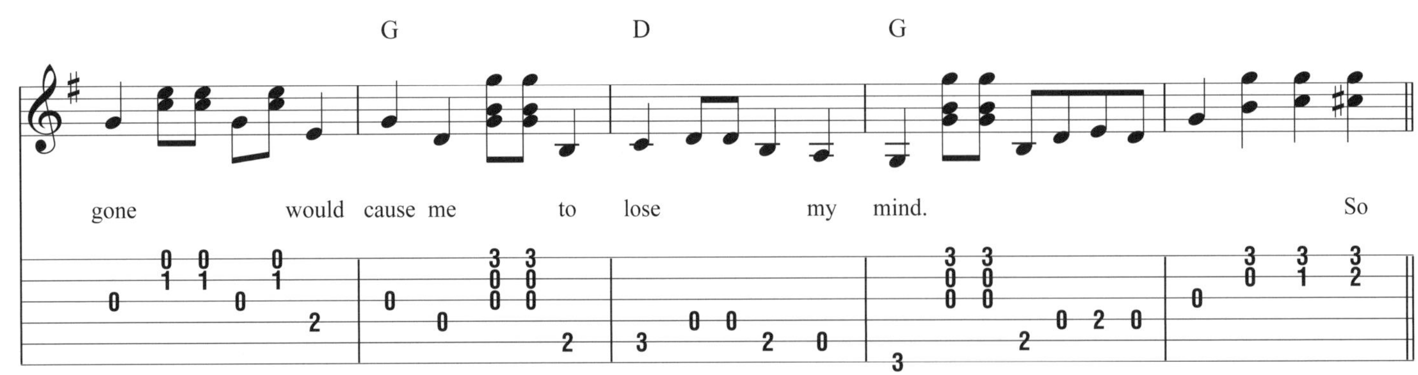

Chorus

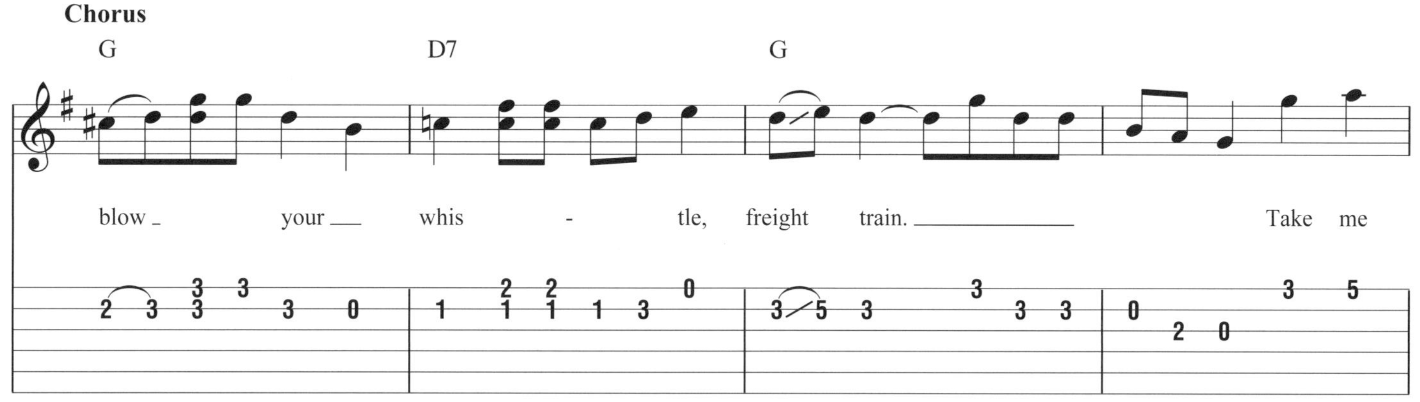

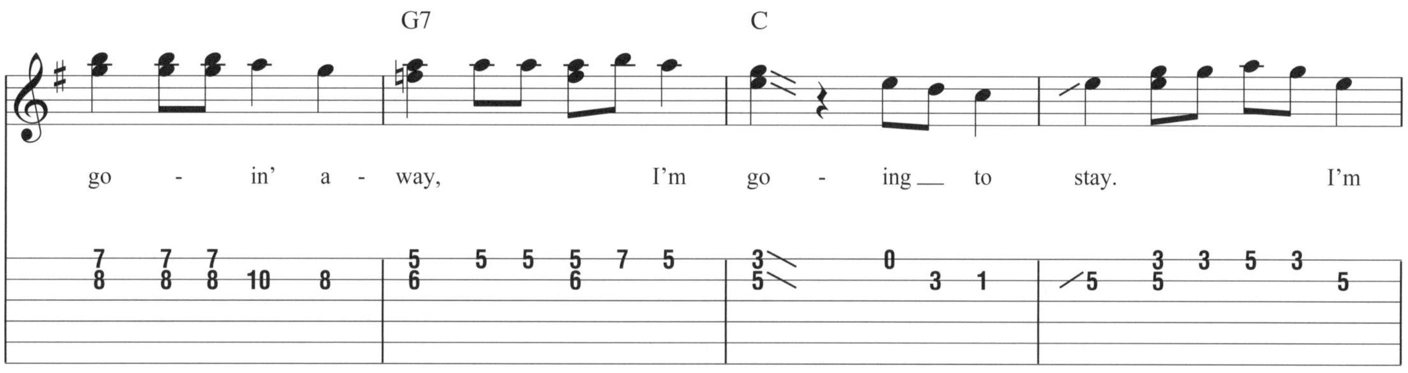

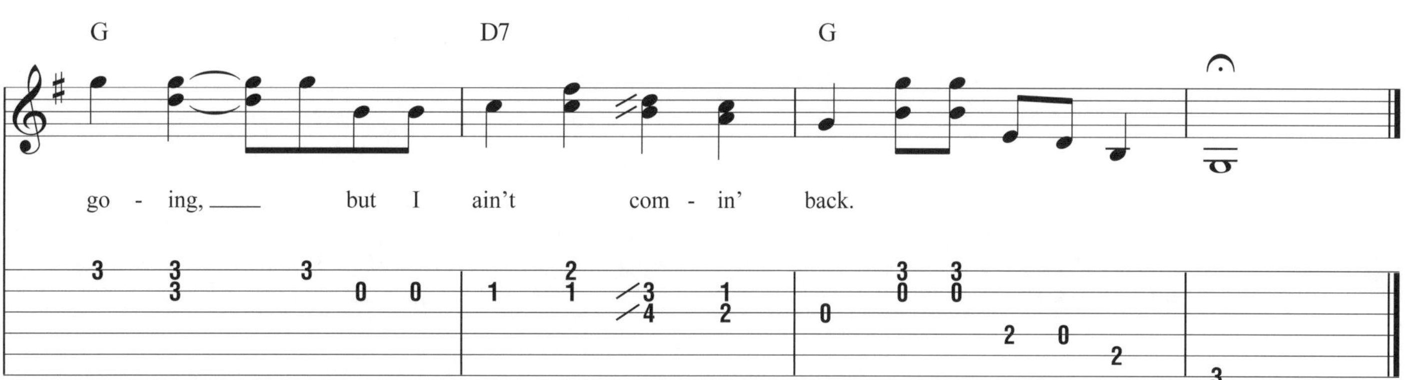

Additional Verse

2. I'd rather be in some dark hollow where the sun don't ever shine,
   Than to be in some big city, in a small room with you upon my mind.

Down the Road

By Lester Flatt and Earl Scruggs

Lester Flatt wrote "Down the Road" and it appeared on Flatt and Scruggs' 1958 Mercury LP, *Country Music.* Notice the odd bar of 3/2 time (two extra beats) at the end of the verse. The following arrangement goes around the tune three times. The third time around, the melody is presented in a lower register and includes melodic variations. This is because the original melody goes down lower than the guitar's low E string.

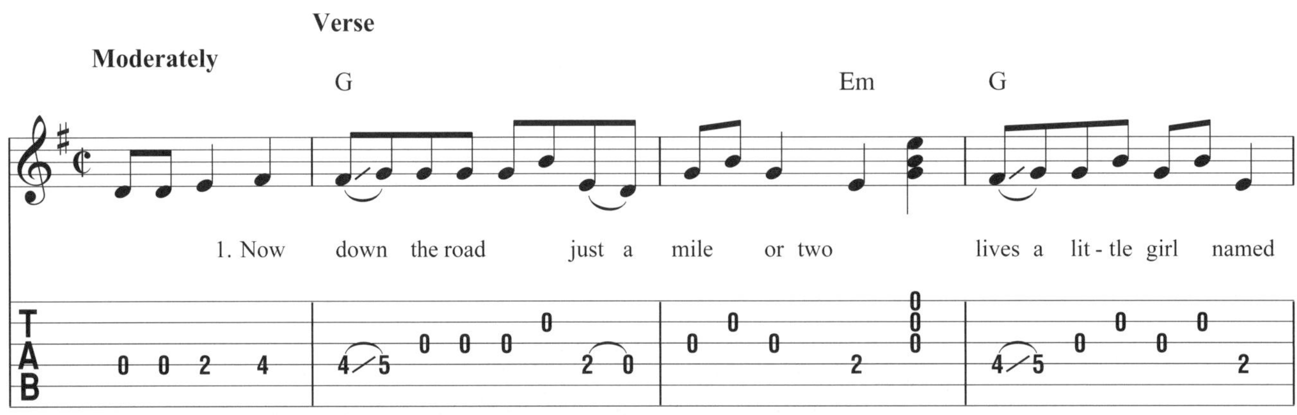

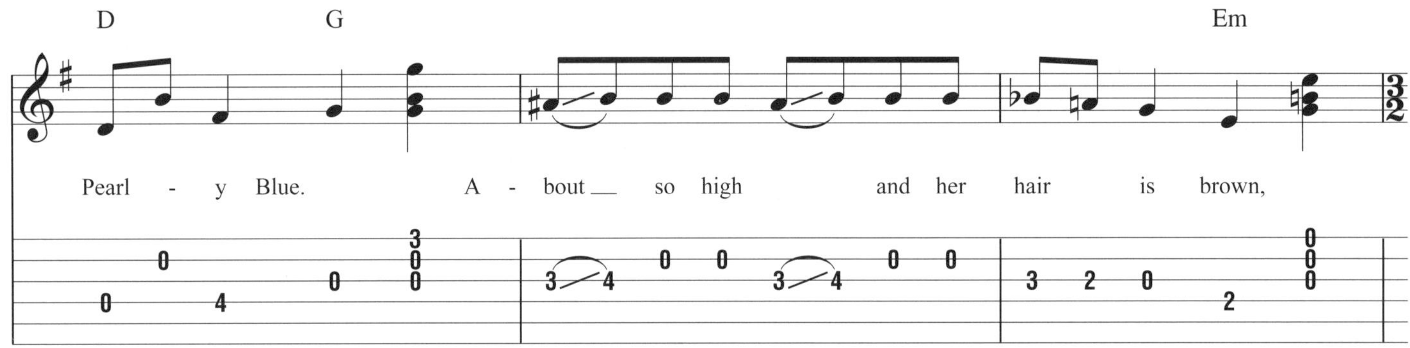

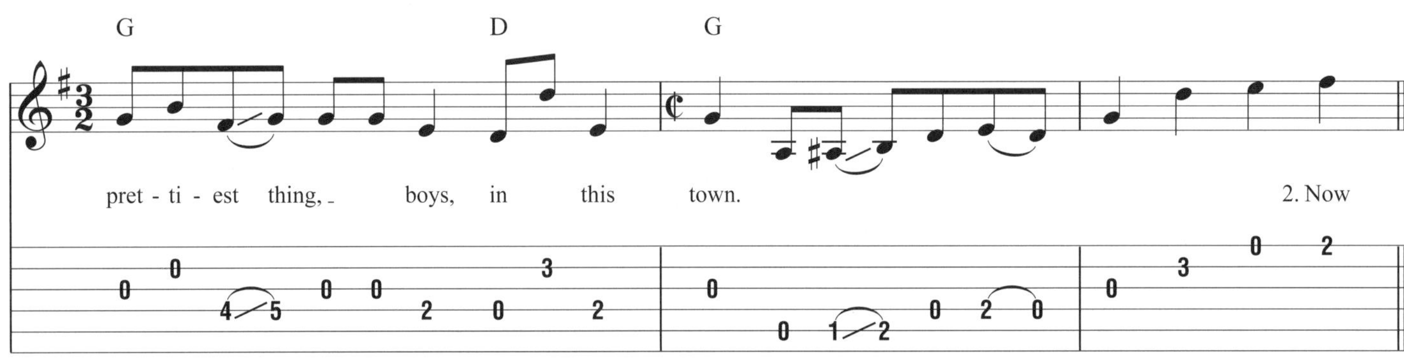

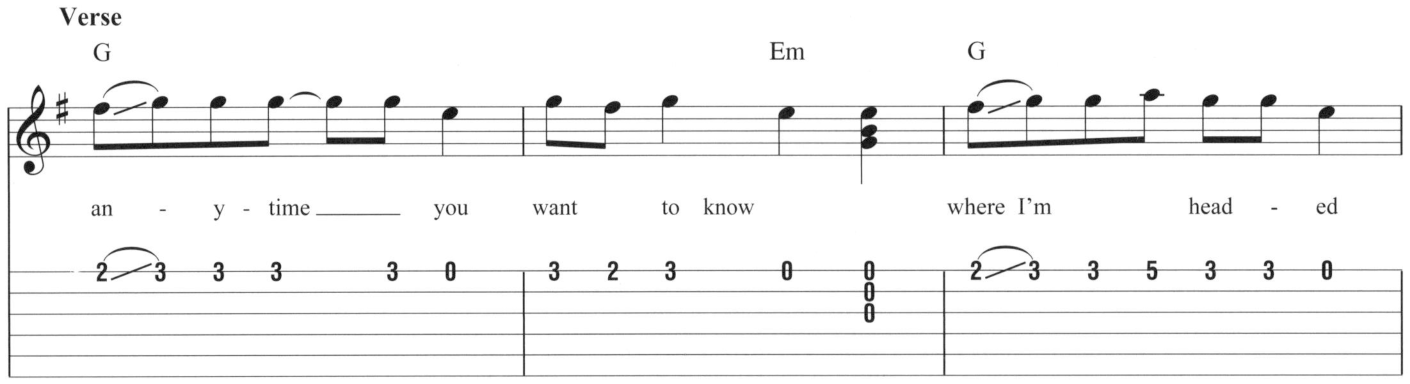

Additional Verses

4. Now, old man Flatt, he owned the farm from the hog lot to the barn.
   From the barn to the rail, he made his living by carrying the mail.

5. Now, every time I get the blues, I walk the soles right off my shoes.
   I don't know why I love her so, that gal of mine lives down the road.

Duelin' Banjos

By Arthur Smith

Arthur "Guitar Boogie" Smith, prolific songwriter/producer/multi-instrumentalist, wrote "Feudin' Banjos" in 1954. When banjoist Eric Weissberg and guitarist Steve Mandell recorded it for the movie *Deliverance* in 1972, they called it "Duelin' Banjos." Their version is one of the few bluegrass tunes to rank high on the pop charts, and it sparked a good deal of interest in bluegrass banjo among the general population. The "duel" consists of a call-and-response pattern between a banjo and a guitar. In the arrangement that follows, the guitar plays lead as well as backup during the banjo "responses."

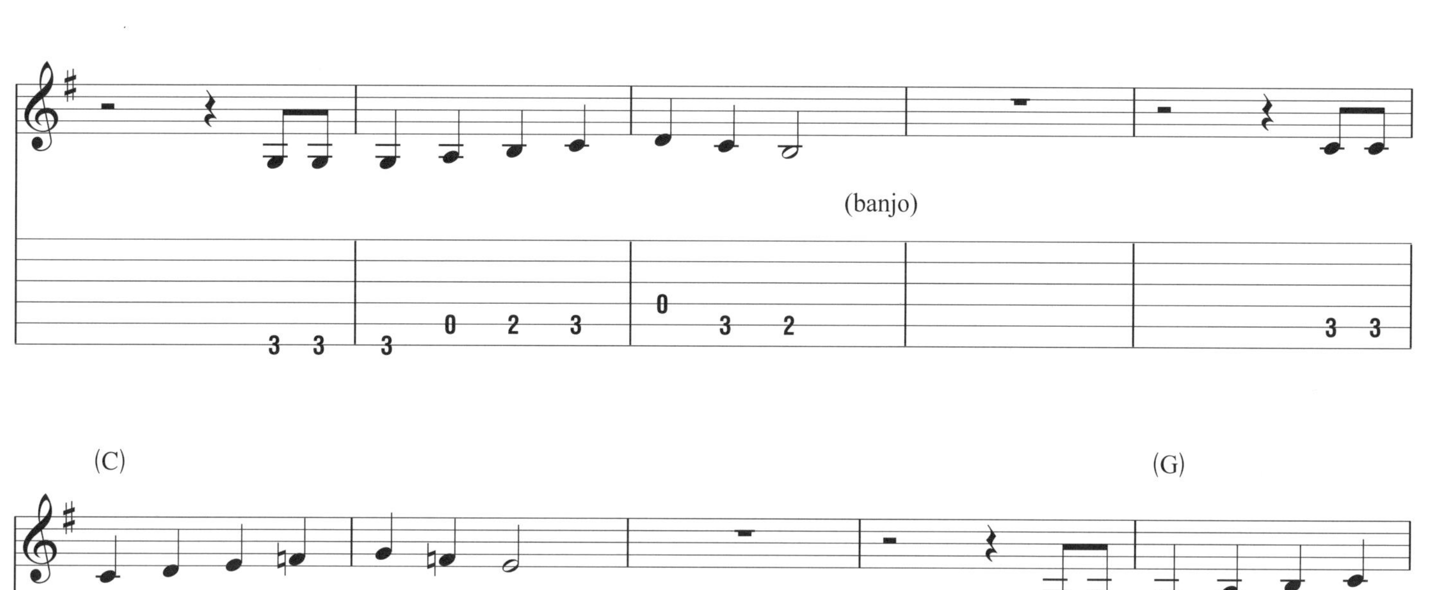
(banjo)
3 3
3 0 2 3
0 3 2
3 3

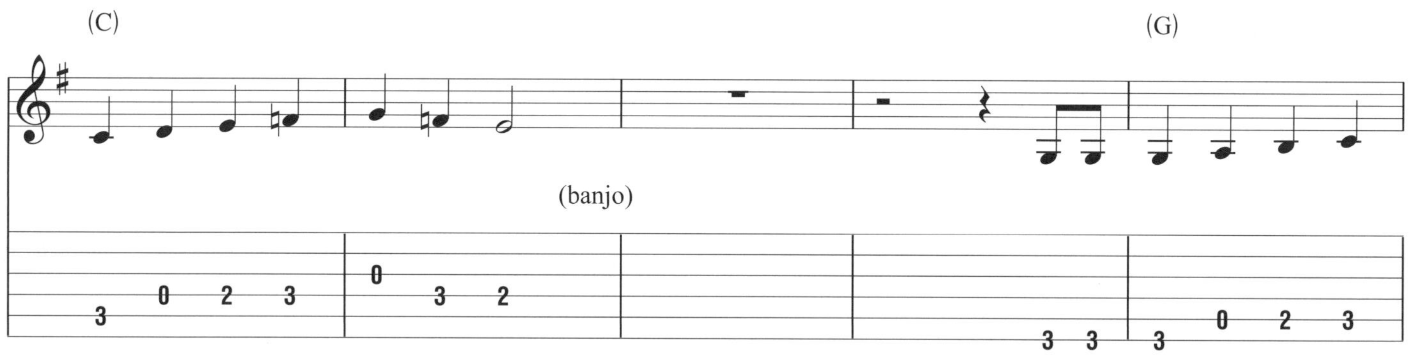
(C)
(G)
(banjo)
3 0 2 3
0 3 2
3 3
3 0 2 3

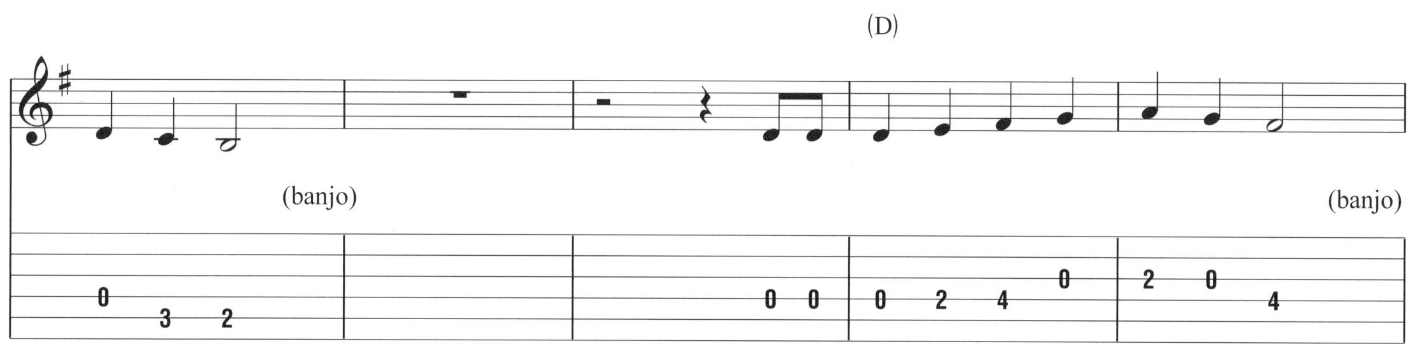
(D)
(banjo)
(banjo)
0 3 2
0 0
0 2 4 0
2 0 4

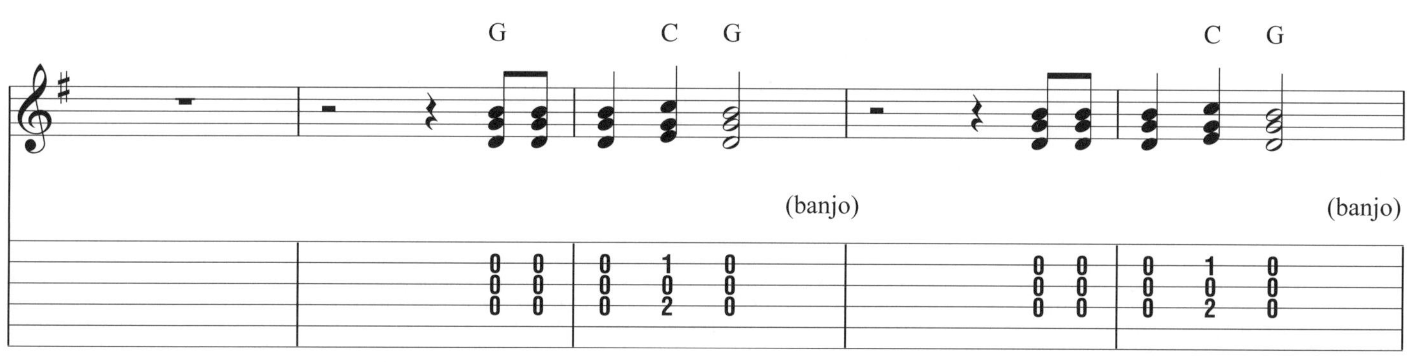
G
C
G
C
G
(banjo)
(banjo)

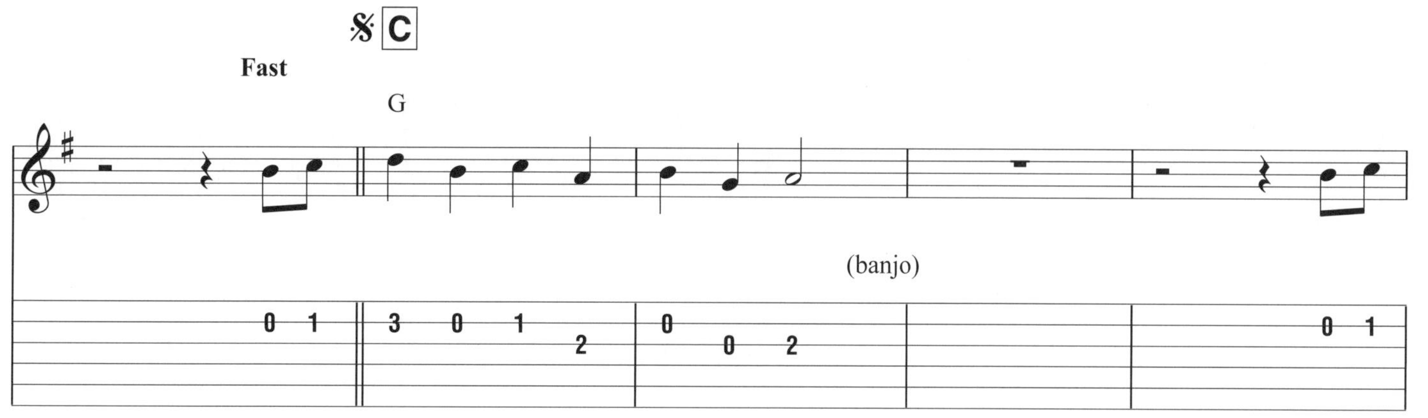
C
Fast
G
(banjo)
0 1
3 0 1 2
0 0 2
0 1

(banjo)
D
C
(banjo)
G
D
1.
2.
To Coda
G
E
G
(banjo answers)

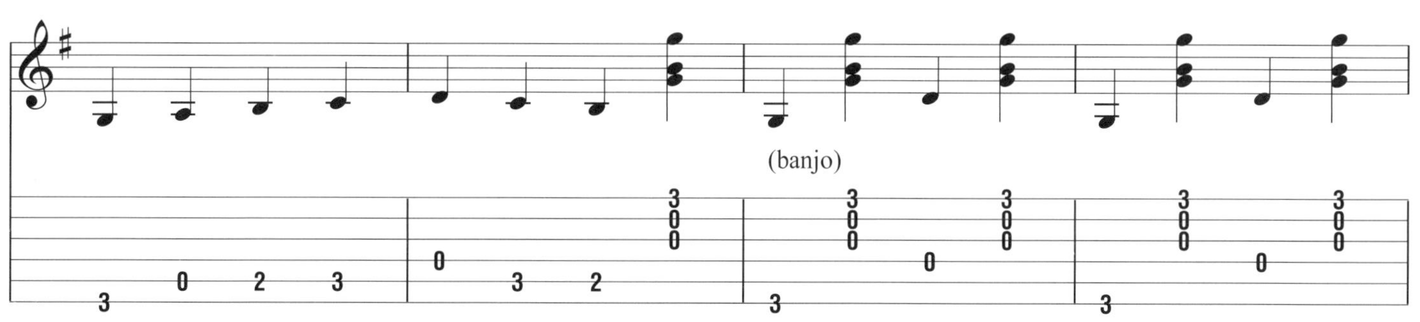
(banjo)

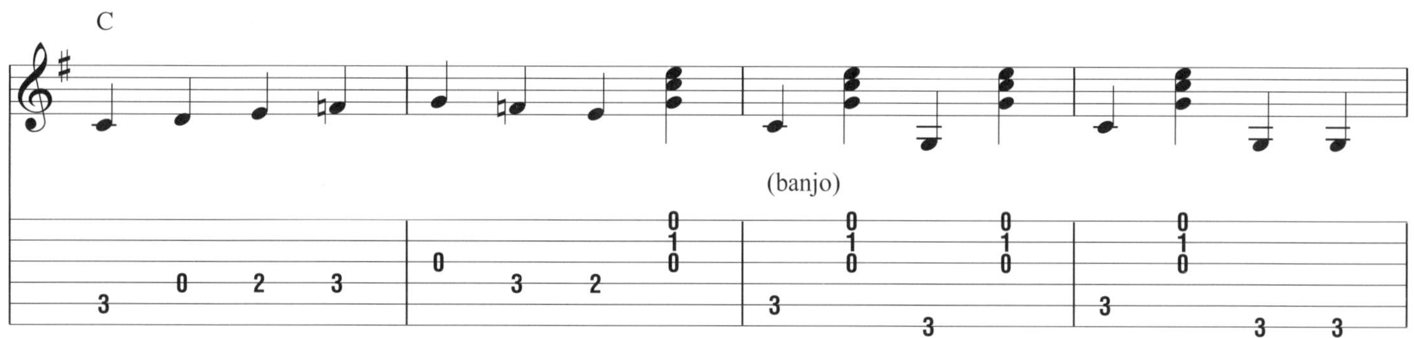
C
(banjo)

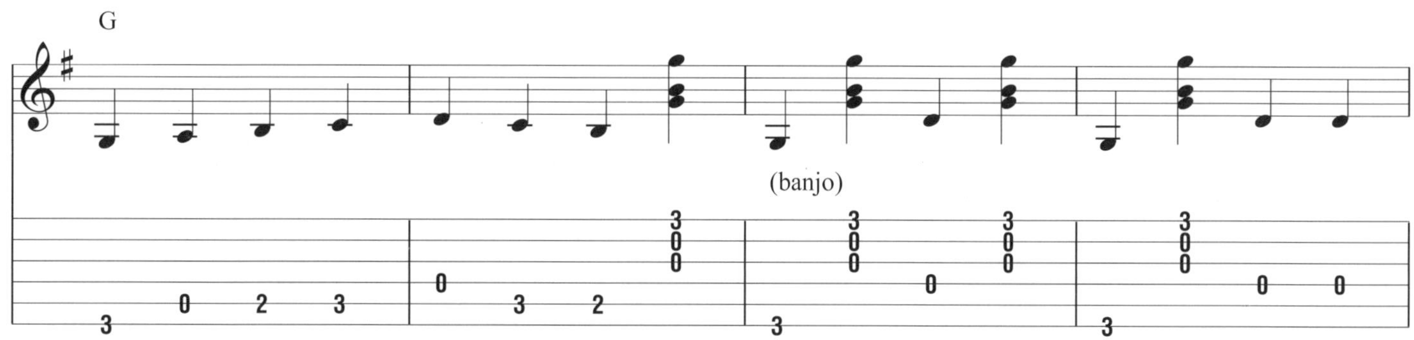
G
(banjo)

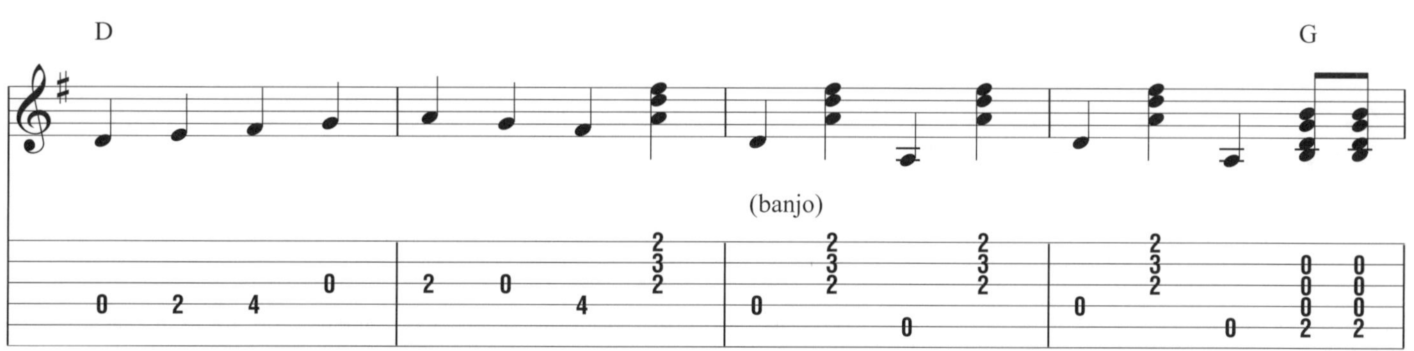
D
G
(banjo)

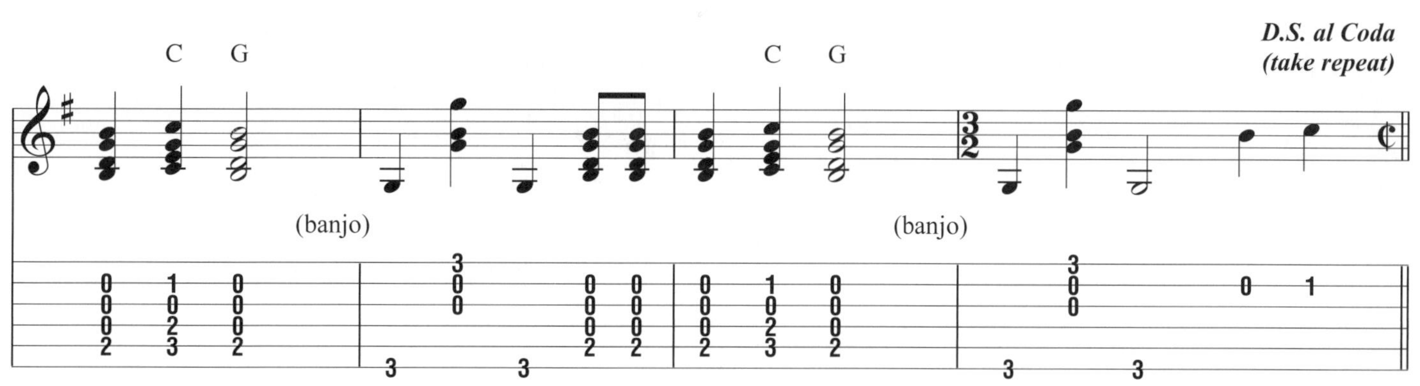
C G
C G
D.S. al Coda
(take repeat)
(banjo)
(banjo)

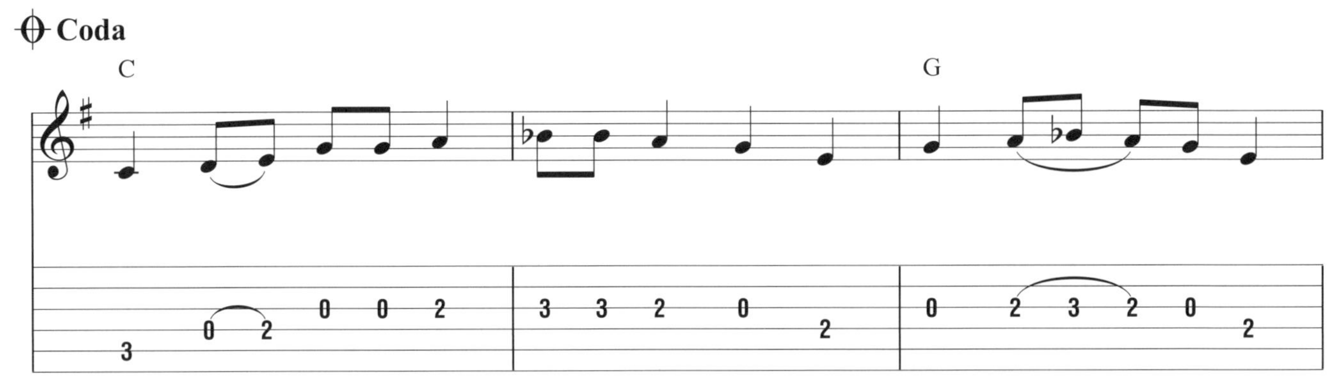
Coda
C
G

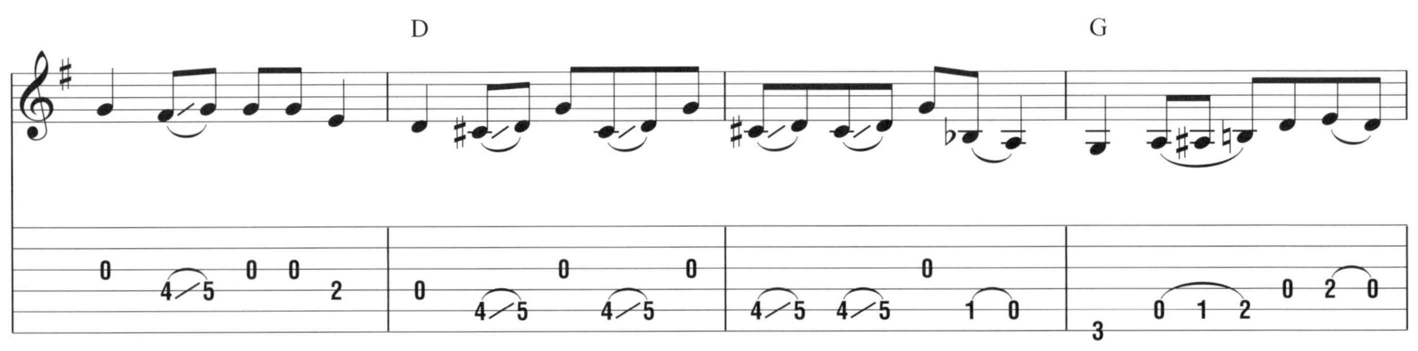
D
G

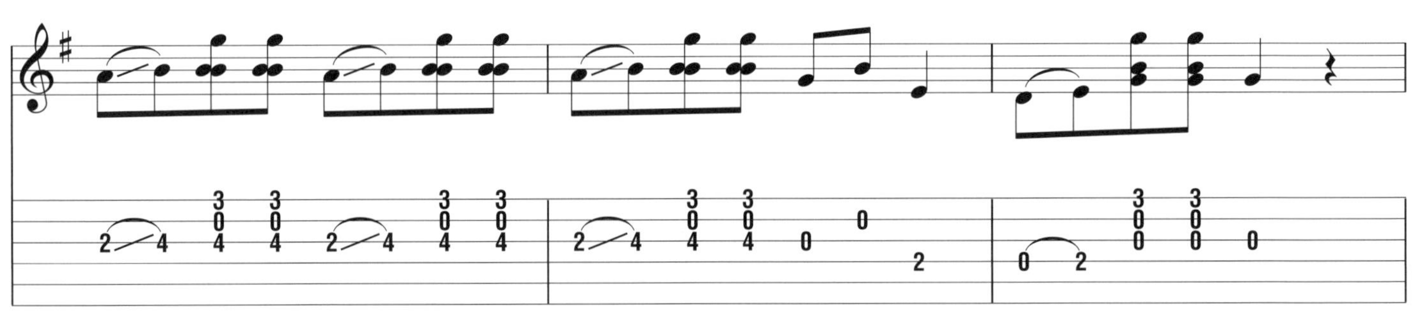

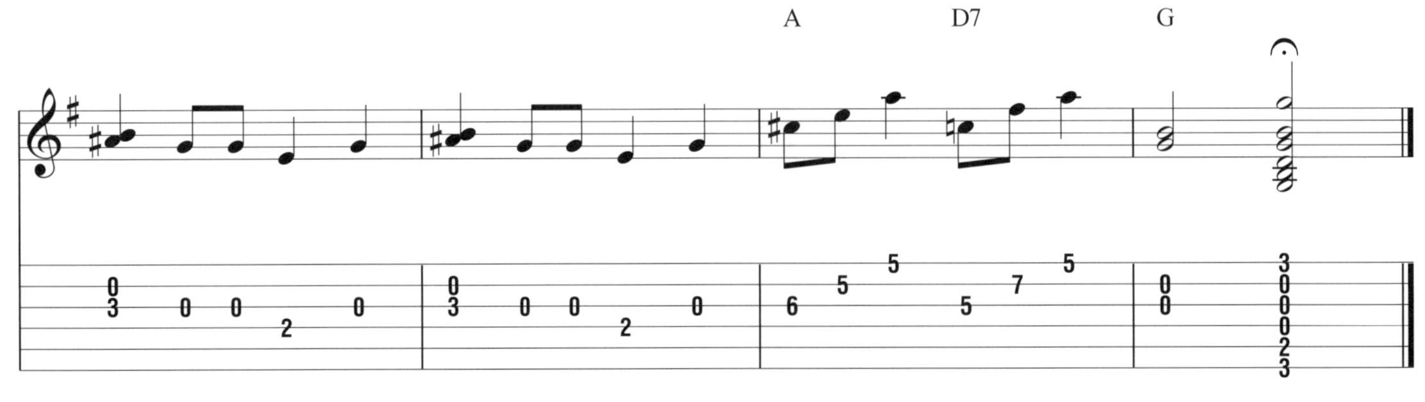
A
D7
G

Whiskey Before Breakfast

Traditional

This fiddle tune is of uncertain origin, though it is just as popular among Irish musicians as it is among bluegrassers. D is the standard key.

Foggy Mountain Breakdown

By Earl Scruggs

In the bluegrass world fast instrumentals are often called *breakdowns*. Earl Scruggs wrote what has since become arguably the most popular banjo instrumental ever, "Foggy Mountain Breakdown," in 1949. Recorded with Lester Flatt and the Foggy Mountain Boys, it was given a second life in 1967 when it was featured in the movie *Bonnie and Clyde*. As it was the first bluegrass instrumental to achieve pop acclaim, learning to play it is a rite of passage for a bluegrass banjoist. In the following arrangement, the repetition of the theme features an improvised melody (not the exact melody), which is what is usually done. For the record, when the guitarist backs up other instruments on this tune, he or she plays an E major chord when the soloist plays an Em chord.

Key of G

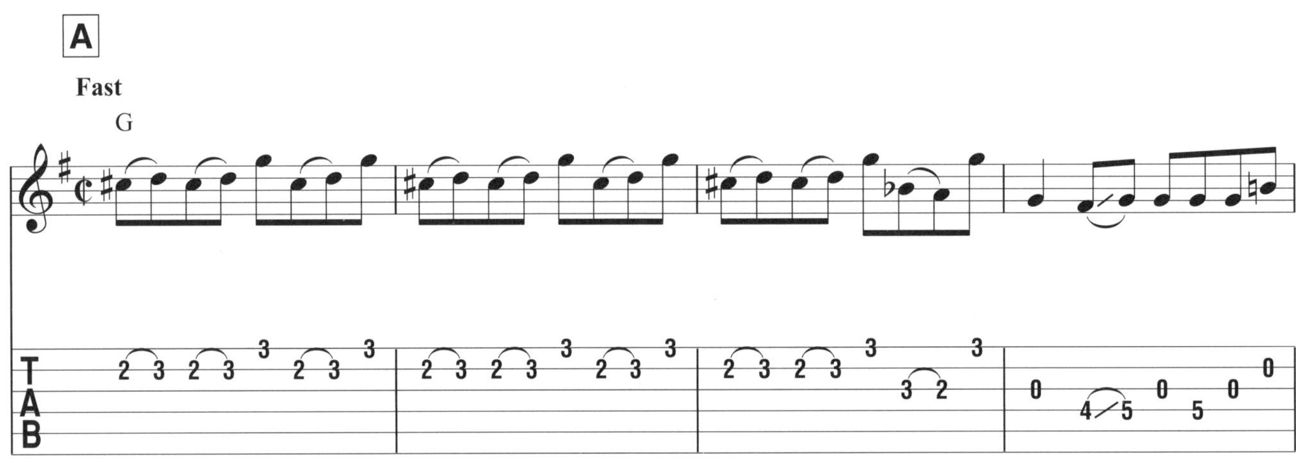

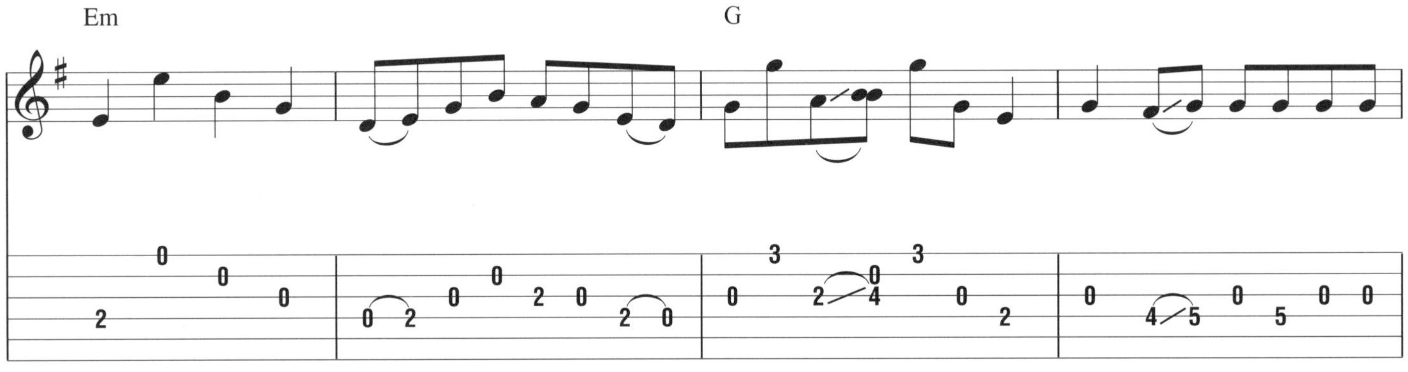

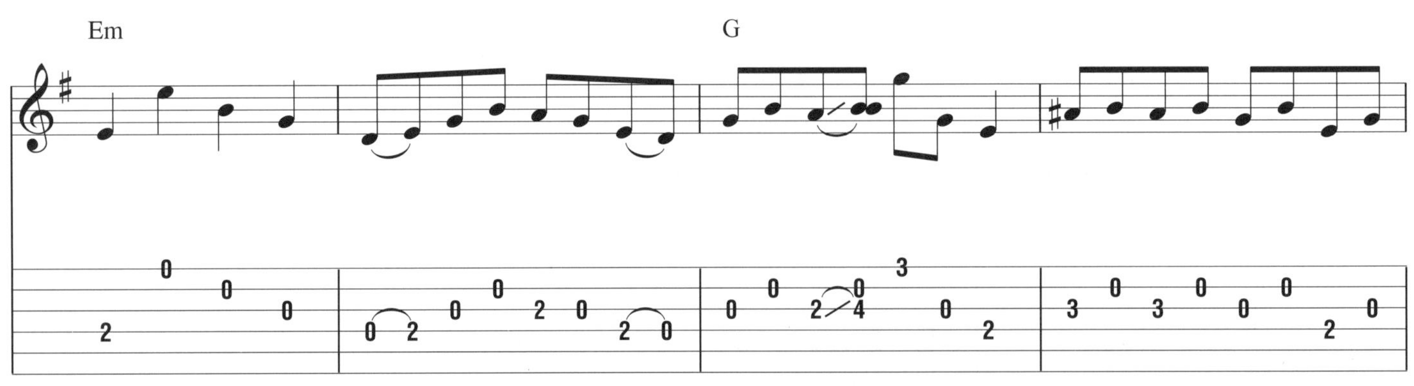

D
G
B
G
Em
G
Em
G
D
G

Footprints in the Snow

Words and Music by Rupert Jones

Bill Monroe's 1945 version of "Footprints in the Snow" led to its status as a bluegrass standard. It was first recorded many years earlier and dates all the way back to around 1880, when it first appeared as a music hall song!

Key of C

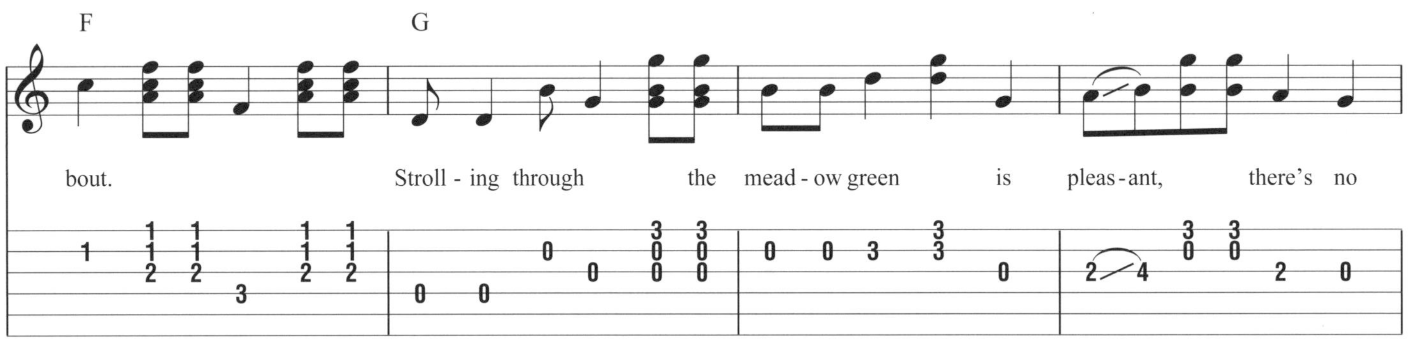

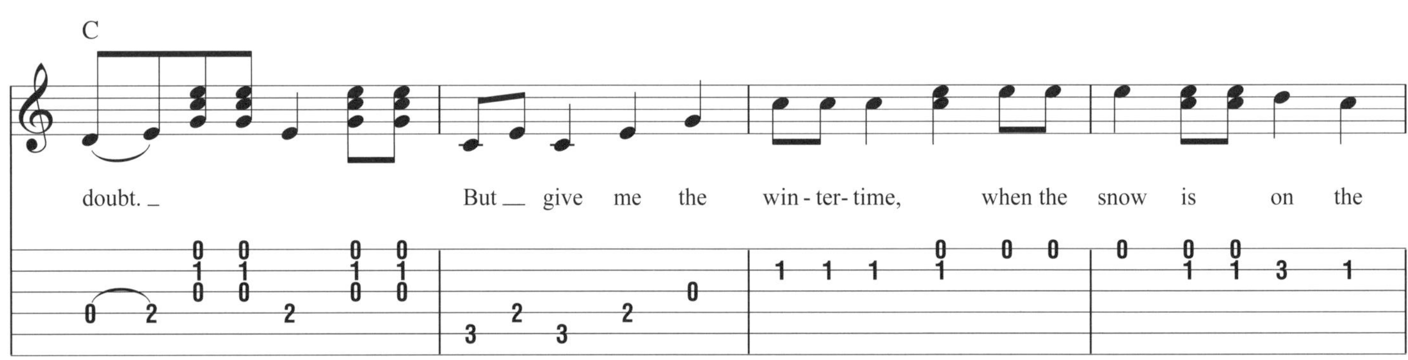

Chorus

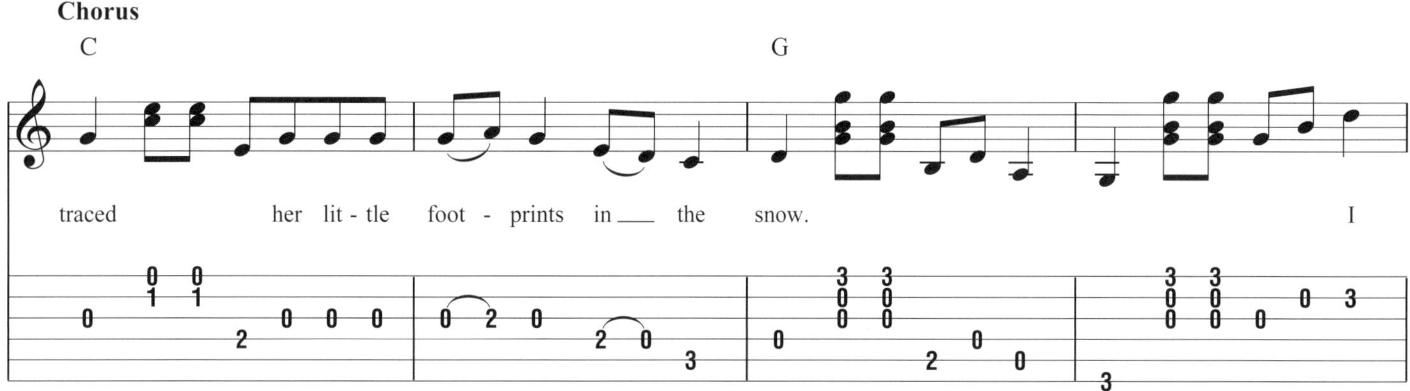

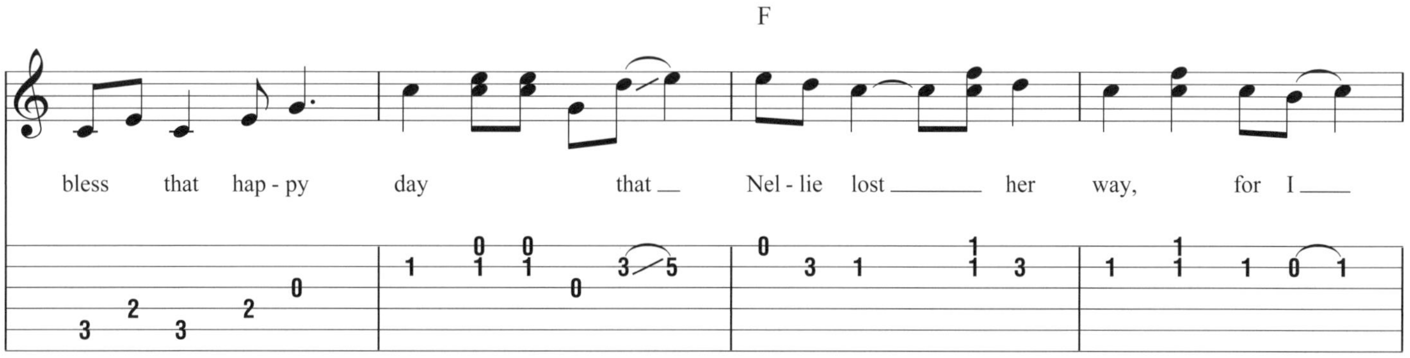

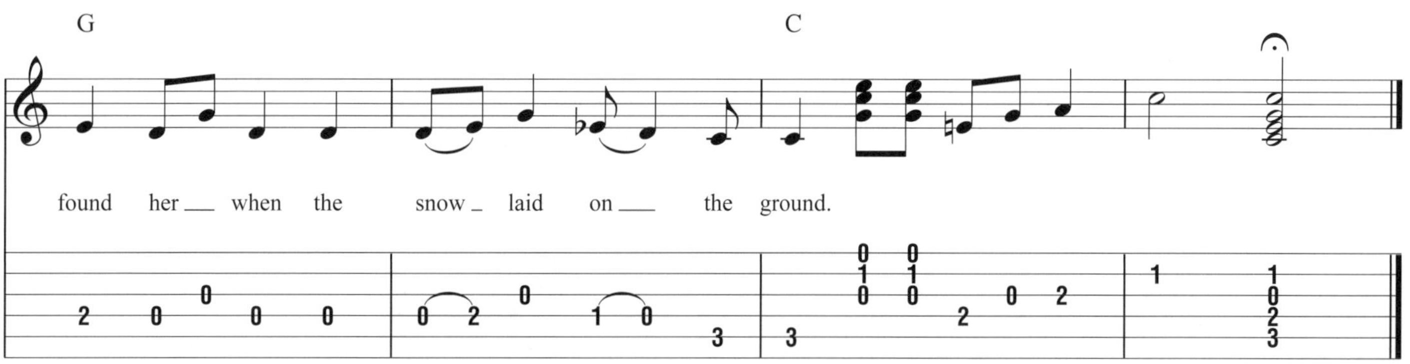

Additional Verses

2. I dropped in to see her, there was a big round moon.
   Her mother said she just stepped out, but would be returning soon.
   I found her little footprints and I traced them through the snow.
   I found her when the snow was on the ground.

3. Now, she's up in heaven, she's with the angel band.
   I know I'm going to meet her in that promised land.
   But every time the snow falls, it brings back memories,
   For I found her when the snow was on the ground.

Hot Corn, Cold Corn

Traditional

The chorus of this old-time tune uses the same melody and chord progression as the verses. In both parts the third from the last bar contains an extra two beats (a bar of 3/2). A note about the lyrics: A *demijohn* is a large jug, often encased in wicker, used for holding liquid—and sometimes used to ferment a "home brew."

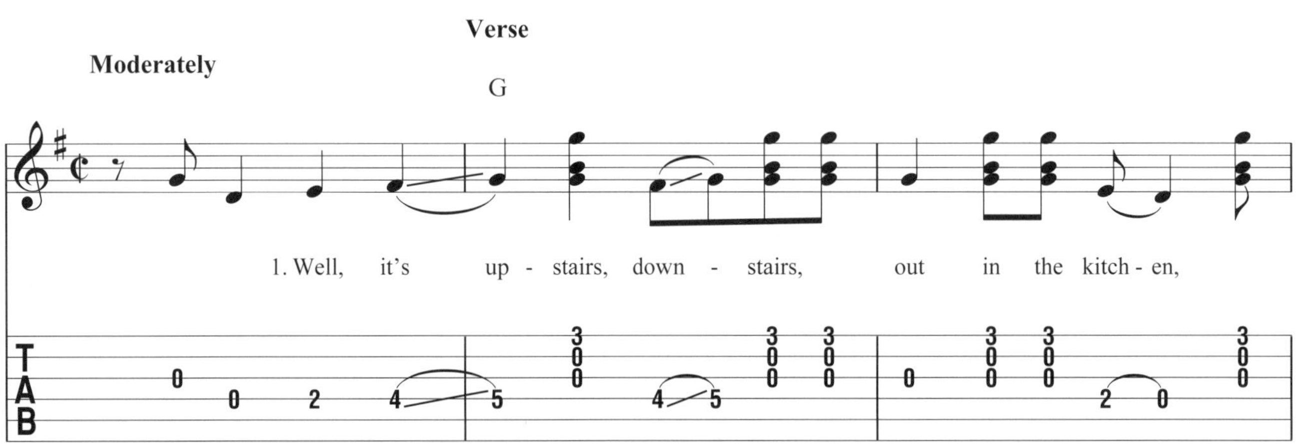

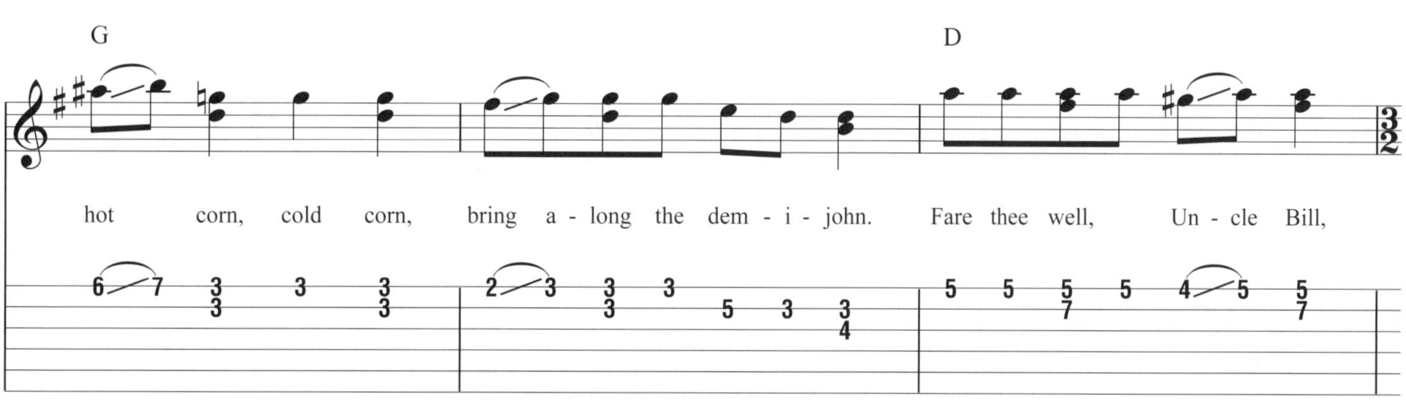

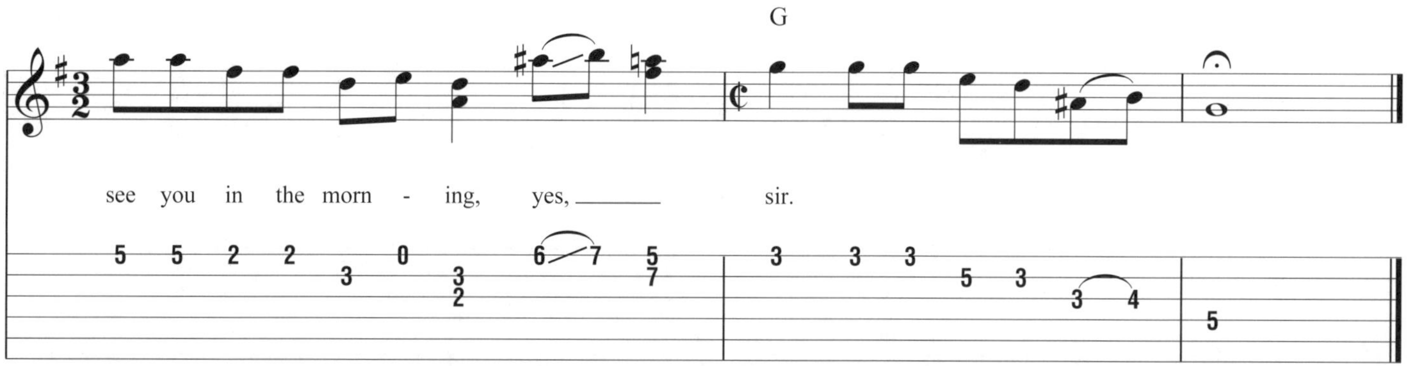

Additional Verses

2. Well, it's old Aunt Peggy, won't you fill 'em up again?
   Old Aunt Peggy, won't you fill 'em up again?
   Old Aunt Peggy, won't you fill 'em up again?
   Ain't had a drink since I don't know when, yes sir.

3. Well, yonder comes the preacher and the children are a-cryin',
   Yonder comes the preacher and the children are a-cryin',
   Yonder comes the preacher and the children are a-cryin',
   Chickens all a-running and the toenails a-flying, yes sir.

How Mountain Girls Can Love

Words and Music by Carter Stanley

"How Mountain Girls Can Love" is one of the Stanley Brothers' most popular compositions. The following arrangement goes around the tune (verse and chorus) twice, first in a high register, then in a lower one.

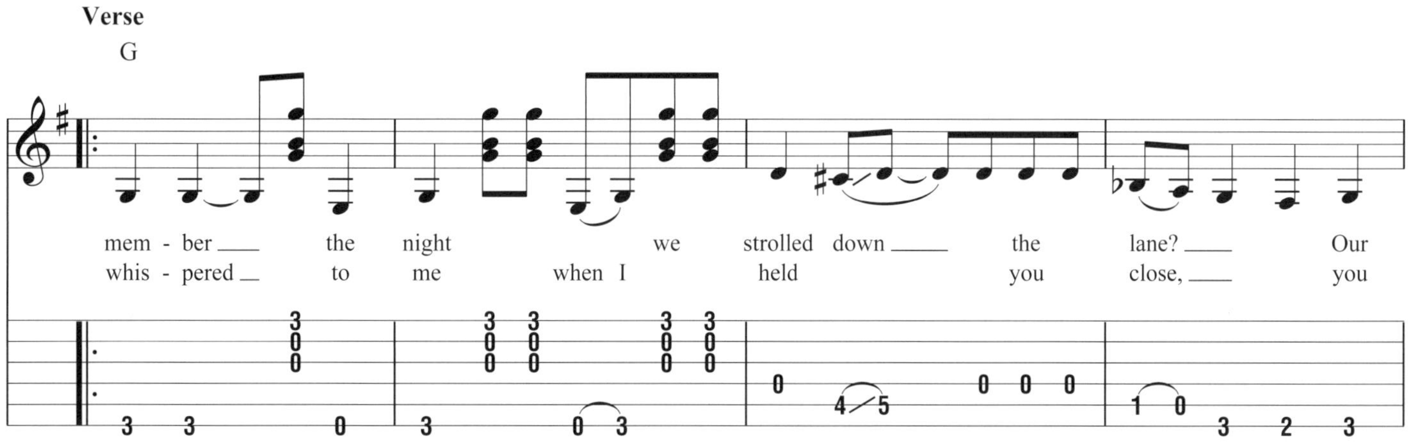
Verse
G
mem - ber the night we strolled down the lane? Our
whis - pered to me when I held you close, you

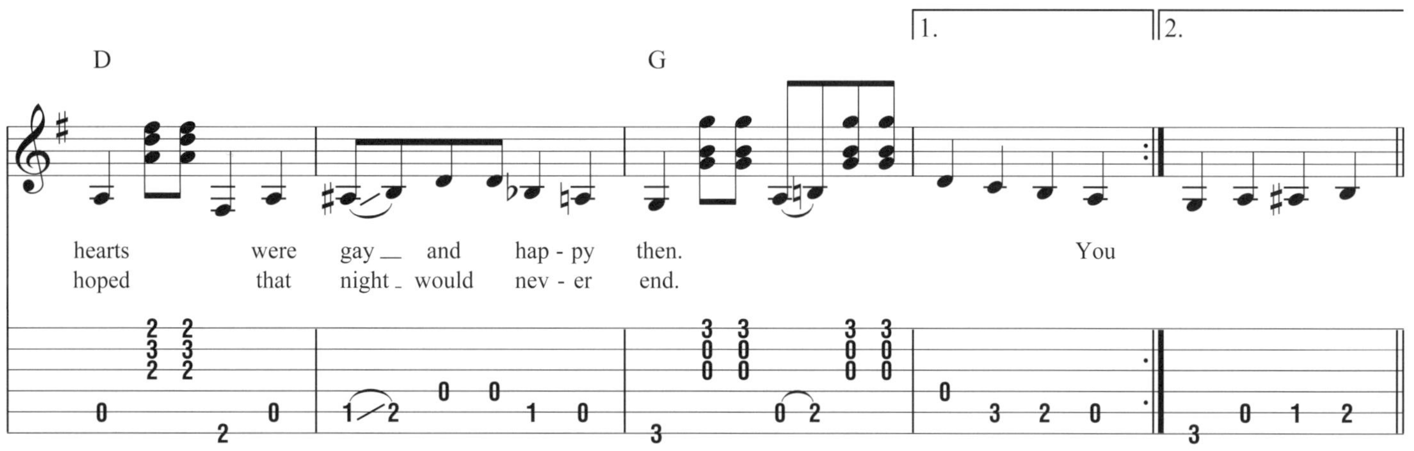
D
G
1.
2.
hearts were gay and hap - py then. You
hoped that night would nev - er end.

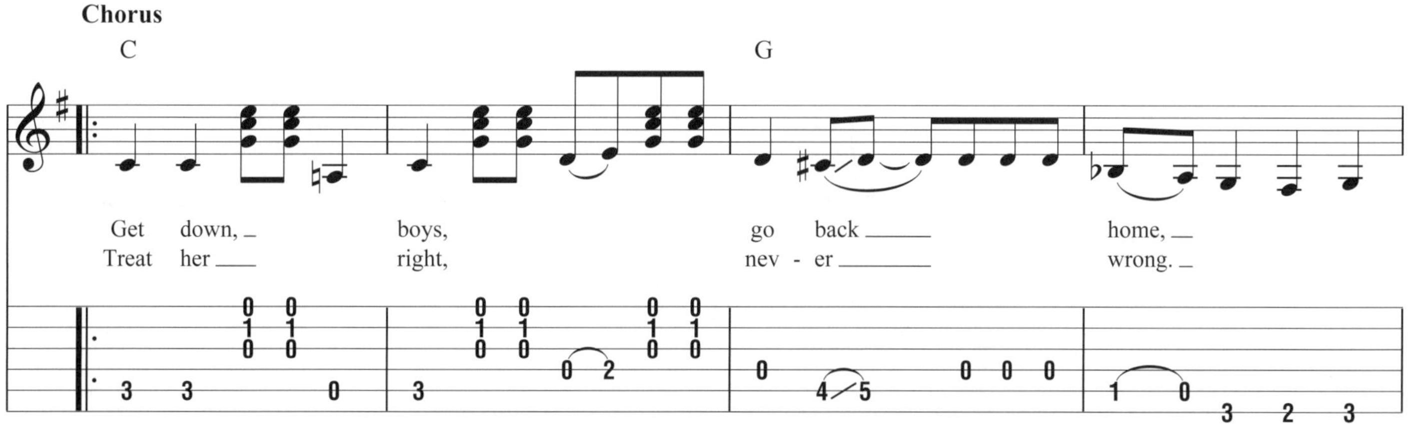
Chorus
C
G
Get down, boys, go back home,
Treat her right, nev - er wrong.

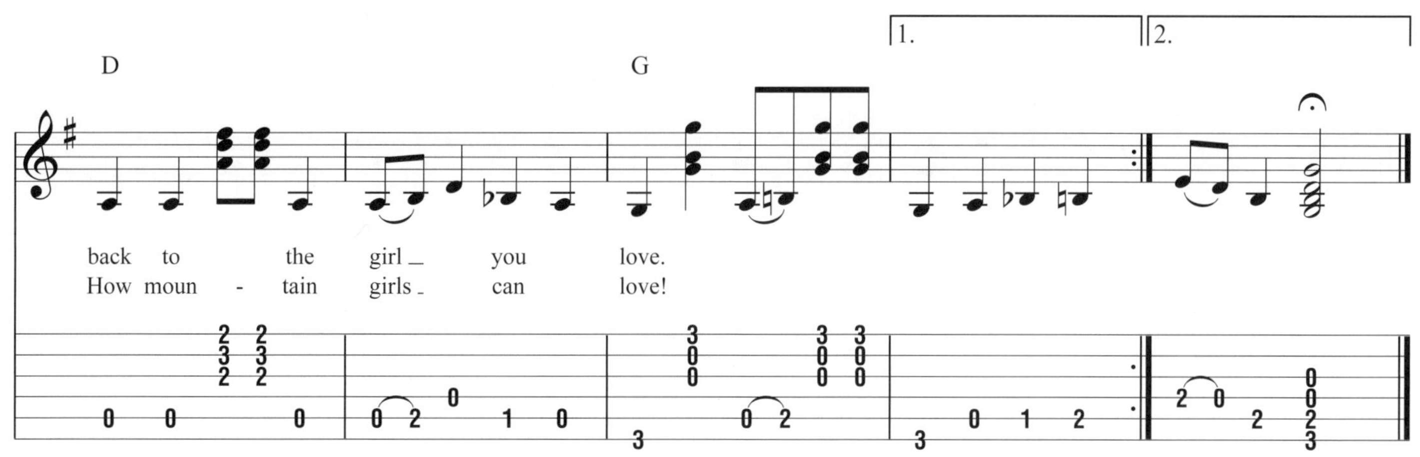
D
G
1.
2.
back to the girl you love.
How moun - tain girls can love!

I Am a Man of Constant Sorrow

Words and Music by Carter Stanley

First published in a songbook in 1913, "I Am a Man of Constant Sorrow" was included on Bob Dylan's first LP nearly 50 years later. However, it was the Stanley Brothers' 1959 recording that served as the template for the million-selling hit version heard in the film *O Brother, Where Art Thou?* in 2000.

Key of E

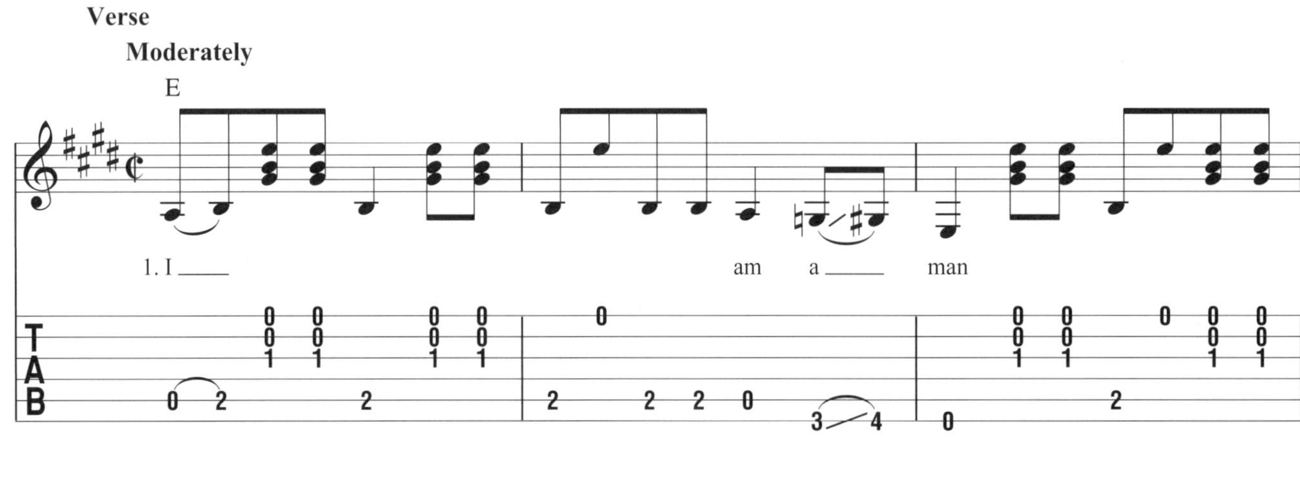

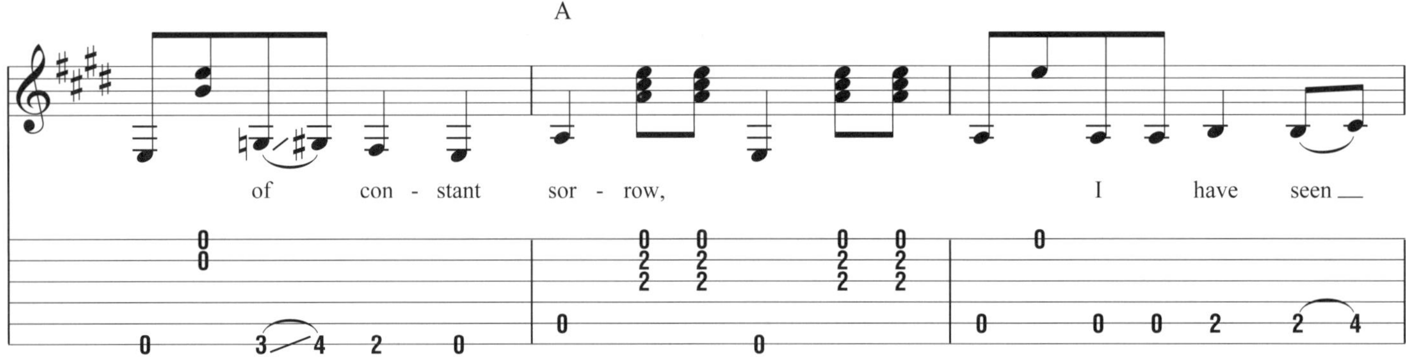

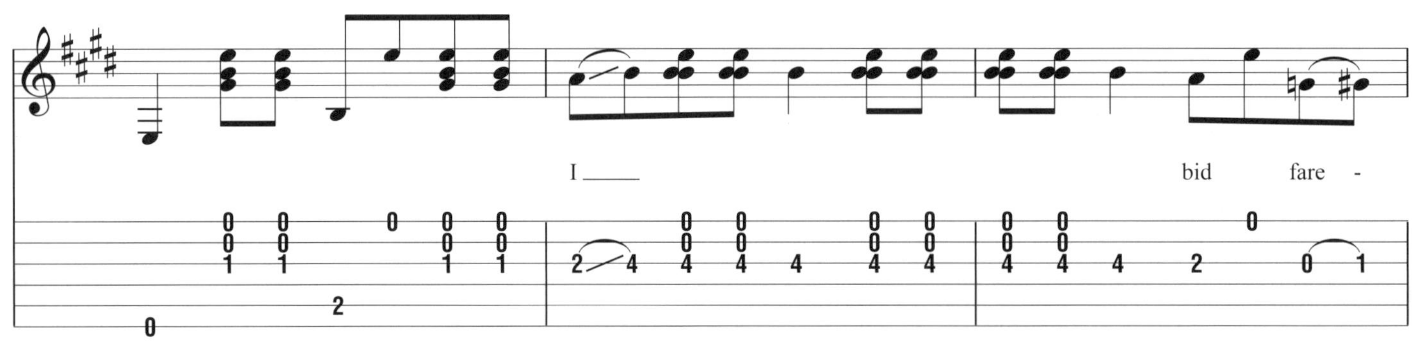

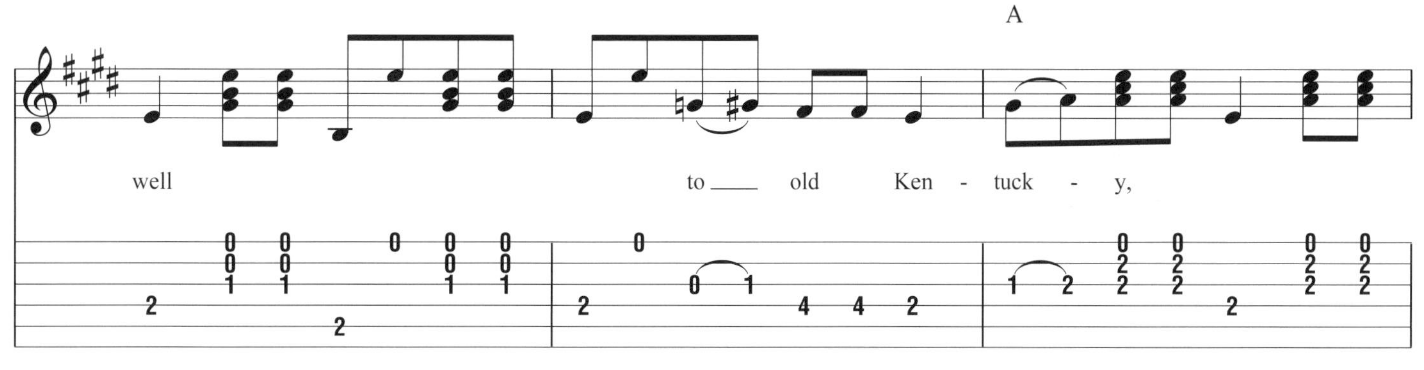

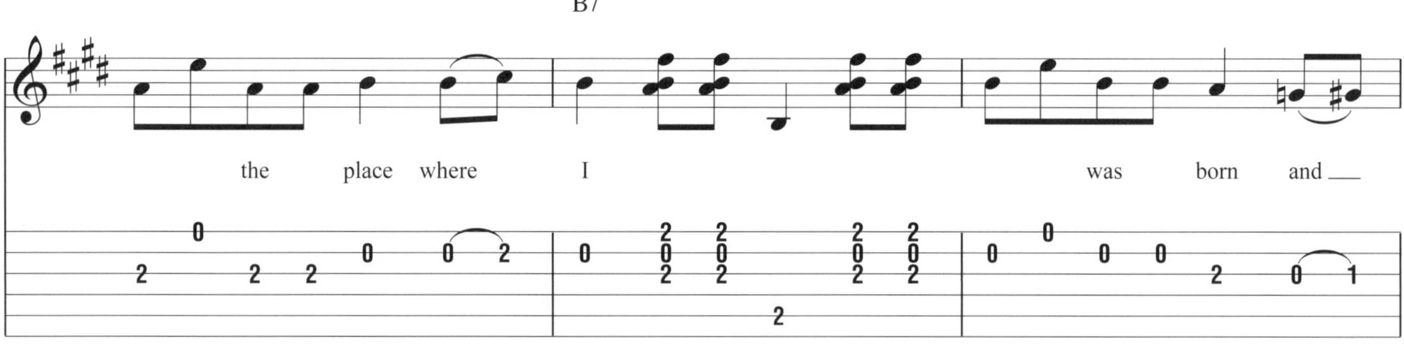

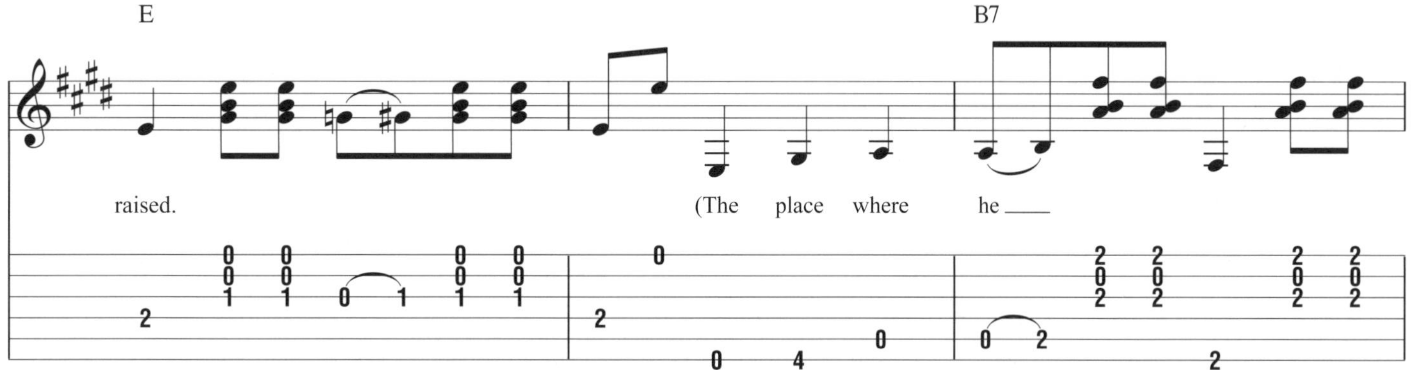

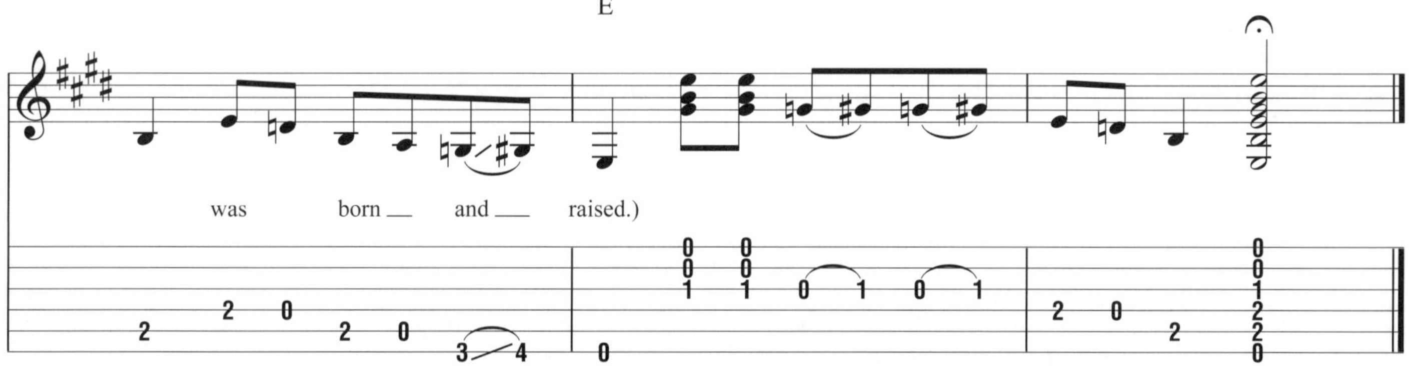

Additional Verses

2. For six long years I've been in trouble, no pleasure here on earth I find.
   For in this world I'm bound to ramble. I have no friends to help me now.
   (He has no friends to help him now.)
3. It's fare thee well, my own true lover. I never expect to see you again.
   For I'm bound to ride that northern railroad. Perhaps I'll die upon this train.
   (Perhaps he'll die upon this train.)
4. You can bury me in some deep valley, for many years where I may lay.
   Then you may learn to love another, while I am sleeping in my grave.
   (While he is sleeping in his grave.)
5. Maybe your friends think I'm just a stranger, my face you never will see no more.
   But there is one promise that is given: I'll meet you on God's golden shore.
   (He'll meet you on God's golden shore.)

I Wonder Where You Are Tonight

Words and Music by Johnny Bond

This tune is a standard in both country and bluegrass music, having been recorded by Hank Snow, Ernest Tubb, and numerous other country legends. (It's often referred to by bluegrassers as "I'll Wear Your Underwear Tonight.")

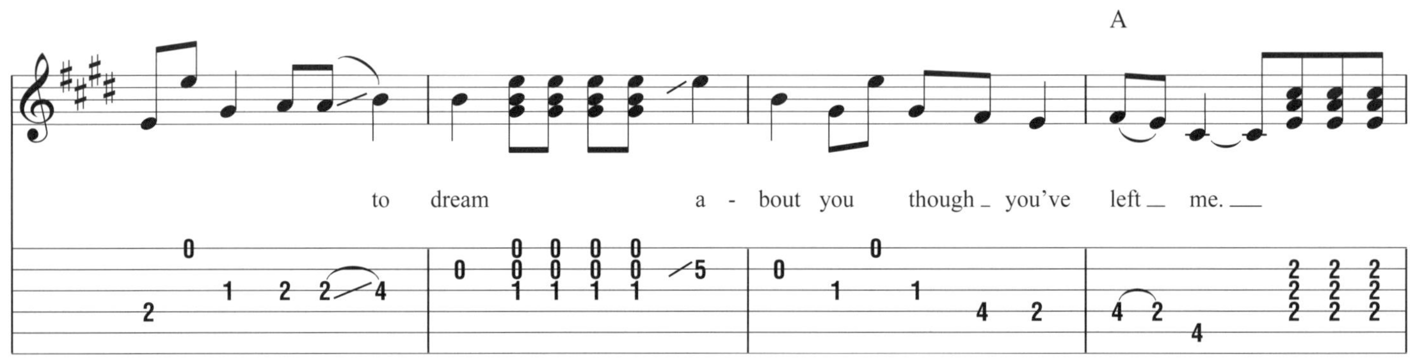

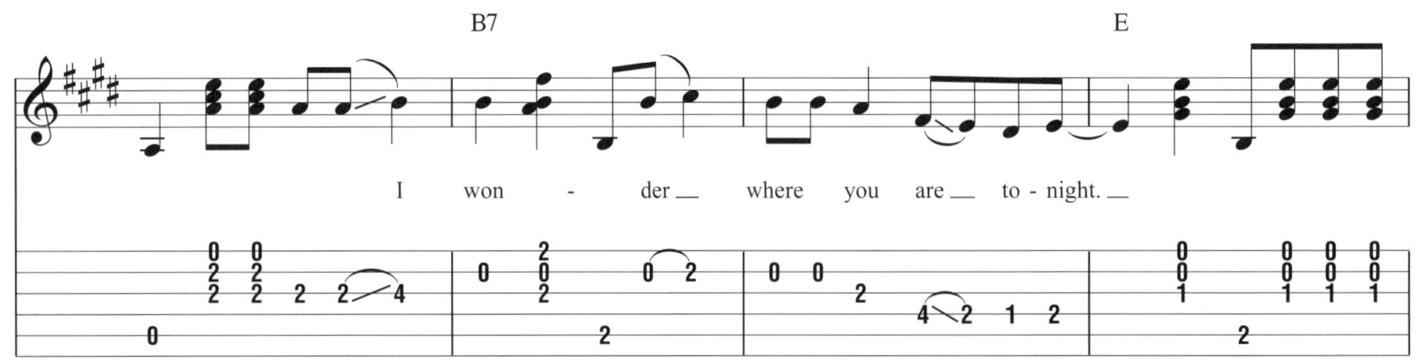

Chorus

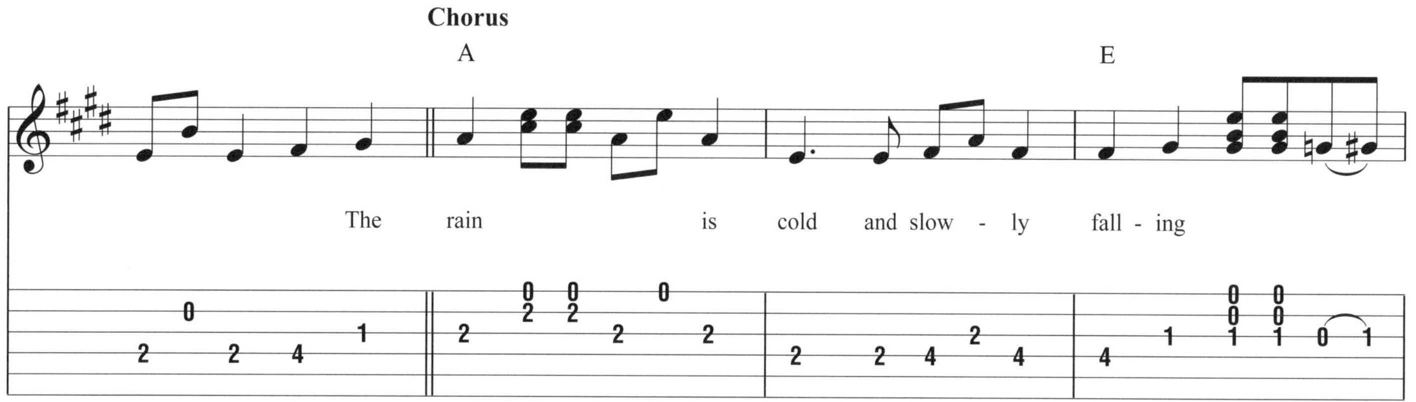

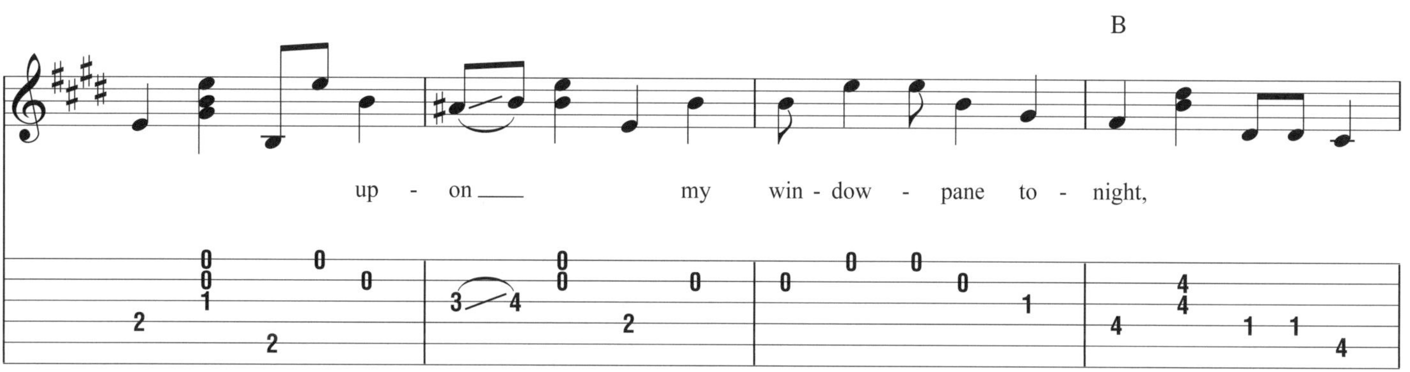

Additional Verses

2. Your heart was cold, you never loved me, though you often said you cared.
   And now you've gone to find another, someone who knows the love I shared.

3. Then came the dawn the day you left me, I tried to smile with all my might.
   But you could see the pain within me that lingers in my heart tonight.

I'll Fly Away

Words and Music by Albert E. Brumley

Possibly the most recorded gospel song of all time (and not just in the bluegrass world), "I'll Fly Away" dates to the 1920s. Its inclusion in the 2000 film *O Brother, Where Art Thou?* gave it new life and inspired new recordings by many artists.

Key of D

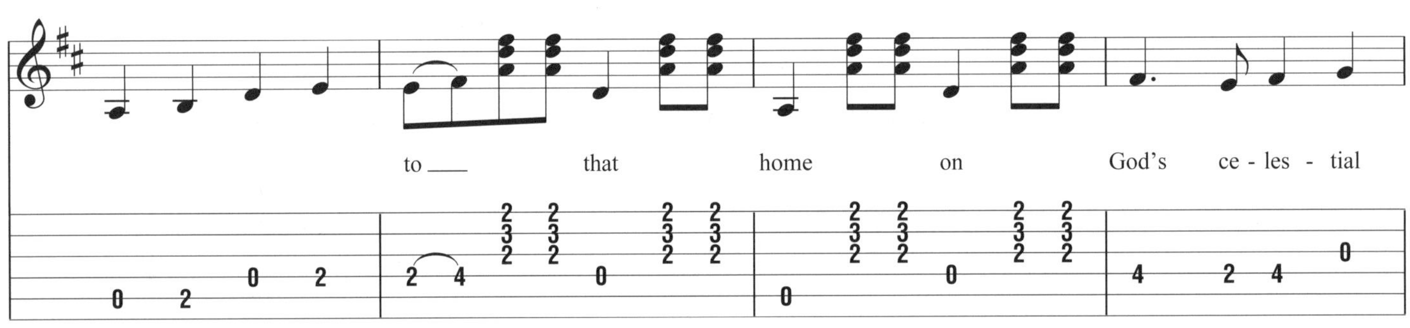

Chorus

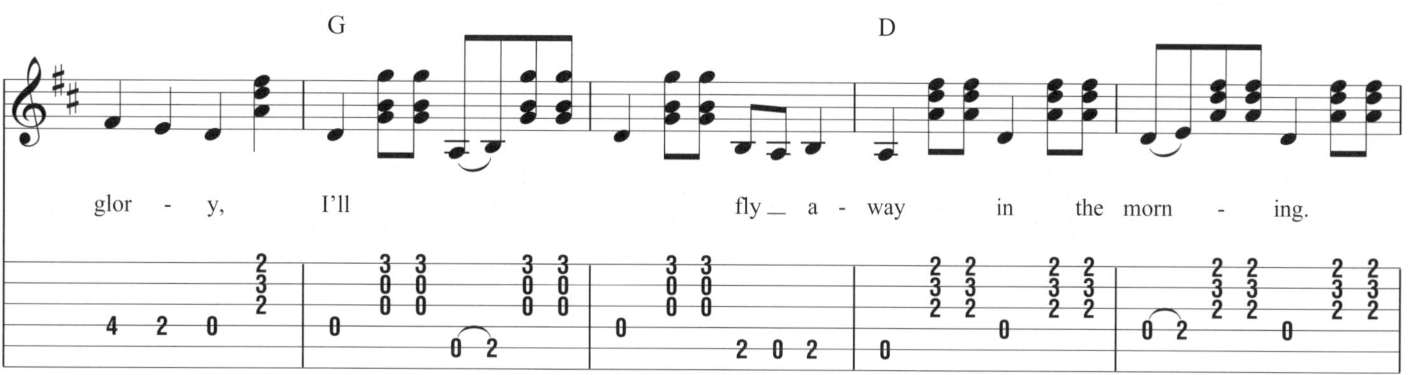

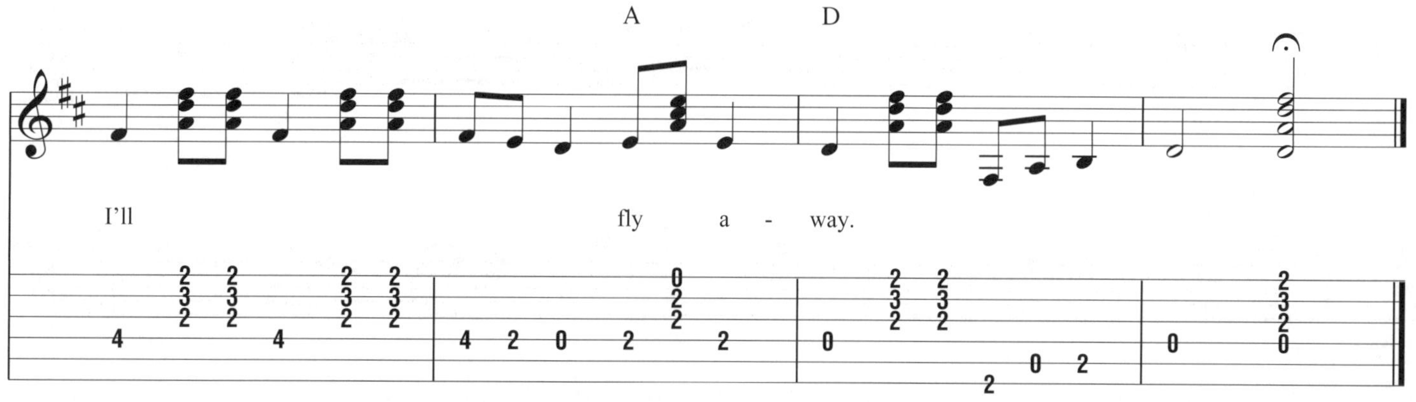

Additional Verses

2. When the shadows of this life have gone, I'll fly away.
   Like a bird from these prison walls, I'll fly, I'll fly away.

3. Oh, how glad and happy when we meet, I'll fly away.
   No more cold iron shackles on my feet, I'll fly away.

4. Just a few more weary days and then, I'll fly away
   To a land where joys will never end, I'll fly away.

In the Pines

Words and Music by Thomas Bryant, Jimmie Davis and Clayton McMichen

Various versions of "In the Pines" have been performed and/or recorded since the late 1800s. Leadbelly popularized it in the 1940s, and Bill Monroe's recording from the 1950s made it a bluegrass standard. The two versions contain very different music but share similar lyrics.

Key of D

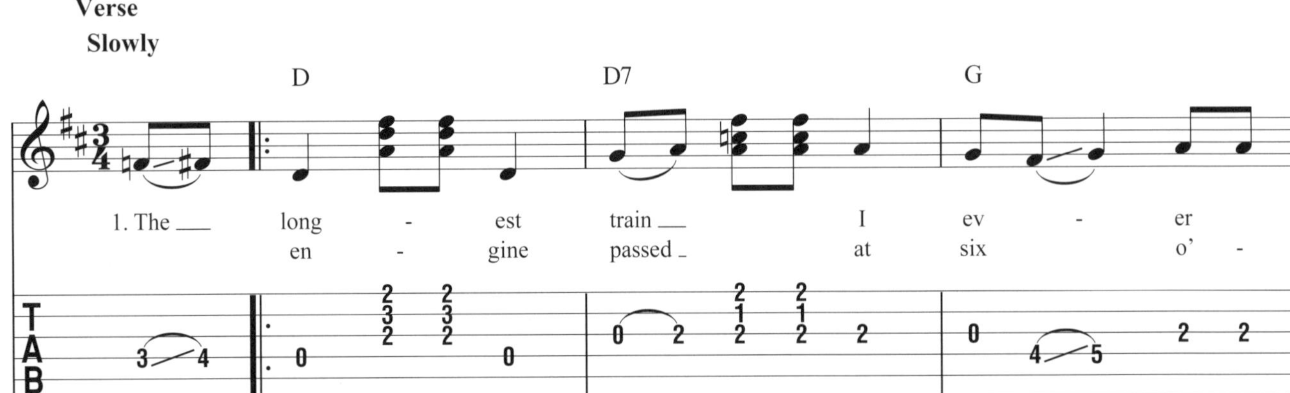

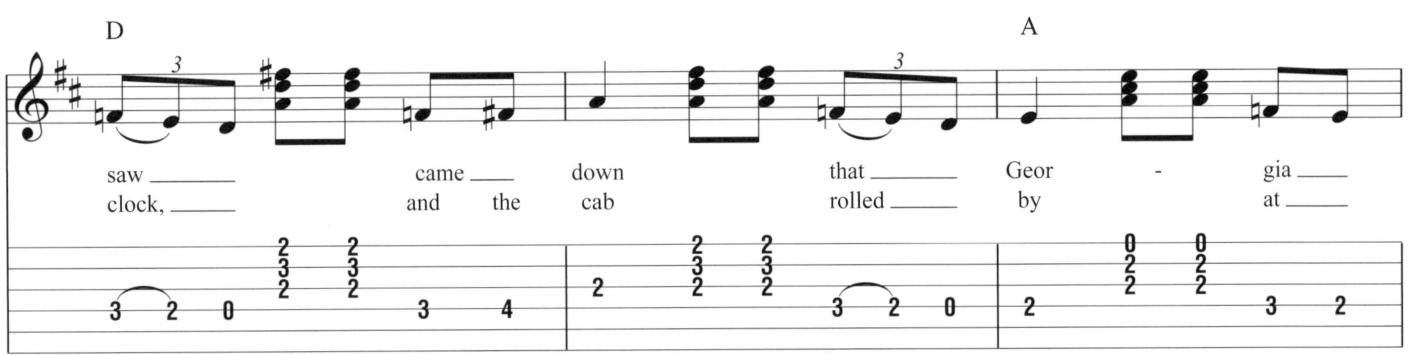

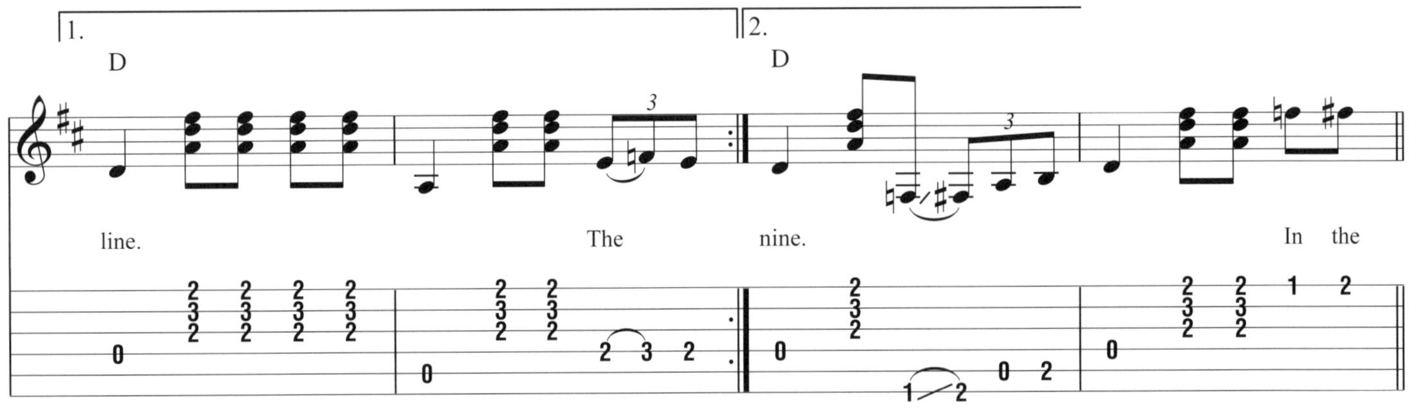

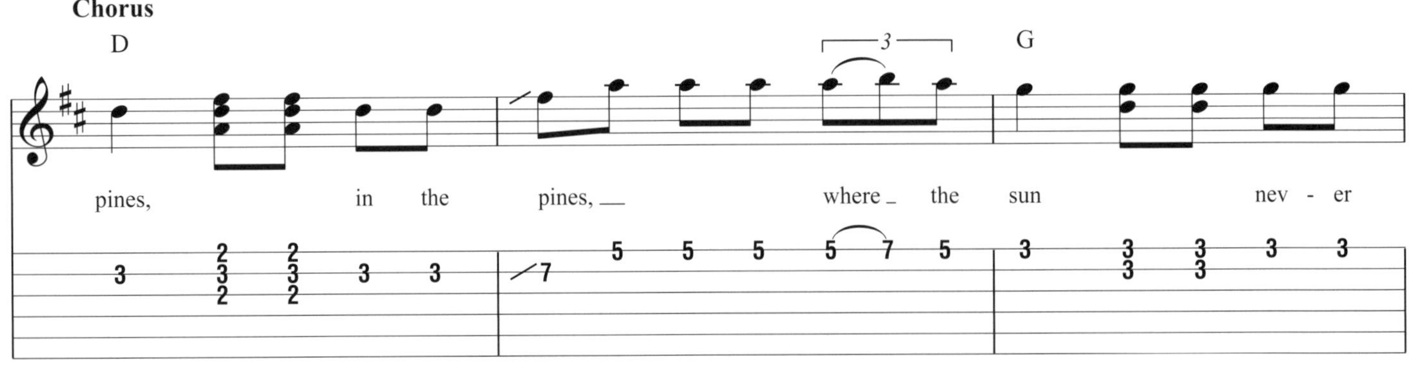

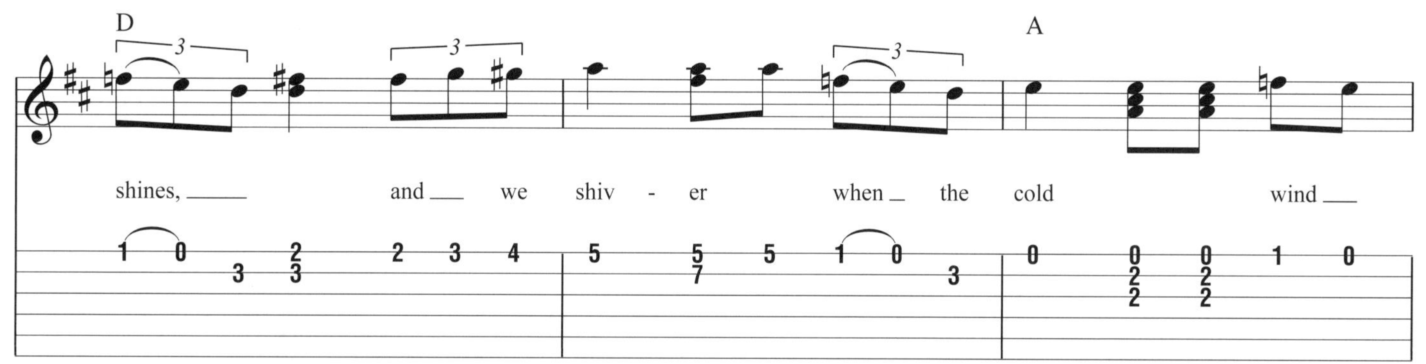

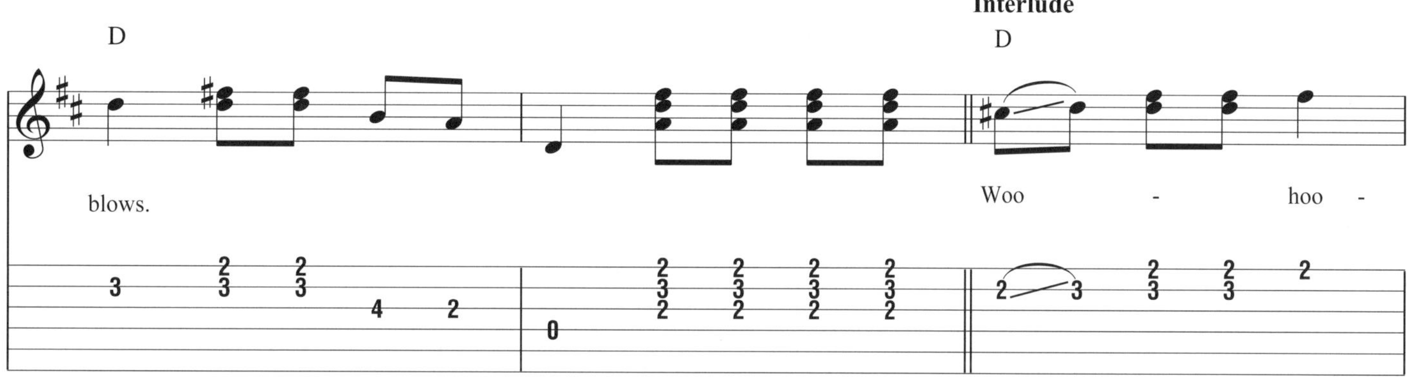

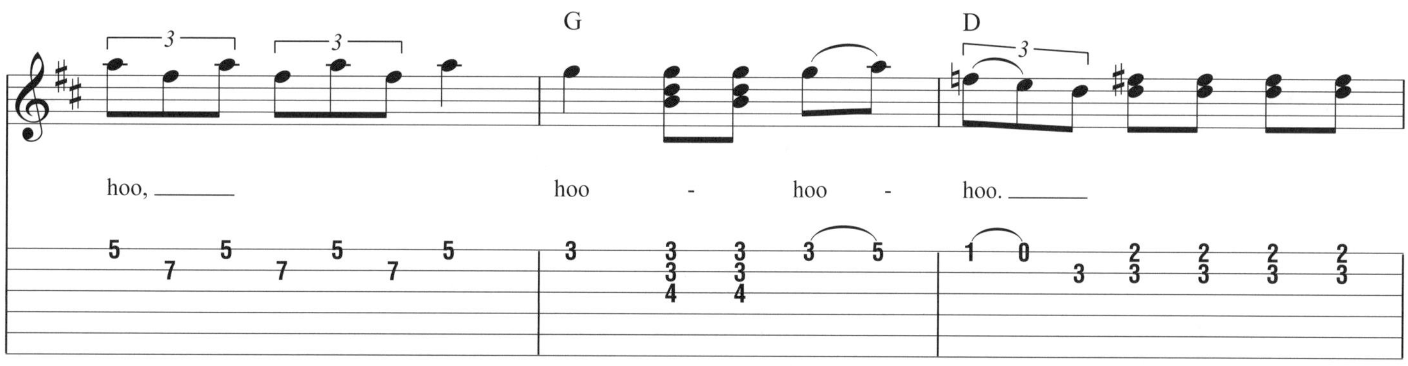

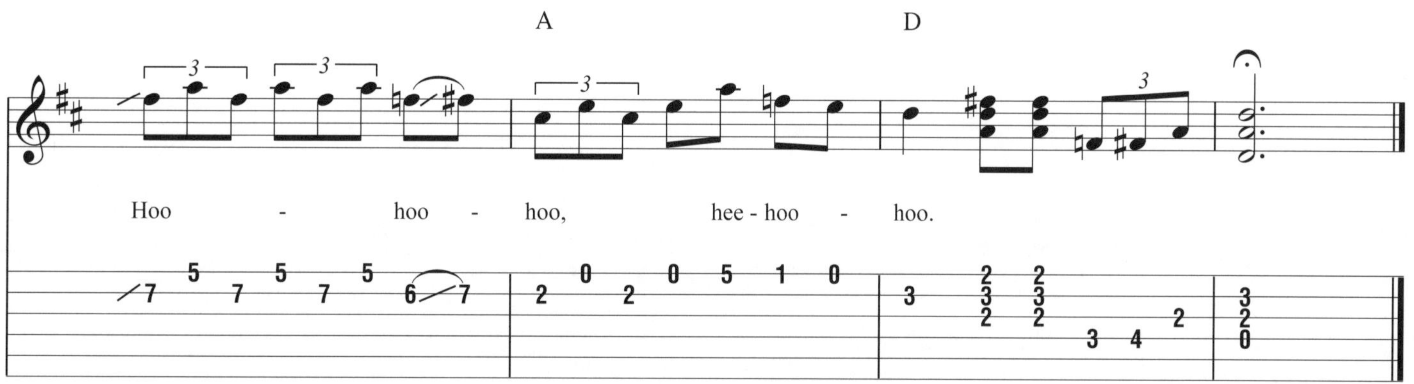

Additional Verses

2. I asked my captain for the time of day. He said he throwed his watch away.
   A long steel rail and a short cross tie, I'm on my way back home.
3. Little girl, little girl, what have I done that makes you treat me so?
   You caused me to weep, you caused me to mourn, you caused me to leave my home.

Jimmie Brown the Newsboy

Words and Music by A.P. Carter

The Carter Family recorded this song in 1929, but the Flatt and Scruggs' 1957 recording on the *Foggy Mountain Jamboree* LP brought it into the bluegrass world.

Key of C

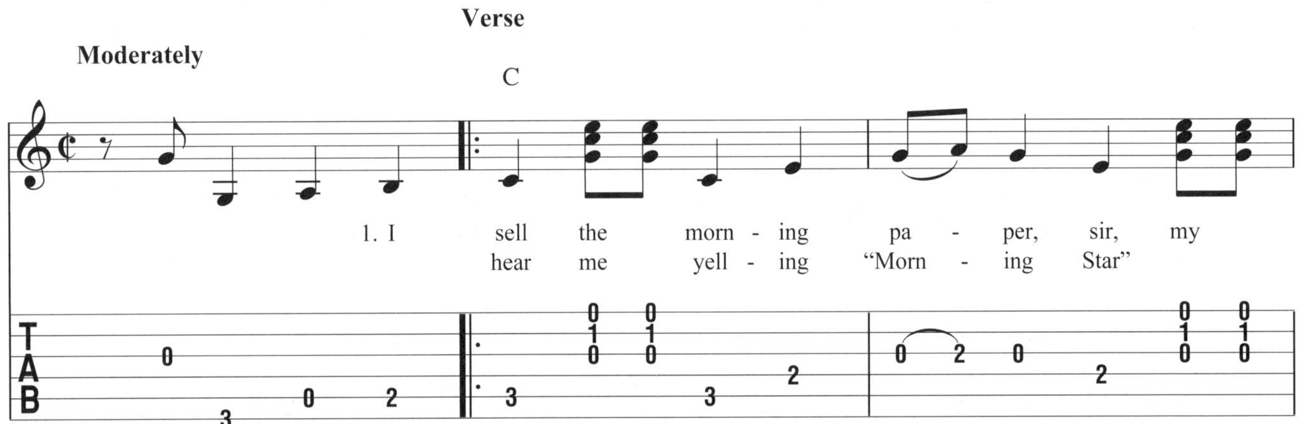

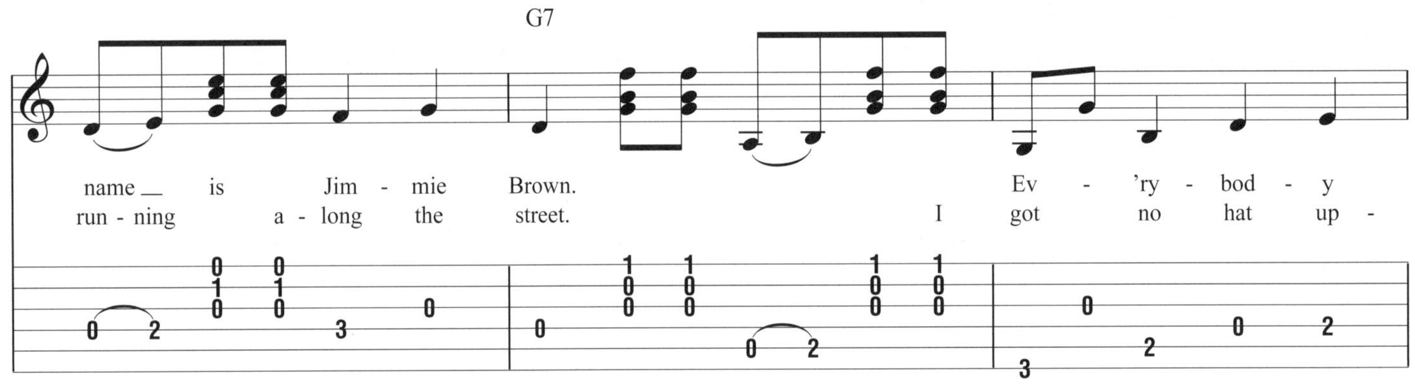

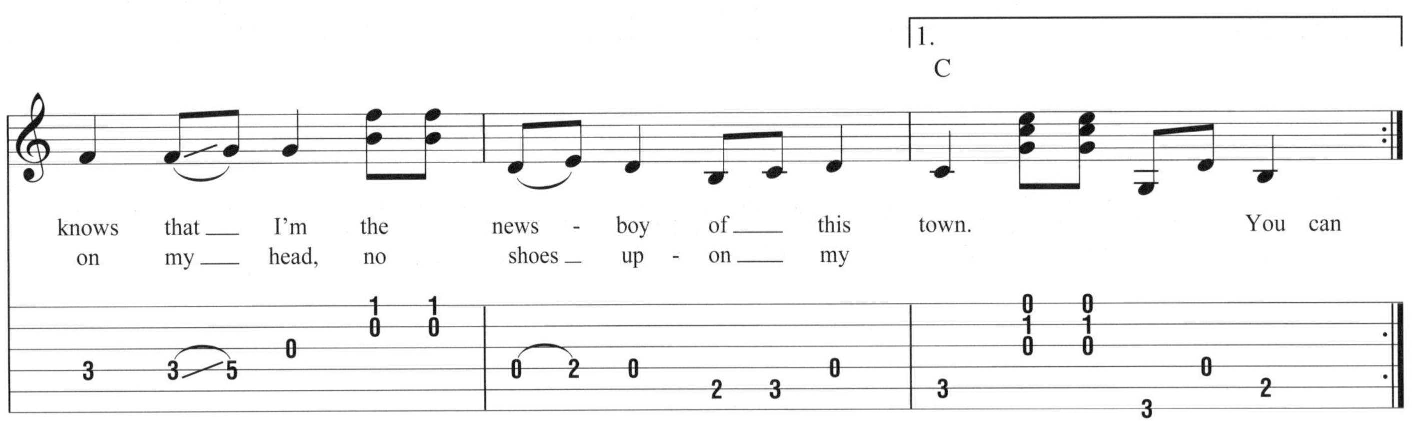

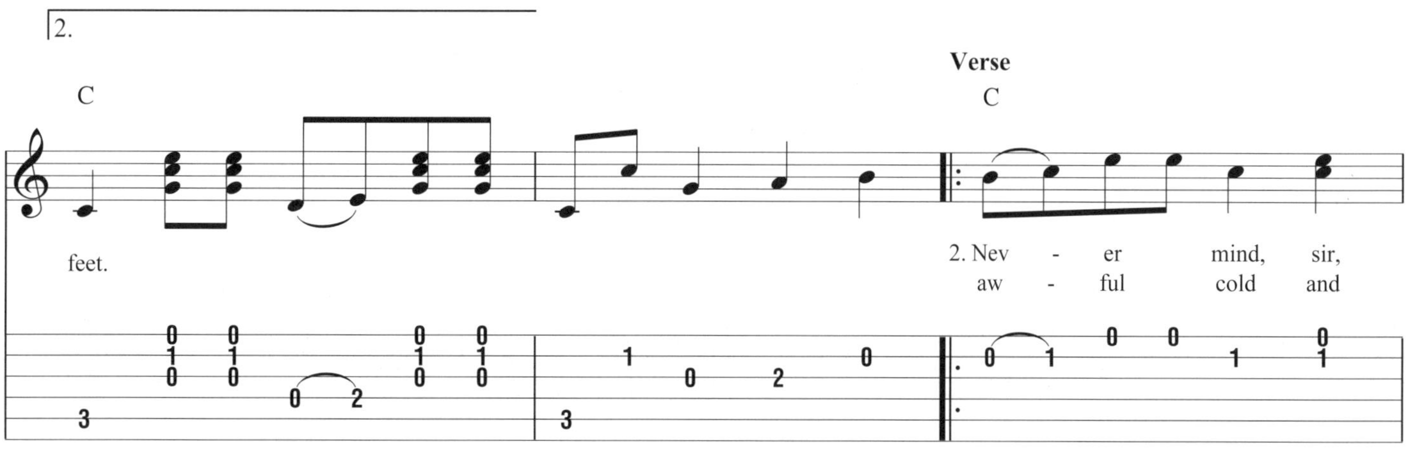

Additional Verse

3. My father died a drunkard, sir, I've heard my mother say.
I am helping Mother, sir, as I journey on my way.
My mother always tells me, sir, I've nothing in the world to lose.
I'll get a place in heaven, sir, to sell the gospel news.

Keep on the Sunny Side

Words and Music by A.P. Carter

Written in 1899, this song was recorded by the Carter Family in 1928 and it eventually became their theme song. The song's composer, Ada Blenkhorn, got the title and idea for "Keep on the Sunny Side" from her disabled nephew, who always wanted his wheelchair pushed on the sunny side of the street.

Chorus

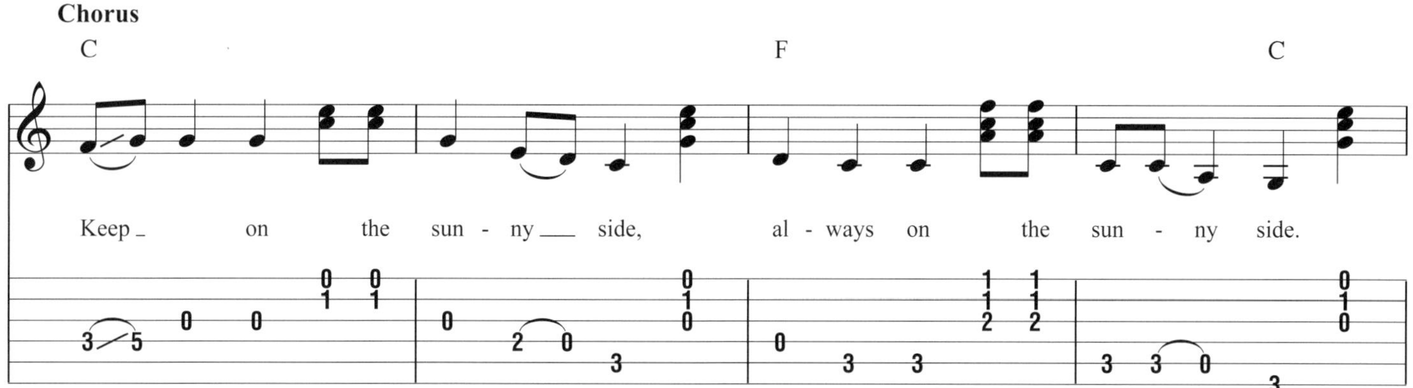

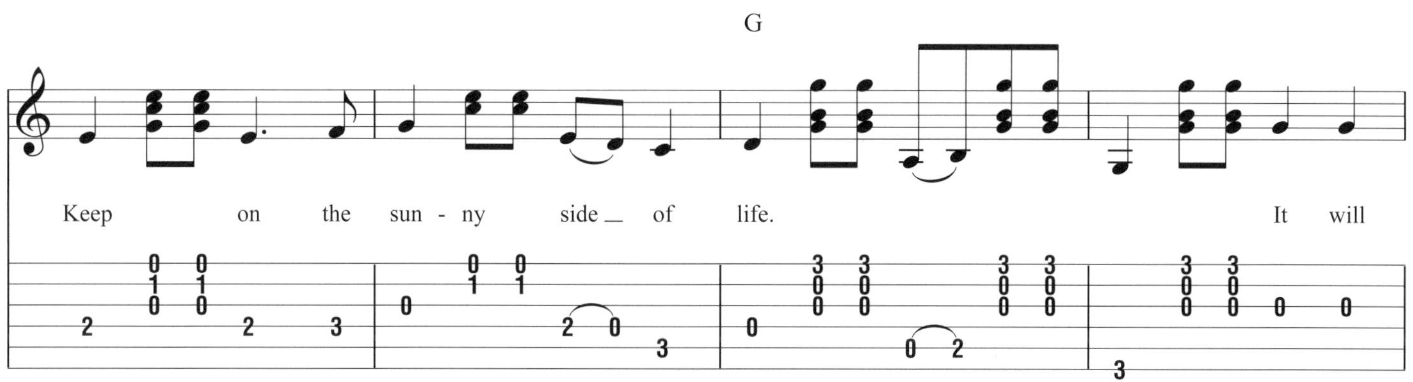

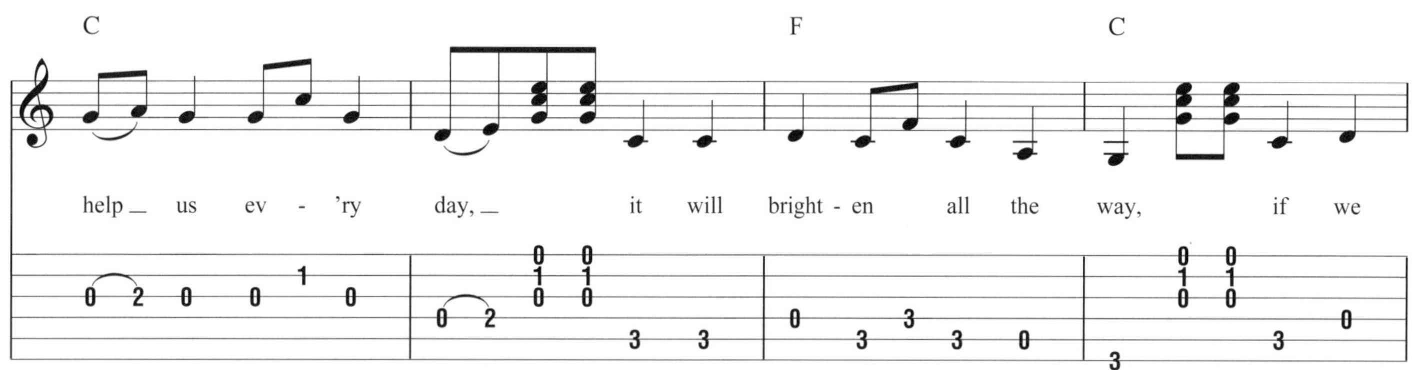

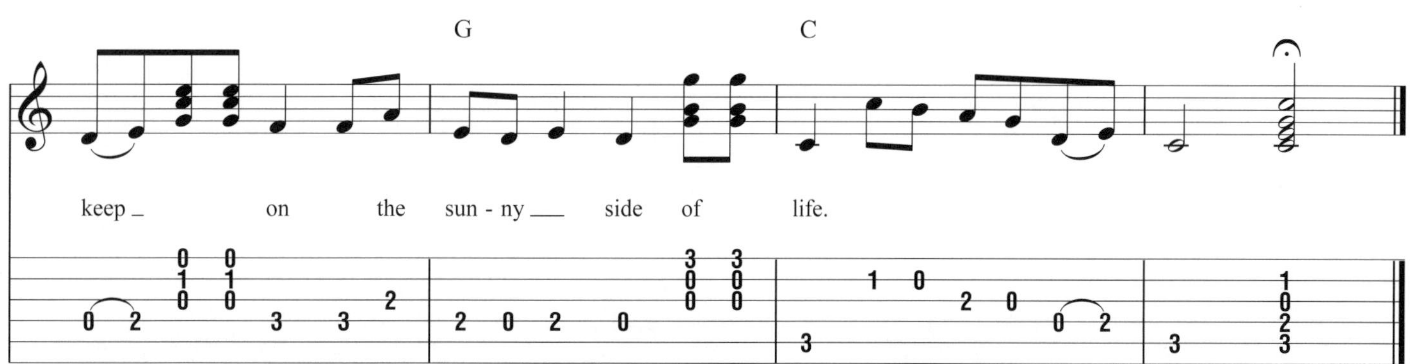

Additional Verses

2. Though a storm and its fury break today, crushing hopes that we cherished so dear,
   Clouds and storm will in time pass away, the sun again will shine bright and clear.
3. Let us greet with a song of hope each day, though the moment be cloudy or fair.
   Let us trust in our Savior away, to keep us, every one, in His care.

Little Cabin Home on the Hill

Words and Music by Lester Flatt and Bill Monroe

Bill Monroe recorded "Little Cabin Home on the Hill" in 1947, when his Bluegrass Boys included Flatt and Scruggs. The recordings made with that lineup served as the original template used by other bluegrass musicians during the "golden age of bluegrass."

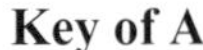

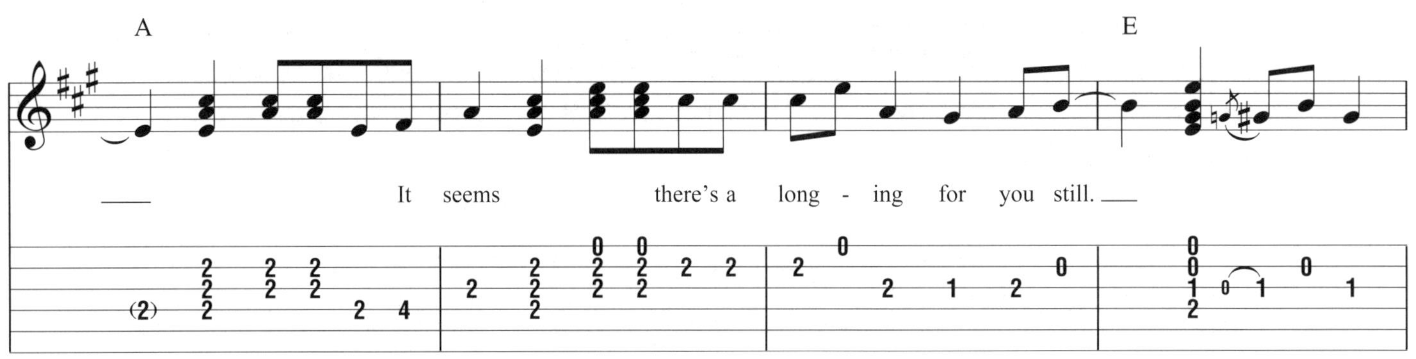

Chorus

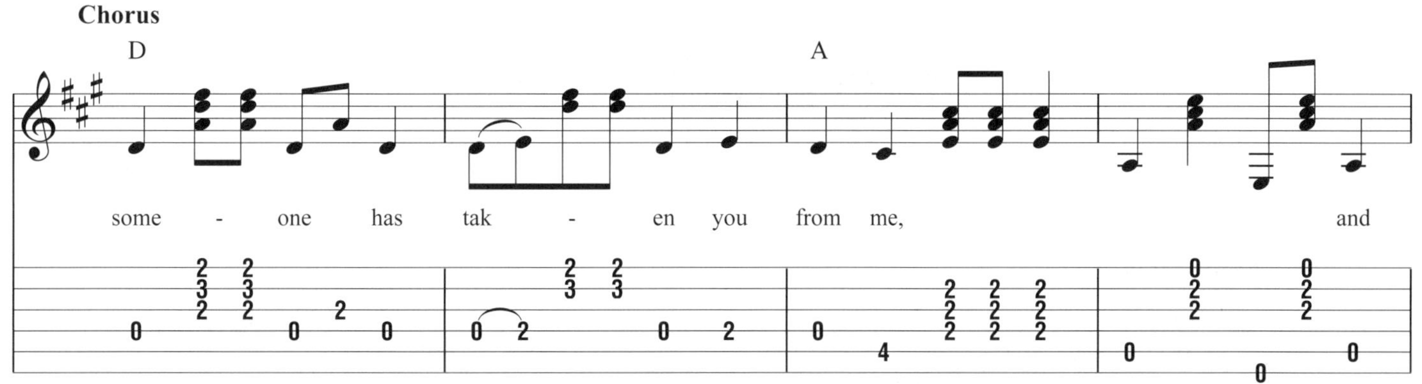

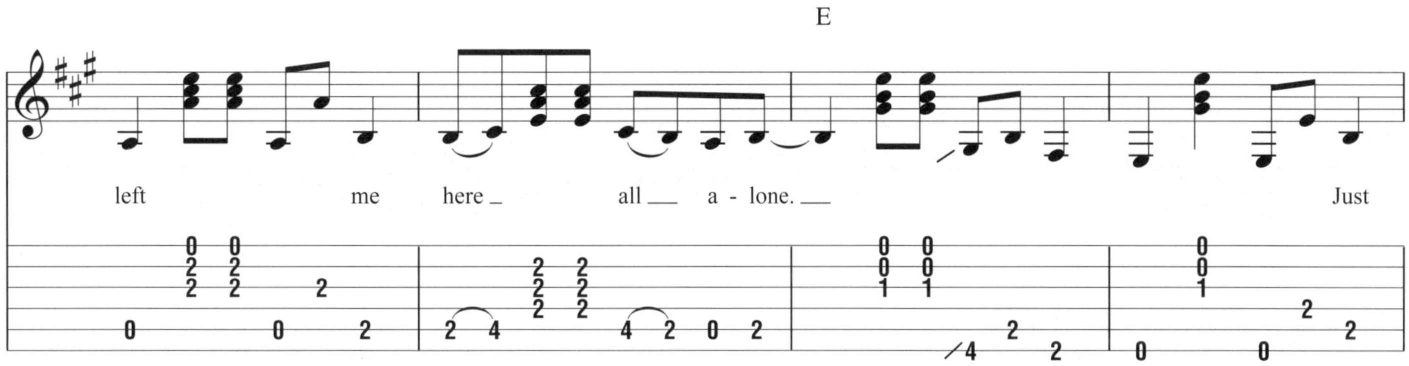

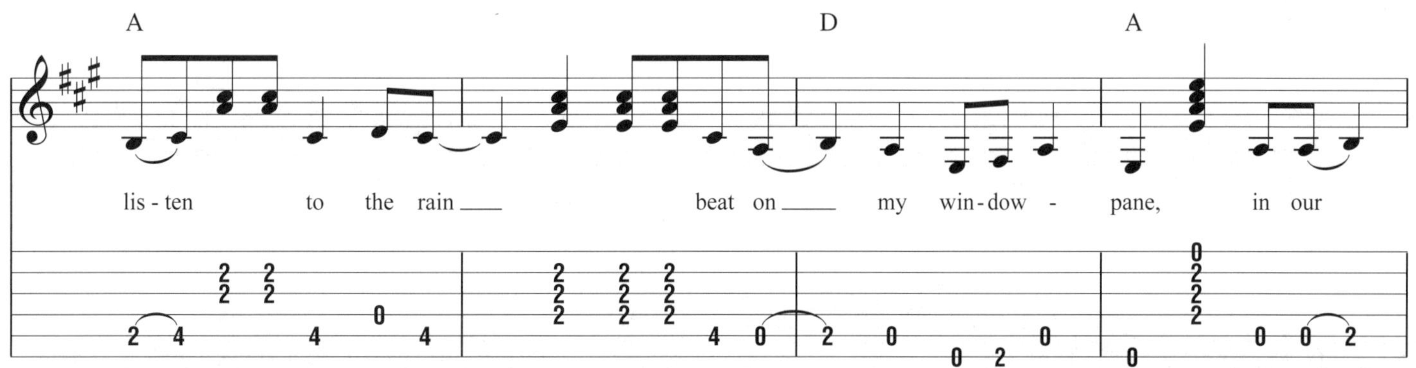

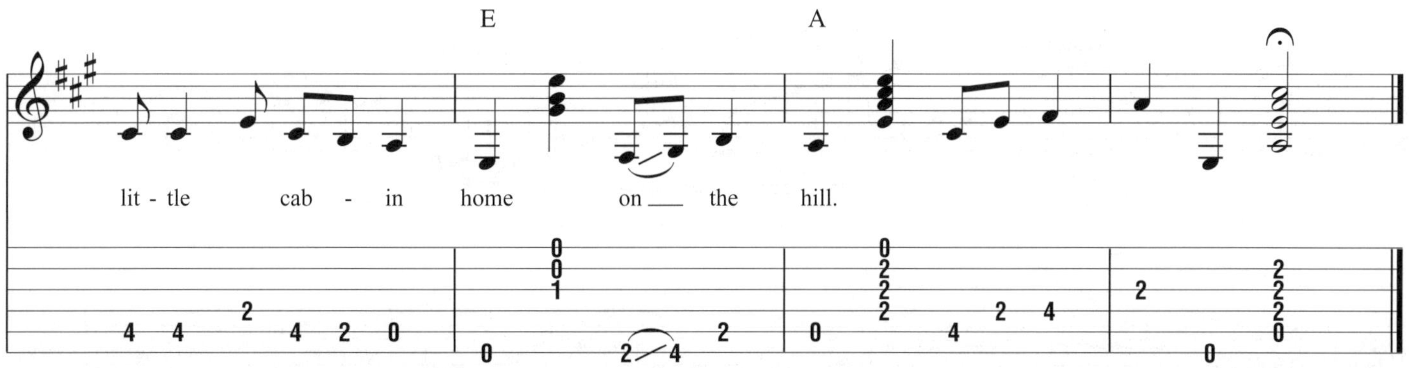

Additional Verses

2. I hope you are happy tonight as you are, but in my heart there's a longing for you still.
   I just keep it there so I won't be alone, in our little cabin home on the hill.

3. Now when you have come to the end of the way, and find there's no more happiness for you,
   Just let your thoughts turn back once more, if you will, to our little cabin home on the hill.

Little Maggie

Traditional

First recorded in 1930, "Little Maggie" is related to another old folk song called "Darling Corey" in that both songs were written about an outlaw woman and share a verse about a gal with a .44 pistol and a banjo (a dangerous combination). "Little Maggie" is one of the first recordings the Stanley Brothers made (in 1948).

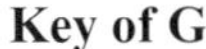

Key of G

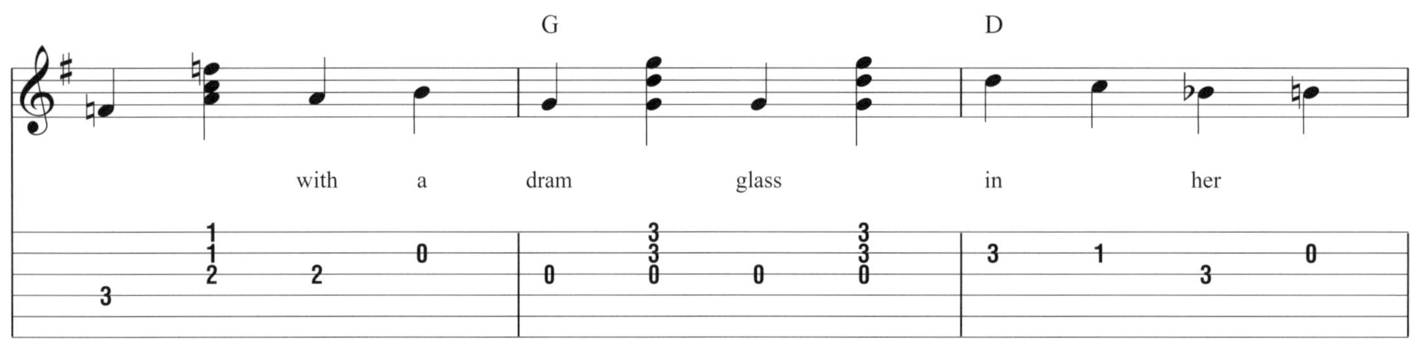

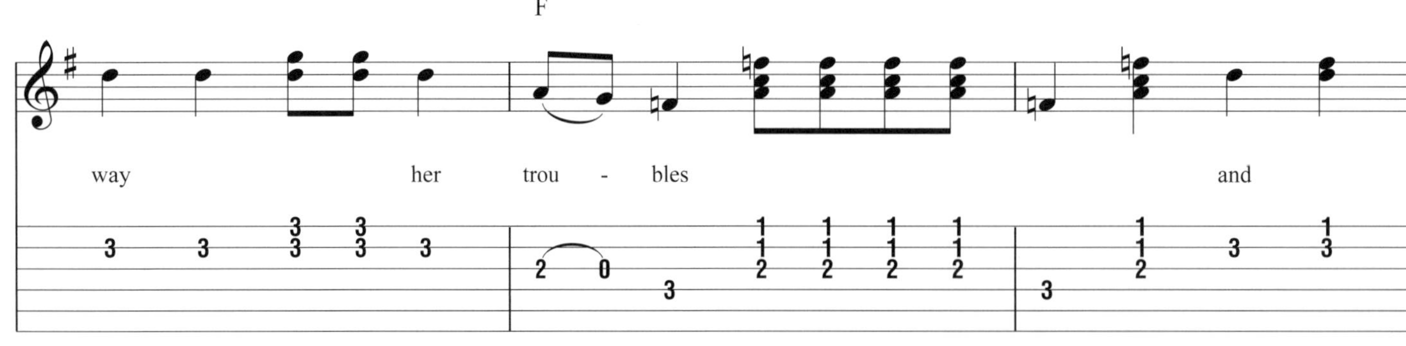

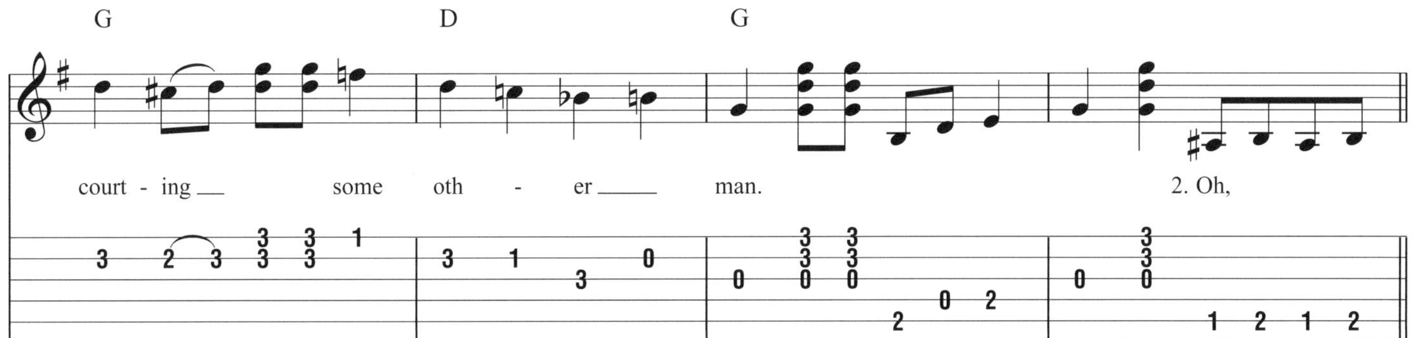

Verse

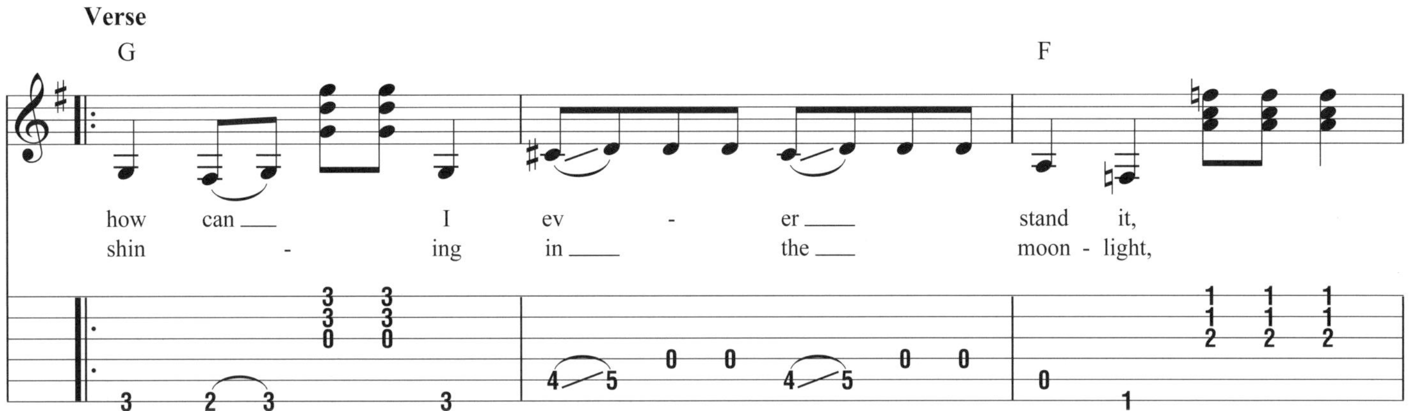

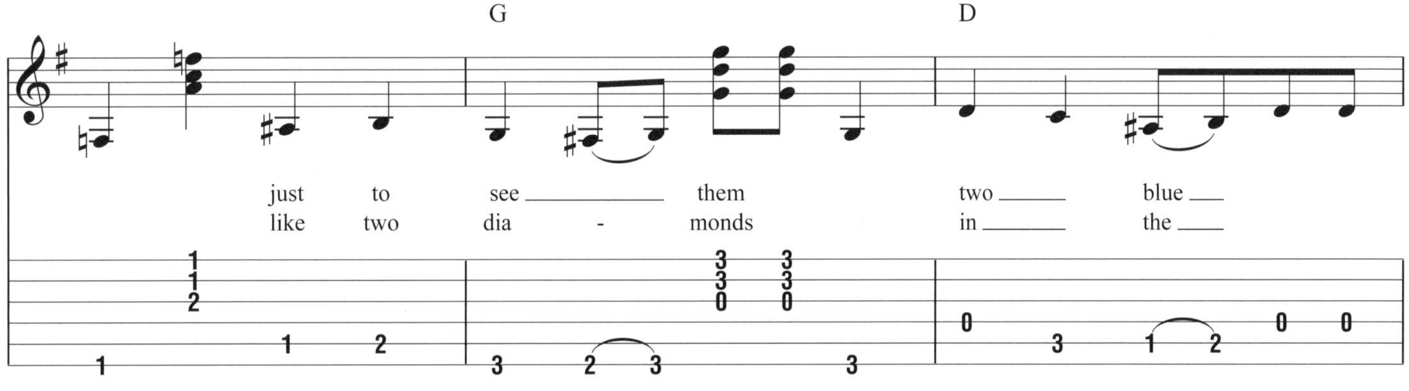

Additional Verses

3. Last time I saw little Maggie, she was sittin' on the banks of the sea
   With a forty-four around her and a banjo on her knee.
4. Lay down your last gold dollar, lay down your gold watch and chain.
   Little Maggie's gonna dance for daddy. Listen to that old banjo ring.
5. Pretty flowers were made for bloomin', pretty stars were made to shine.
   Pretty women were made for lovin'. Little Maggie was made to be mine.

Long Journey Home

Traditional

The old folk song "Long Journey Home" was recorded in 1936 by the Monroe Brothers (Bill Monroe's band with his brother Charlie) and it is still one of the most-performed bluegrass songs today.

Key of A

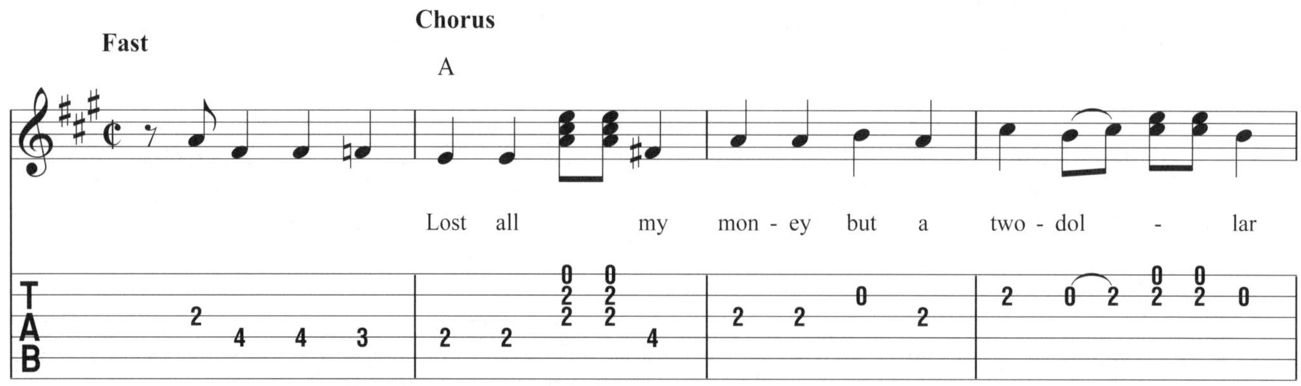

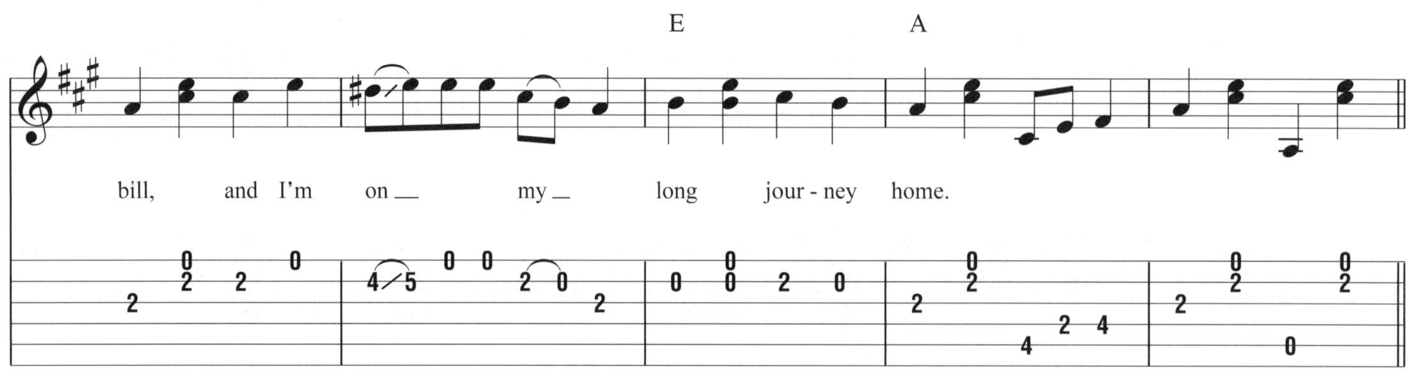

Verse

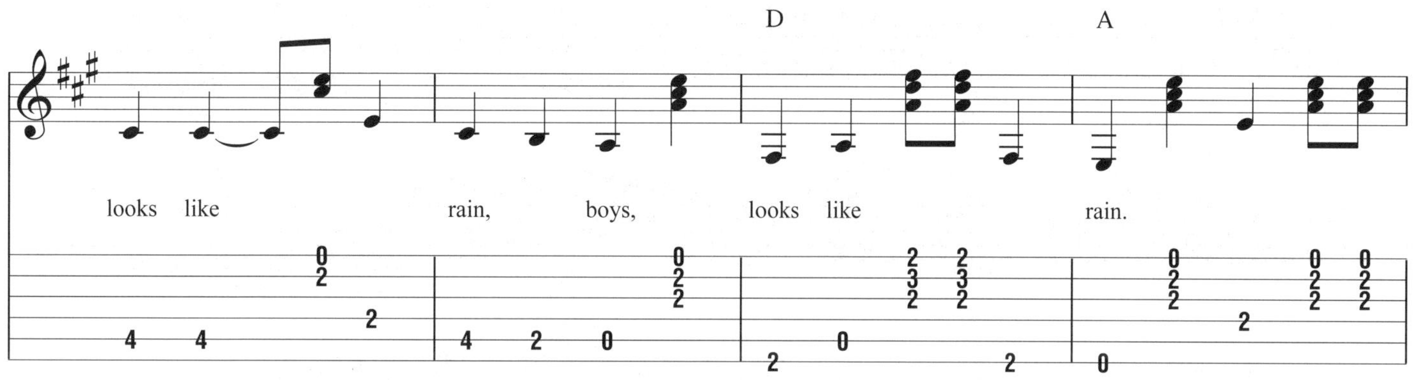

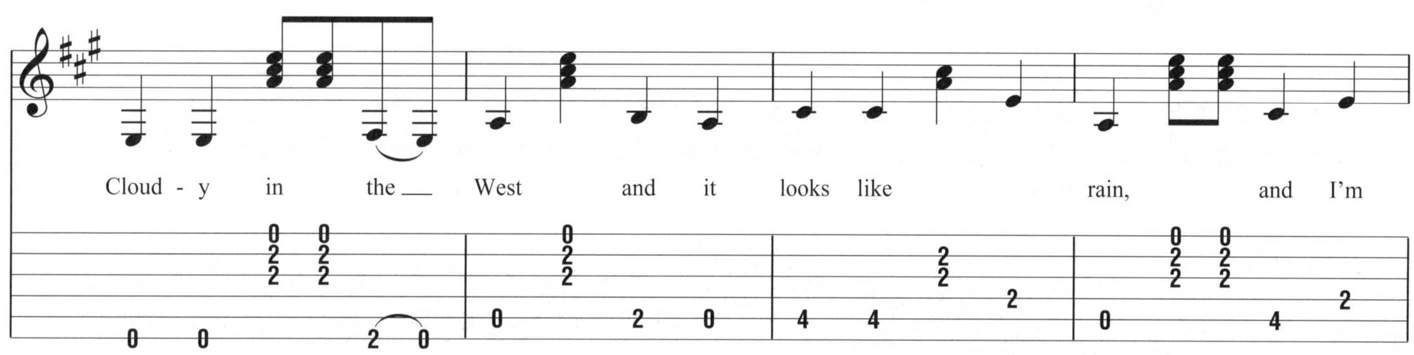

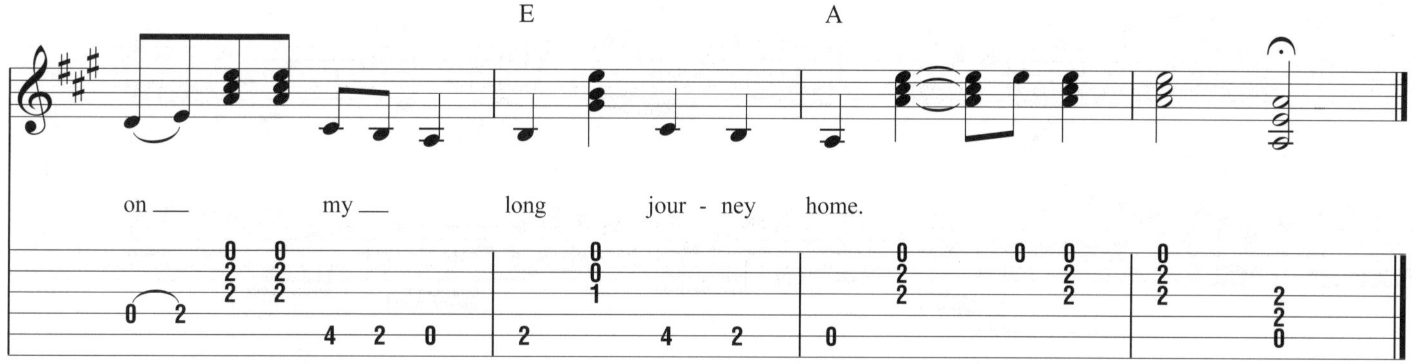

Additional Verses

2. It's dark and a-raining and I got to go home, got to go home, boys, got to go home.
   It's dark and a-raining and I got to go home. I'm on my long journey home.
3. Homesick and lonesome and I'm feeling kind of blue.
   Feeling kind of blue, boys, feeling kind of blue.
   Homesick and lonesome and I'm feeling kind of blue. I'm on my long journey home.
4. There's black smoke a-rising and it surely is a train. Surely is a train, boys, surely is a train.
   There's black smoke a-rising and it surely is a train. I'm on my long journey home.

Love Please Come Home

Words and Music by Leon Jackson

This one was popularized by Reno and Smiley, one of the first bluegrass groups active in the 1950s.

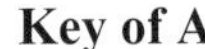

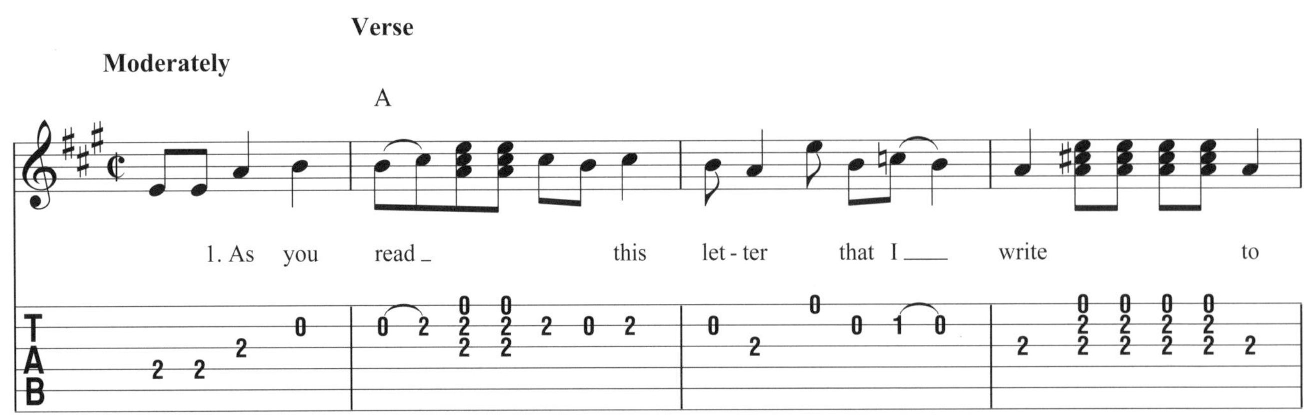

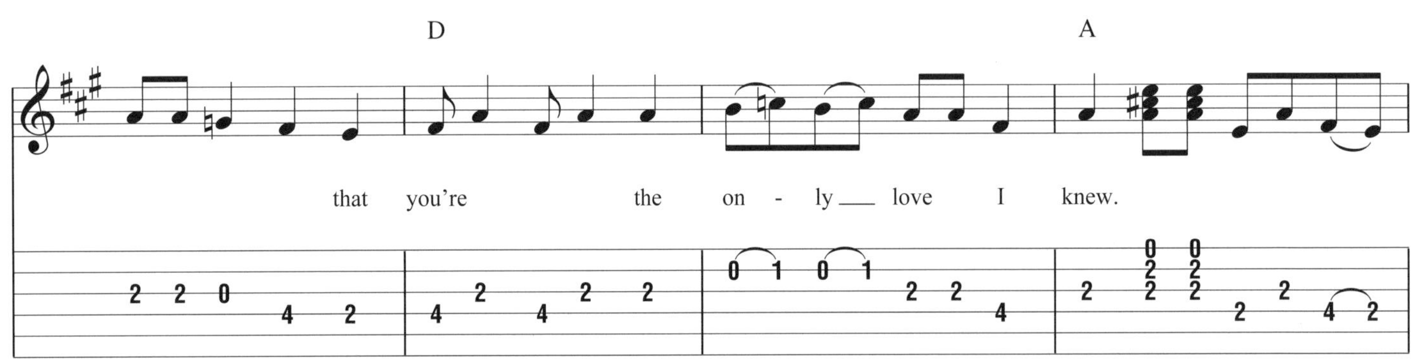

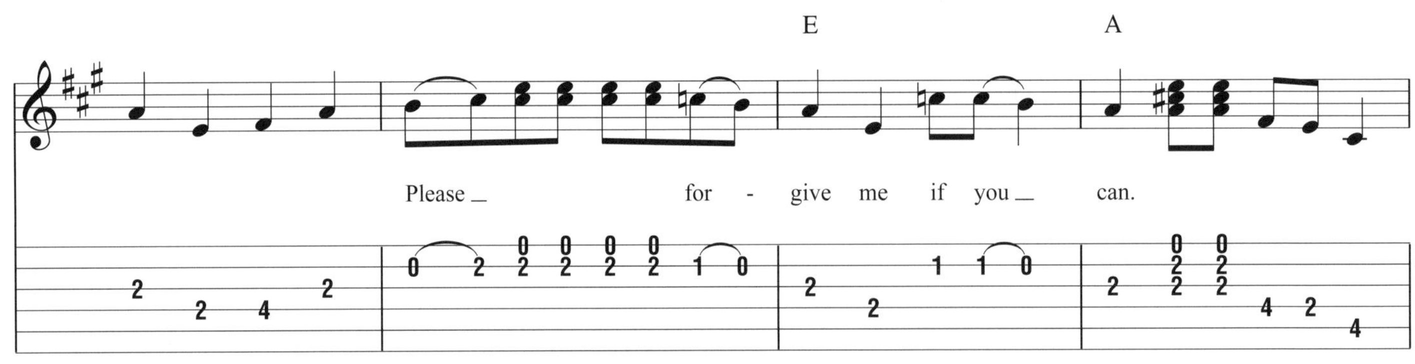

Chorus

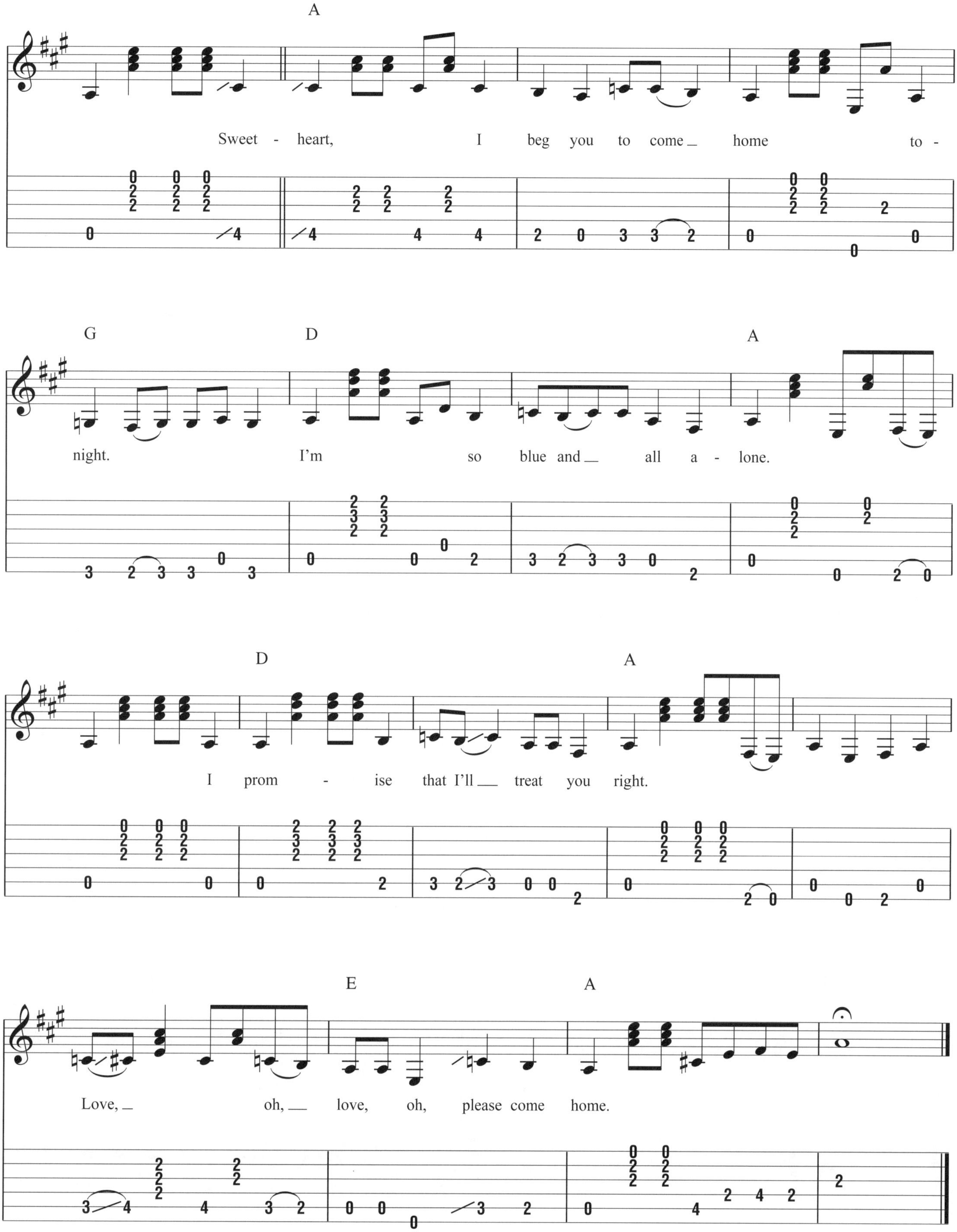

A

Sweet - heart, I beg you to come home to -

G D A

night. I'm so blue and all a - lone.

D A

I prom - ise that I'll treat you right.

Additional Verse

2. That old wind is cold and slowly creeping 'round, and the fire is burning low.
The snow has covered up the ground. Your baby's hungry, sick, and cold.

Molly and Tenbrooks

Words and Music by Bill Monroe

A fictionalized version of an actual horse race that occurred in 1878, this song was written shortly after the event. The version that impacted the bluegrass world was Bill Monroe's 1947 recording. During his 1946 debut performance with Bill Monroe and His Bluegrass Boys at the Grand Ol' Opry, Earl Scruggs caused a sensation with his solo on "Molly and Tenbrooks." Having never heard banjo playing like that, the audience applauded wildly and made him play it over and over again… and banjo picking has never been the same.

Additional Verses

3. Tenbrooks said to Molly, "What makes your head so red?"
   "Running in the hot sun with a fever in my head.
   Fever in my head, oh Lord, fever in my head."

4. Molly said to Tenbrooks, "You're looking mighty squirrel."
   Tenbrooks said to Molly, "I'm leaving this old world.
   Leaving this old world, oh Lord, leaving this old world."

5. Out in California where Molly done as she pleased,
   she come back to old Kentucky, got beat with all ease.
   Beat with all ease, oh Lord, beat with all ease.

6. The women's all a-laughing, the children all a-crying,
   Men all a-hollering old Tenbrooks a-flying.
   Old Tenbrooks a-flying, Lord, old Tenbrooks a-flying.

7. Kiper, Kiper, you're not riding right,
   Molly's beating old Tenbrooks clear out of sight.
   Clear out of sight, oh Lord, clear out of sight.

8. Kiper, Kiper, Kiper my son.
   Give old Tenbrooks the bridle and let old Tenbrooks run.
   Let old Tenbrooks run, oh Lord, let old Tenbrooks run.

9. Go and catch old Tenbrooks and hitch him in the shade.
   We're gonna bury old Molly in a coffin readymade.
   In a coffin readymade, oh Lord, in a coffin readymade.

Nine Pound Hammer

Traditional African-American

This work song was recorded by string bands in the 1920s and by the Monroe Brothers in the 1930s. Bill Monroe continued to record and perform it later with his Bluegrass Boys, and Merle Travis' 1947 fingerpicking guitar version also helped popularize the tune.

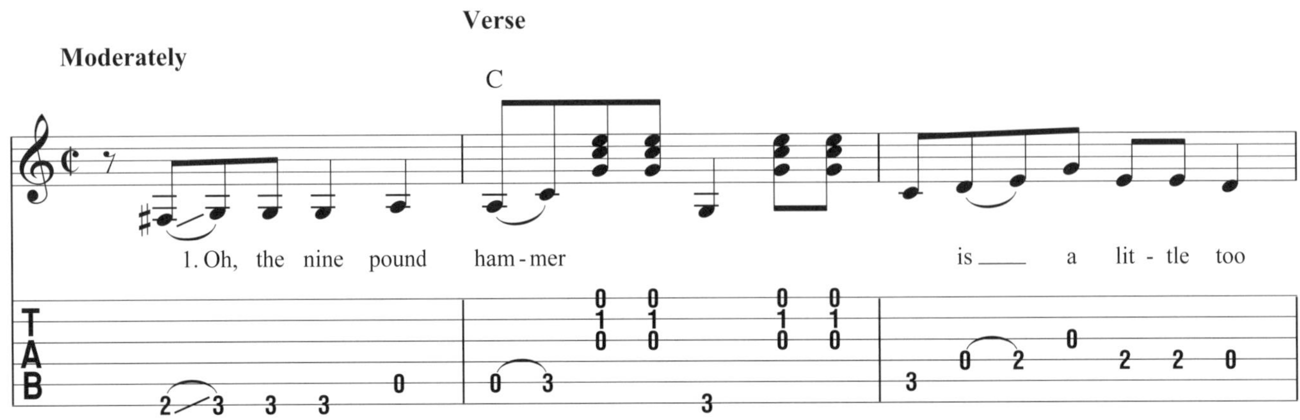

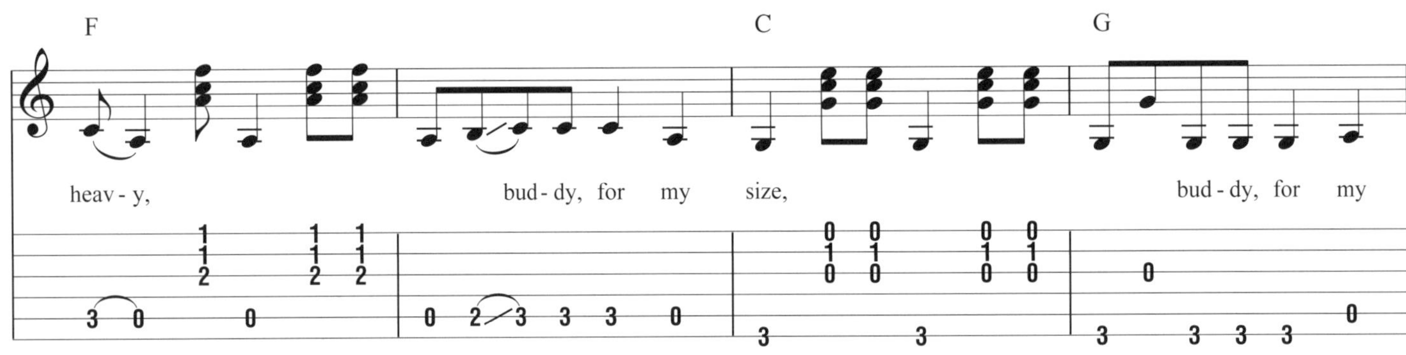

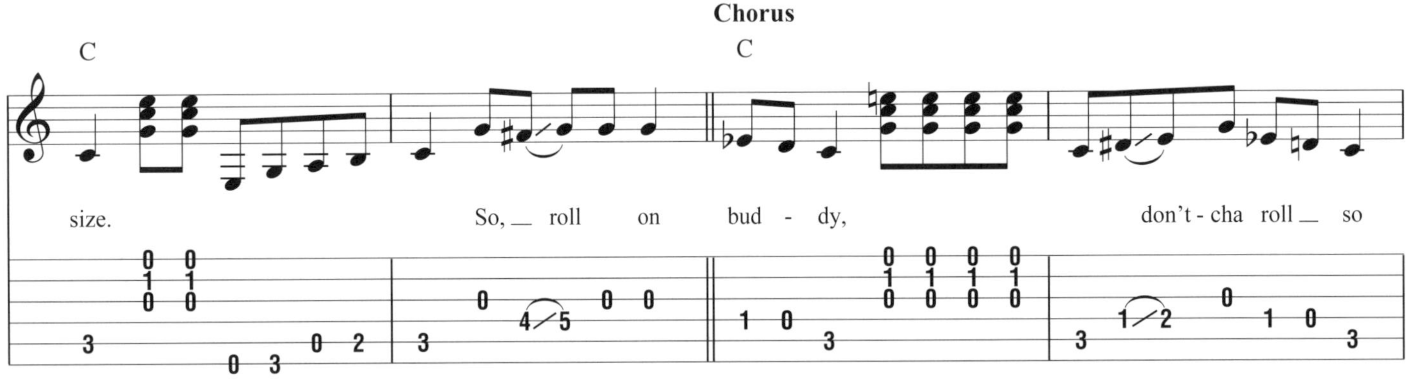

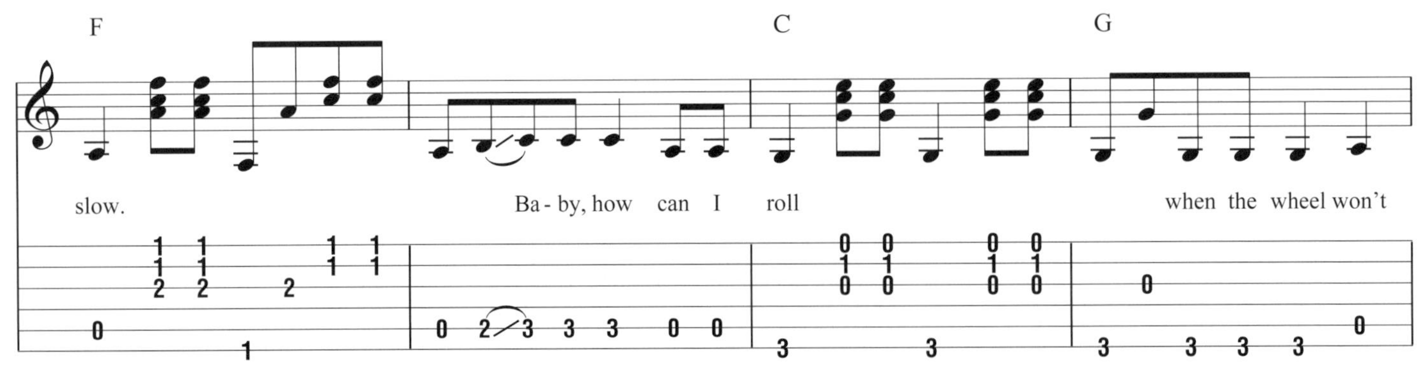

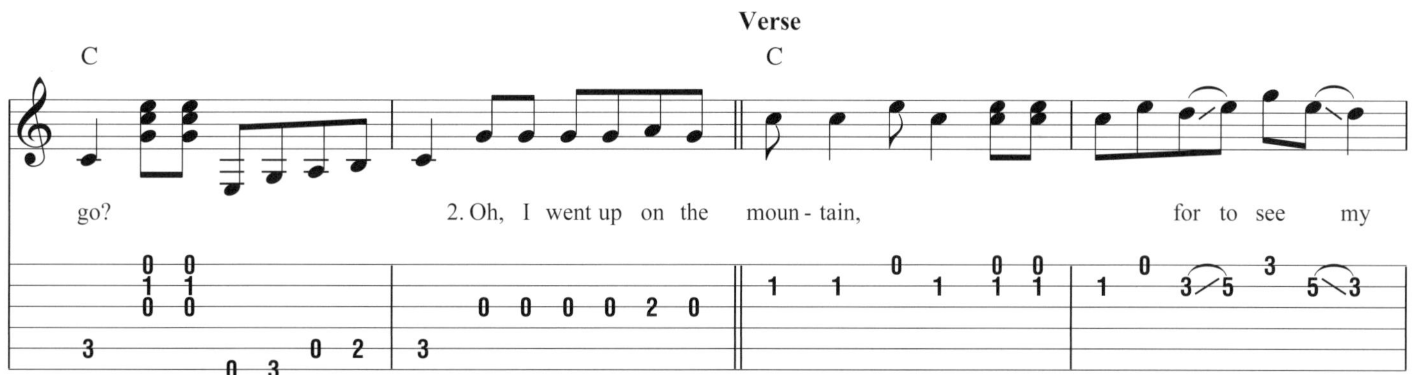

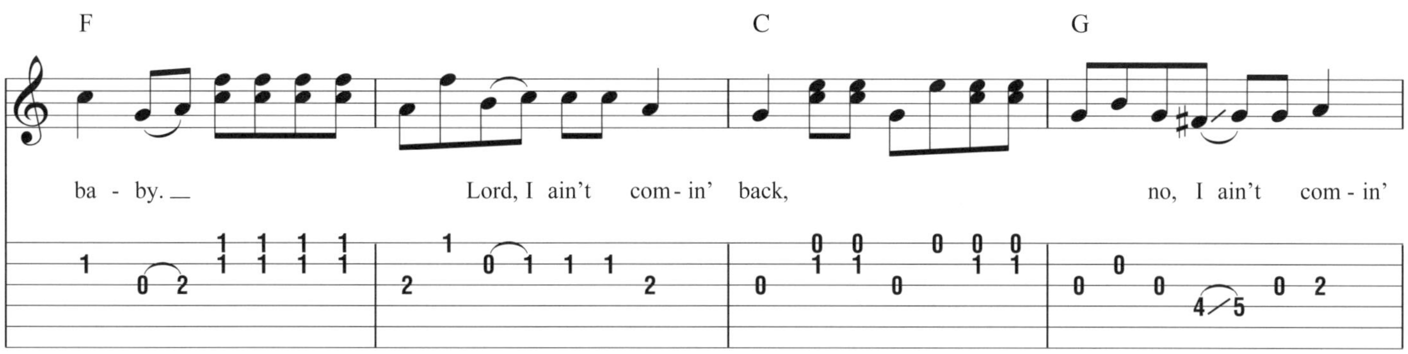

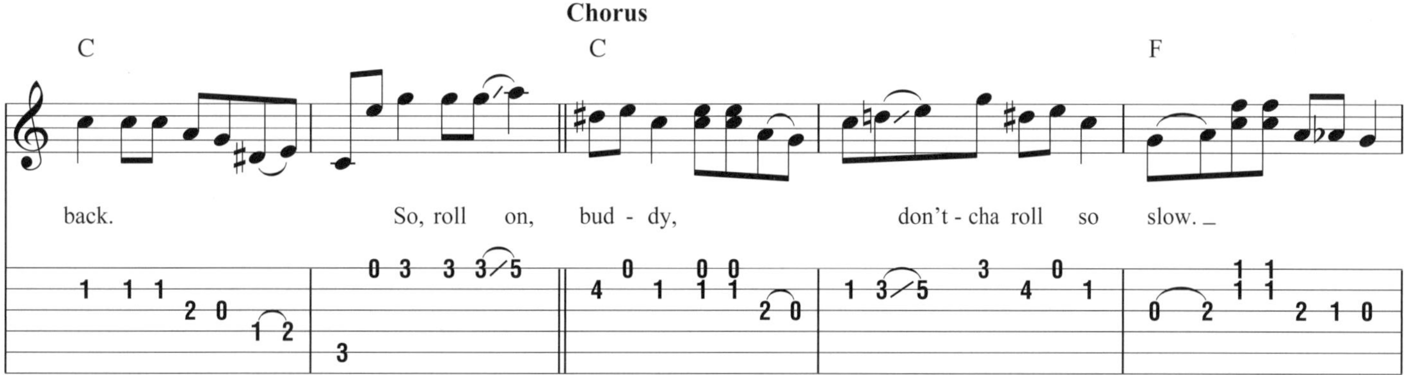

Additional Verses

3. There ain't one hammer in this tunnel
   That'll ring like mine, that'll ring like mine.

4. Rings like silver, and it shines like gold.
   Rings like silver, and it shines like gold .

5. Oh, the nine pound hammer, that killed John Henry,
   Ain't a-gonna kill me, it ain't gonna kill me.

Old Home Place

Words by Mitchell F. Jayne
Music by Rodney Dillard

The Dillards (known to many as "The Darlings"—as they were called when they appeared on Andy Griffith TV shows) introduced this song in the early 1960s. Since then it has become a bluegrass standard. It tells a story often told in bluegrass tunes: A young man leaves his rural home, lured by the big city, and returns to find everything gone to seed. Two other classic examples that tell a similar story are: "The Fields Have Turned Brown" (great metaphor) and "Rank Stranger."

Key of G

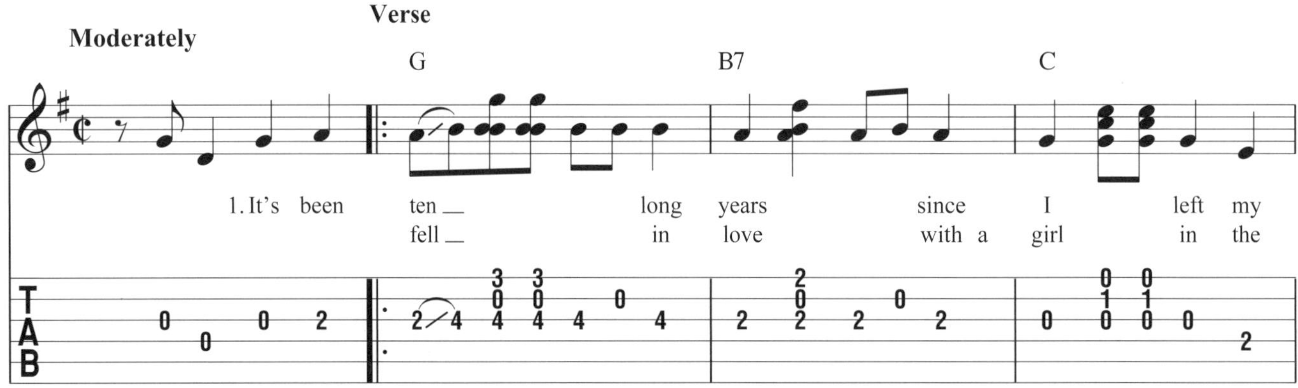

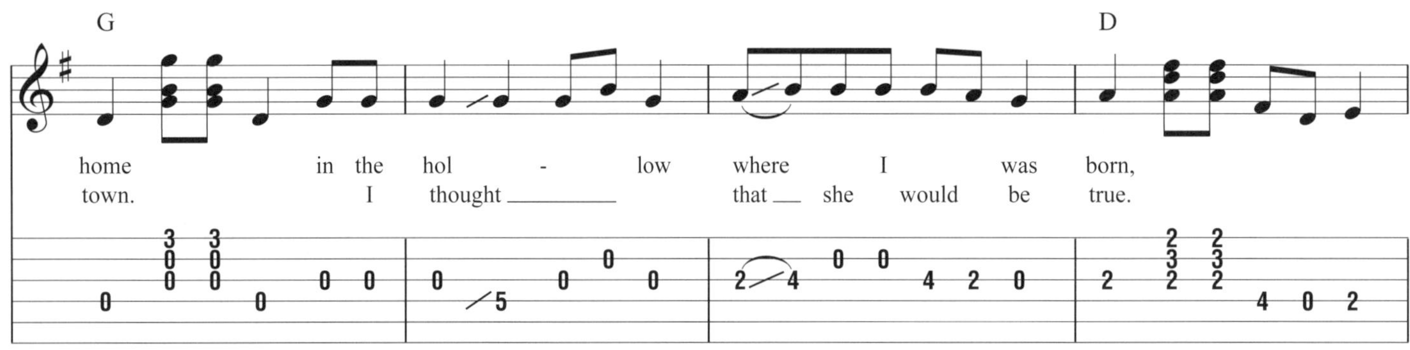

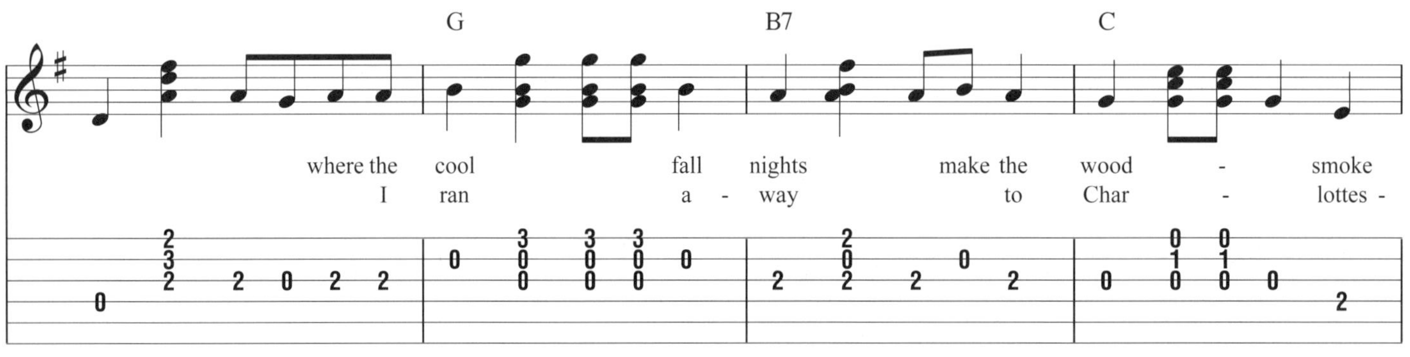

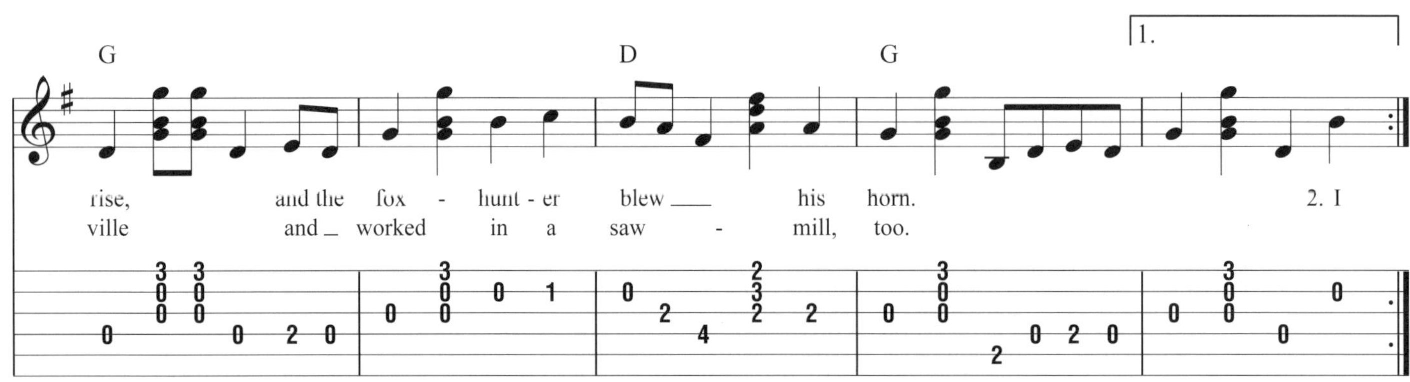

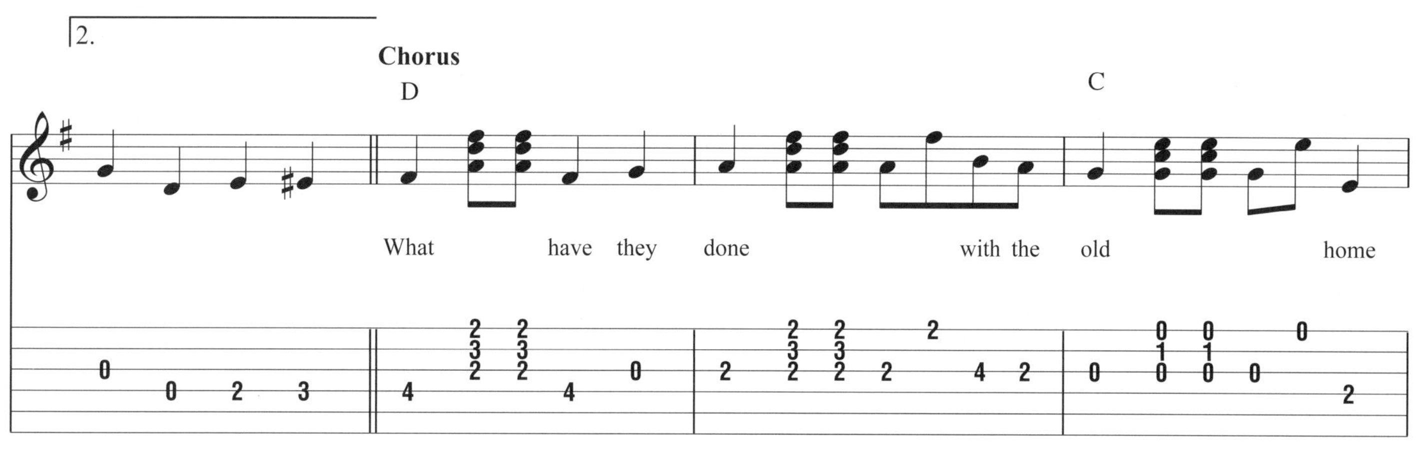

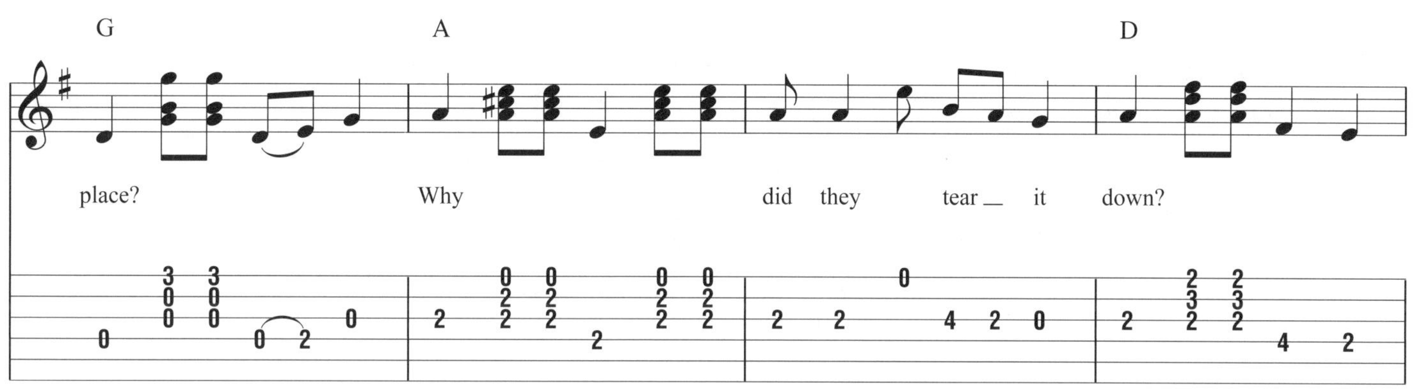

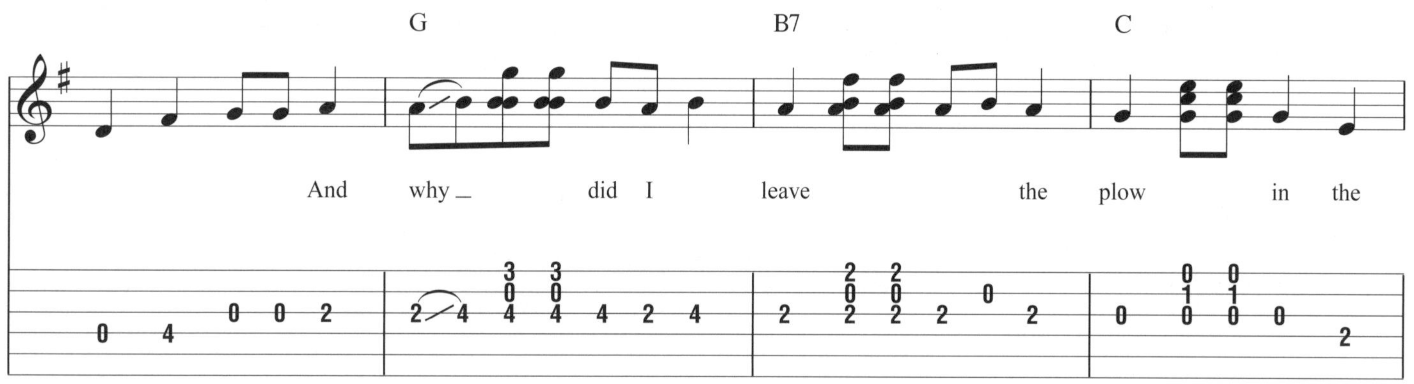

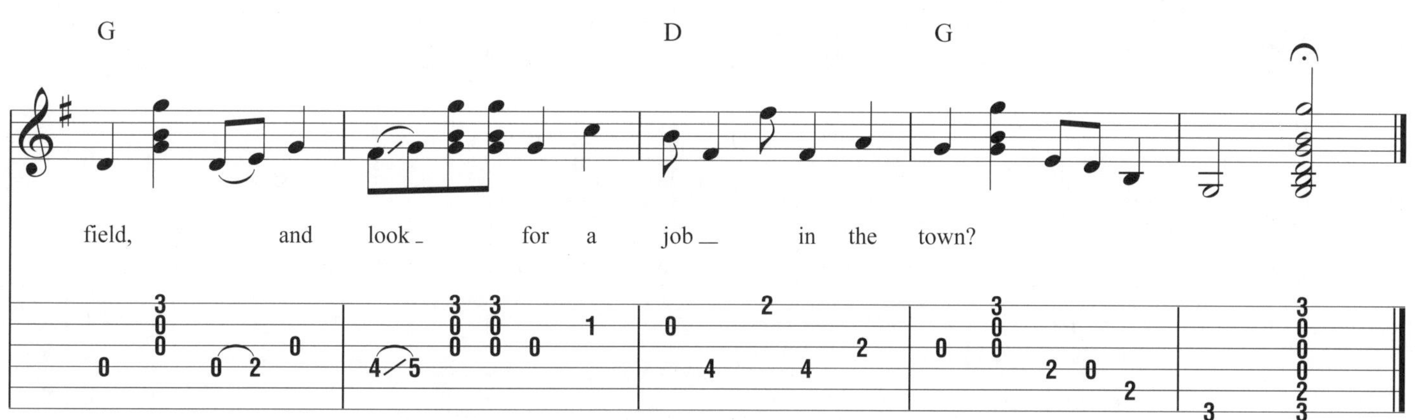

Additional Verses

3. Well, my girl she ran off with somebody else. The taverns took all my pay.
   And here I stand where the old home stood, before they took it away.

4. Now, the geese they fly south and the cold wind blows, as I stand here and hang my head.
   I've lost my love, I've lost my home, and now I wish that I was dead.

Old Joe Clark

Tennessee Folksong

One of the most popular fiddle tunes in the bluegrass tradition, "Old Joe Clark" goes back as far as the 1800s. The 90 or more verses indicate its possible origin as a children's song. There are many conflicting stories about who the "real" Joe Clark was: He was a civil war soldier from Kentucky, a murderer from Virginia, or somebody else entirely. Bluegrassers rarely sing the verses, rather playing it as an instrumental in the key of A. (A typical verse: "I wouldn't marry an old schoolteacher, tell you the reason why… She'd blow her nose in old cornbread and call it pumpkin pie!")

Key of G (Capo II for key of A)

1.
2.
D
G
G
A
G
D
1.
2.
G
D
G
G
B
G
F
1.
2.
G
D
G
G

Pig in the Pen

Words and Music by Ralph Stanley and Carter Stanley

The Stanley Brothers may have been the first bluegrass band to record "Pig in the Pen," but there's a much older recording by "Fiddlin'" Arthur Smith (not to be confused with Arthur "Guitar Boogie" Smith), who wrote many country hits and may have written this tune as well. Deadheads know the tune because it was one of Jerry Garcia's favorites and he included it on his 1975 bluegrass LP, *Old and In the Way* (one of the best-selling bluegrass LPs of all time).

Key of G

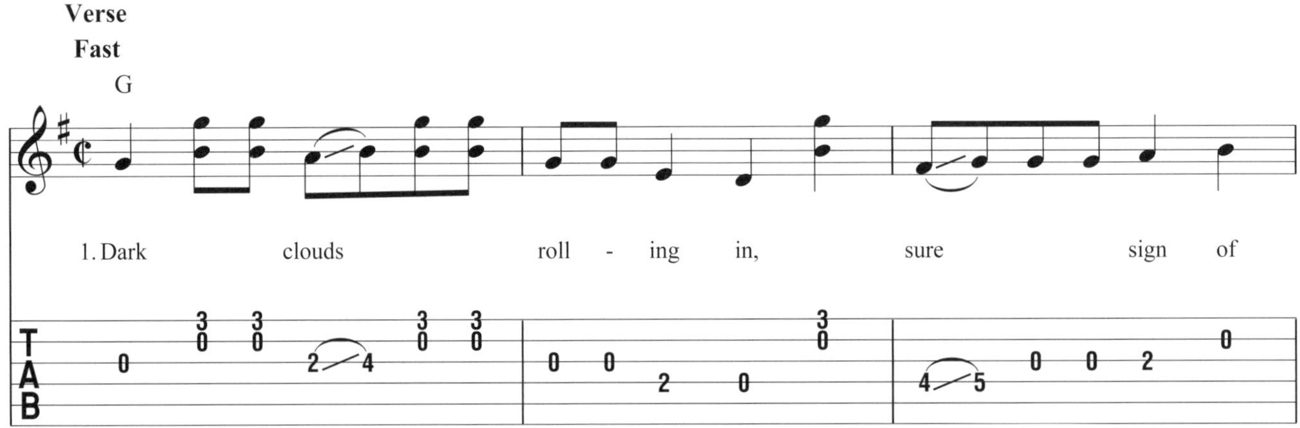

Chorus

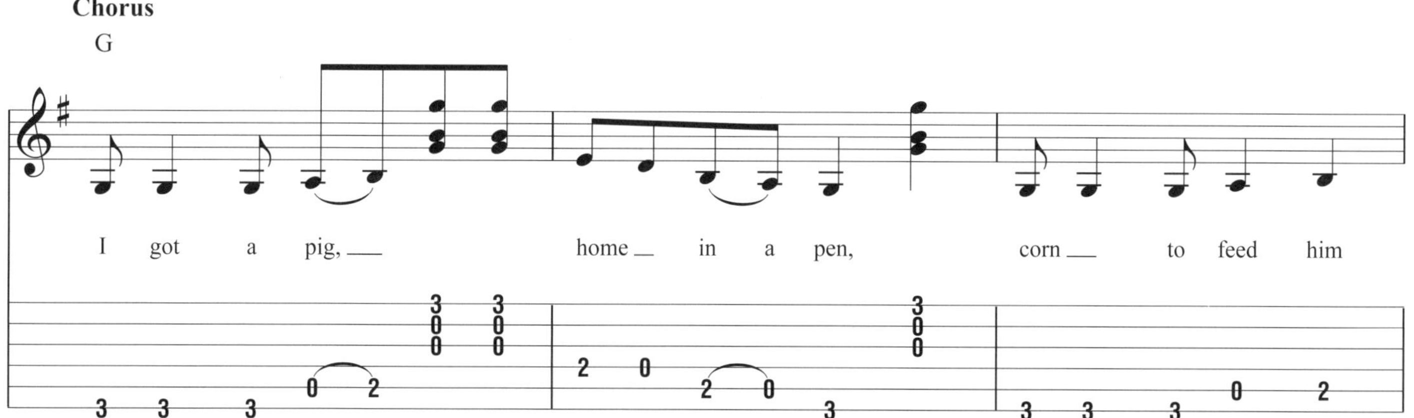

Additional Verses

2. Goin' on the mountain to sow a little cane.
   Raise a barrel of sorghum to sweeten lil' Liza Jane.
3. Yonder comes that gal of mine, how you think I know?
   I can tell by that gingham gown hangin' down so low.
4. Bake them biscuits, baby, bake 'em good n' brown.
   When you get them biscuits baked, we're Alabamy bound.
5. When she sees me comin', she wrings her hands and cries,
   Says, "Yonder comes the sweetest boy that ever lived or died."
6. Now when she sees me leavin', she wrings her hands and cries,
   "Yonder goes the meanest boy that ever lived or died."

The Red Haired Boy

Old Time Fiddle Tune

Many American fiddle tunes that are favorites among bluegrass bands originated in the British Isles. "The Red Haired Boy," also called "The Red Headed Irishman," is an Irish reel that crossed over into bluegrass territory. Its history can be traced back at least as far as the 1800s.

Key of G (Capo II for Key of A)

1.
2.
A
D
G
D
G
G
C
G
F
G
C
1.
2.
B
G
D
G
D
G
F
C
G
F
G
1.
2.
C
G
D
G
D
G

Reuben

By Earl Scruggs

When Earl Scruggs was ten years old, sitting on the floor, picking the old song "Reuben's Train" on the banjo, he stumbled upon the three-finger rolls that became the foundation of his bluegrass banjo or "Scruggs' Picking" style. Today, every bluegrass banjo player gets started by learning rolls, licks, and solos; bluegrass bands usually play "Reuben" the way Earl recorded it (as an instrumental). There are countless versions of "Reuben's Train" dating all the way back to the very early days of recording. The song seems to be about a real train designed by Reuben Wells in the 1860s, and several verses are the basis for the folk song "Nine Hundred Miles" (also known as "Five Hundred Miles"). In the following arrangement, some lyrics are included even though they are not in the Flatt and Scruggs recording. Also, this arrangement features solos that roughly imitate Scruggs' banjo variations.

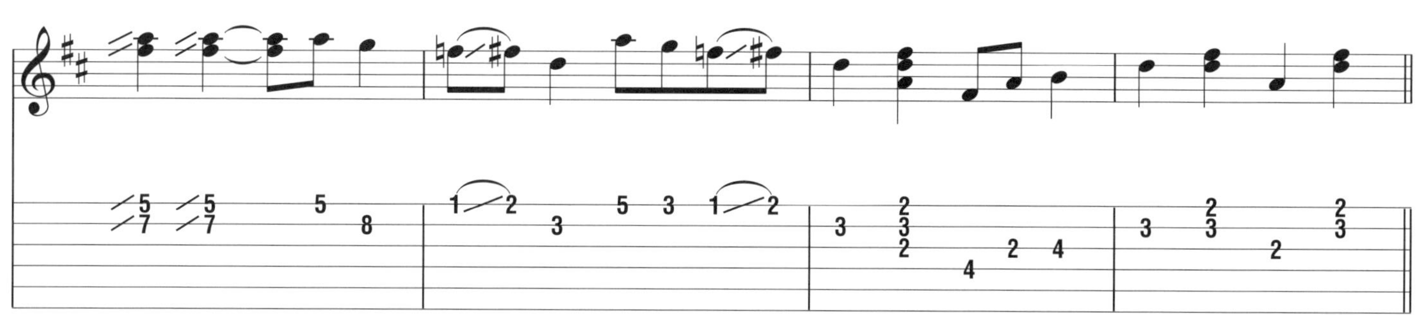

D7

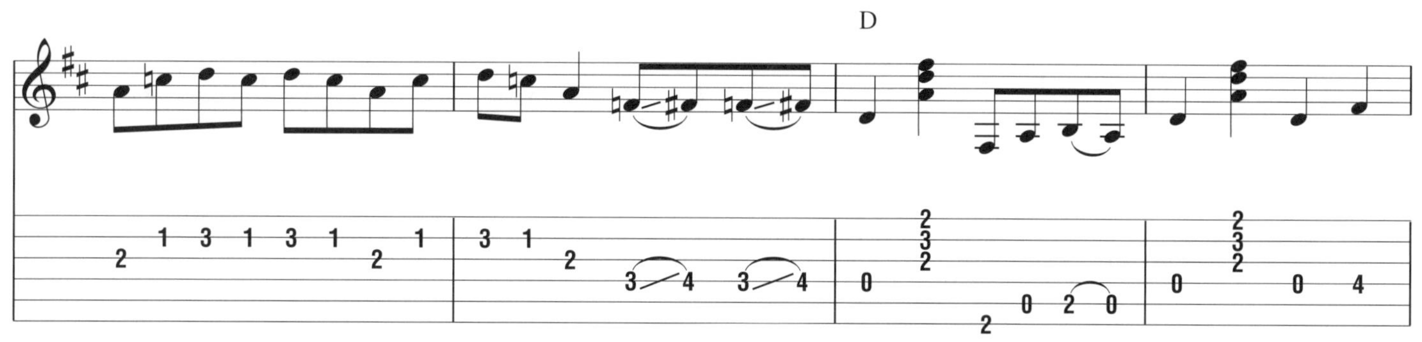
D

D7
D

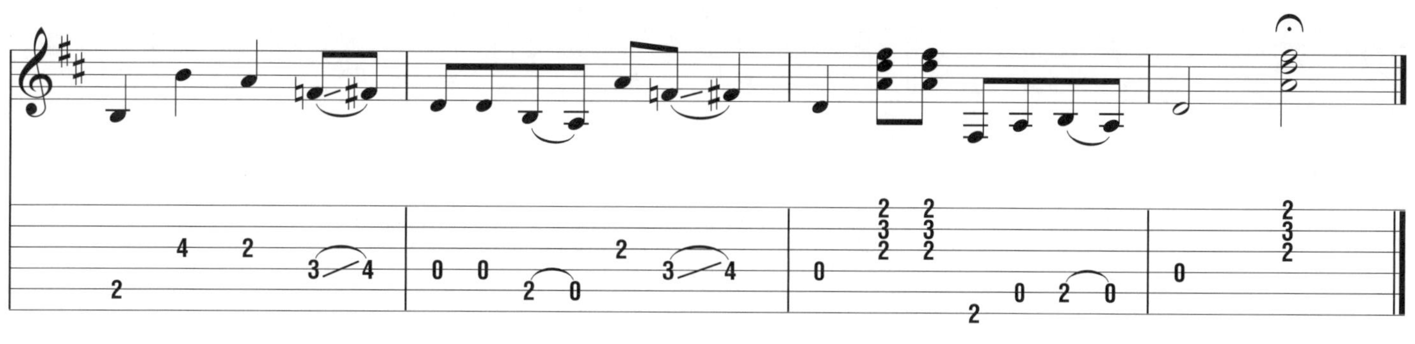

Rocky Top

Words and Music by Boudleaux Bryant and Felice Bryant

Felice and Boudleaux Bryant were the songwriting couple responsible for hits like "All I Have to Do Is Dream" and "Bye Bye Love" (Everly Brothers), "Love Hurts" (Roy Orbison), "Raining in My Heart" (Buddy Holly), "You're the Reason God Made Oklahoma," and many more. They wrote "Rocky Top" in 1967 and later that year the Osborne Brothers' rendition became one of the few bluegrass recordings ever to reach the country charts. (Lynn Anderson's cover charted again in 1970.)

Key of G

Brightly

Verse

G C G

1. Wish _ that I was on old Rock - y Top,
Ain't _ no smog - gy smoke on Rock - y Top,

Em D 1. G 2. G

down _ in the Ten - nes - see Hills. bills.
ain't _ no tel - e - phone

Verse

G C G

2. Once _ I had a girl _ on Rock - y Top,
Wild _ as a mink, but sweet _ as so - da pop,

Em D 1. G 2. G

half _ bear, the oth - er half cat. _ that.
I _ still dream a - bout

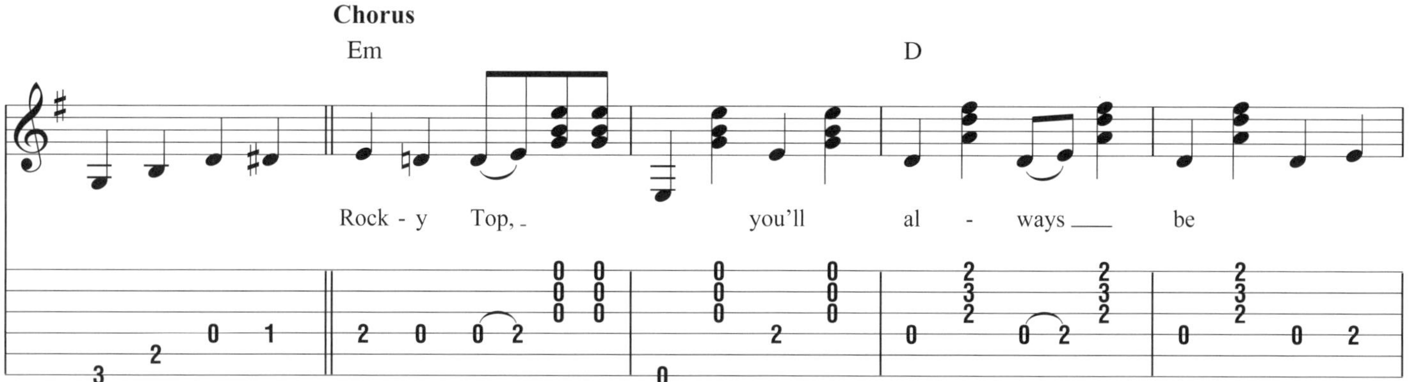

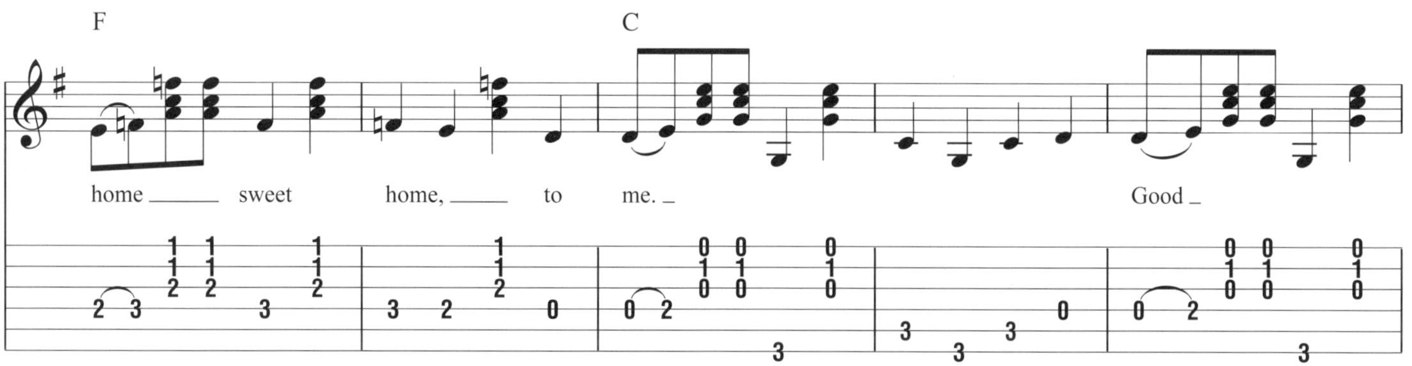

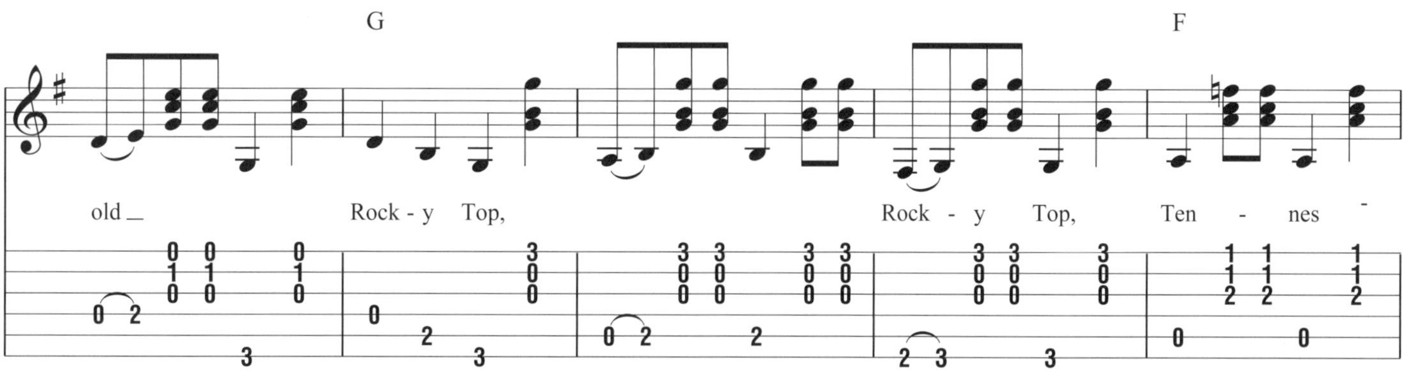

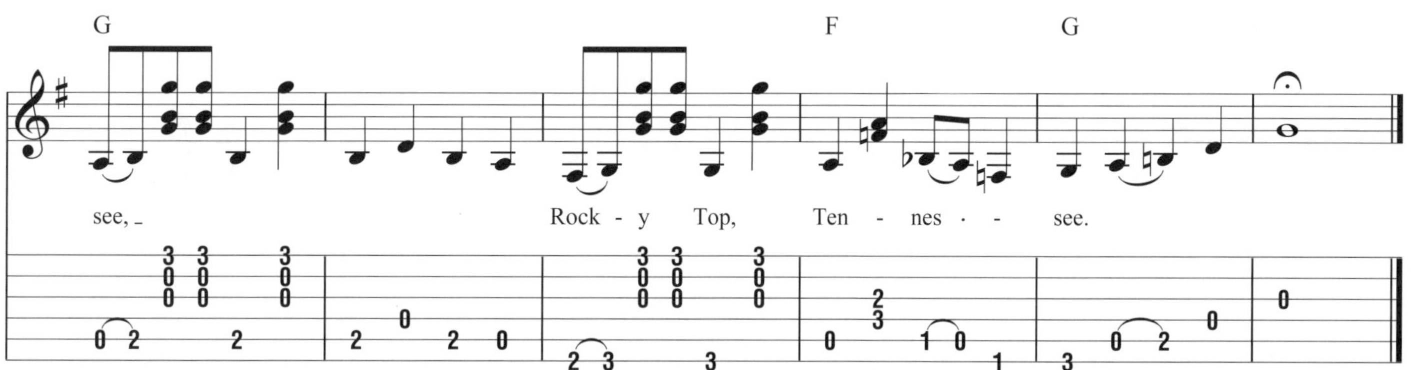

Additional Verses

3. Once two strangers climbed old Rocky Top, looking for a moonshine still.
   Strangers ain't come down from Rocky Top. Reckon they never will.

4. Corn won't grow at all on Rocky Top, dirt's too rocky by far.
   That's why all the folks on Rocky Top get their corn from a jar.

5. I've had years of cramped up city life, trapped like a duck in a pen.
   All I know is, it's a pity life can't be simple again.

Roll in My Sweet Baby's Arms

Traditional

Posey Rorer, Buster Carter, and Preston Young recorded a version of this old folk song in 1931. The Flatt and Scruggs' 1951 arrangement has been covered by countless bluegrass and country artists.

Additional Verses

2. Now, where was you last Friday night while I was lyin' in jail?
   Walkin' the streets with another man, you wouldn't even go my bail.
3. I know your parents don't like me, they drove me away from your door.
   If I had my life to live over again, I'd never go there anymore.
4. Mama's a beauty operator, sister can weave and can spin.
   Dad's got an interest in the old cotton mill, just watch the money roll in.

Salt Creek

By Bill Monroe and Bradford Keith

In 1929 old-time fiddler Clark Kessinger recorded "Salt River," a fiddle tune named after a river in Kentucky. In 1964, when banjo player Bill Keith was in Bill Monroe's band, the two Bills reworked the tune and recorded it with the name "Salt Creek" (named after the creek in Indiana where Monroe held the annual bluegrass Bean Blossom Festival). Both Bills are gone now, but the festival continues, and "Salt Creek" is still performed by bluegrass bands.

Key of A

A

Brightly

A D G

E A D E

B

A A G

A G E A

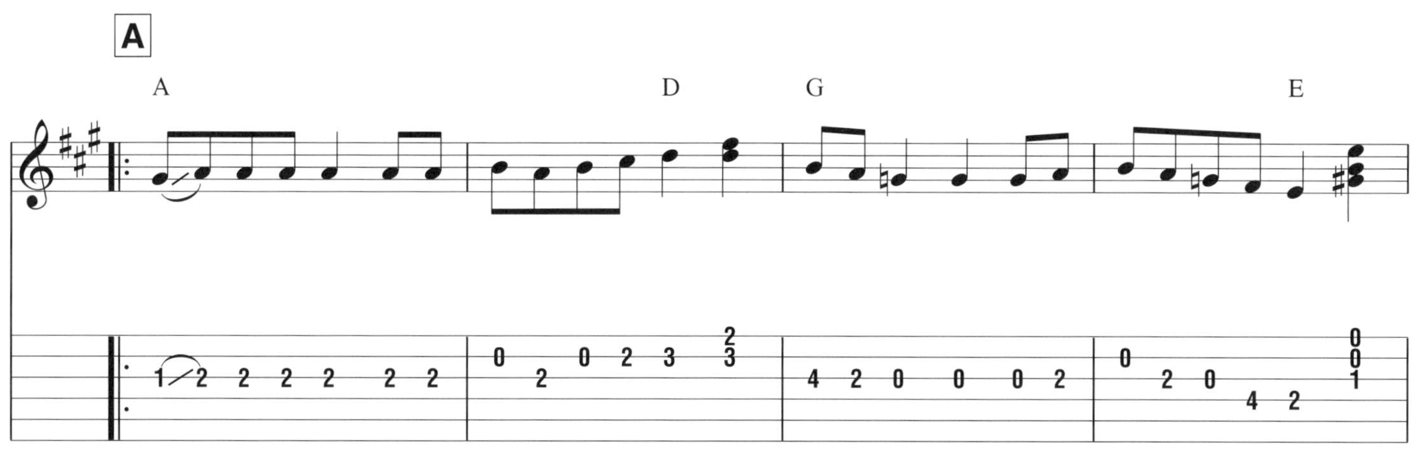
A
A
D
G
E

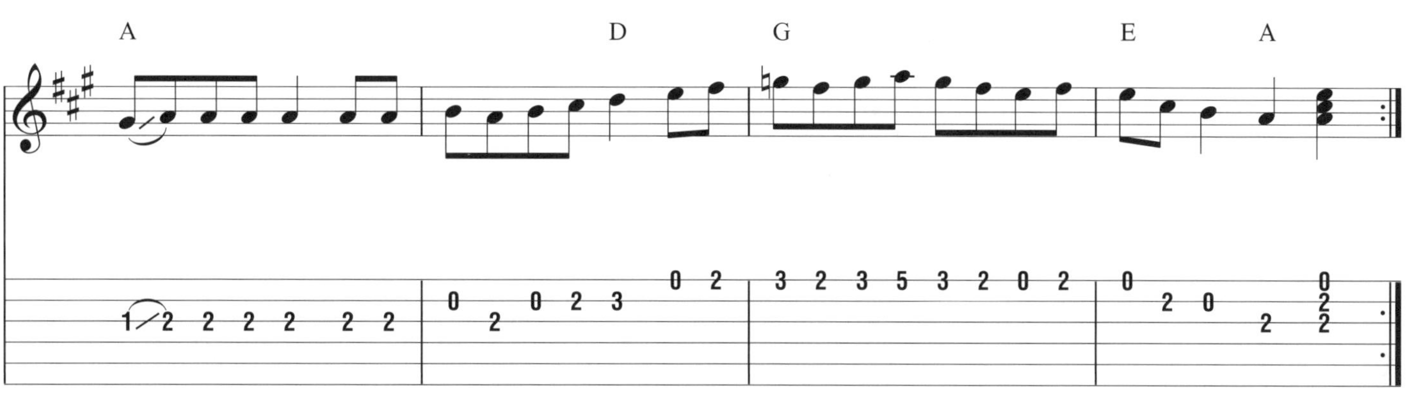
A
D
G
E
A

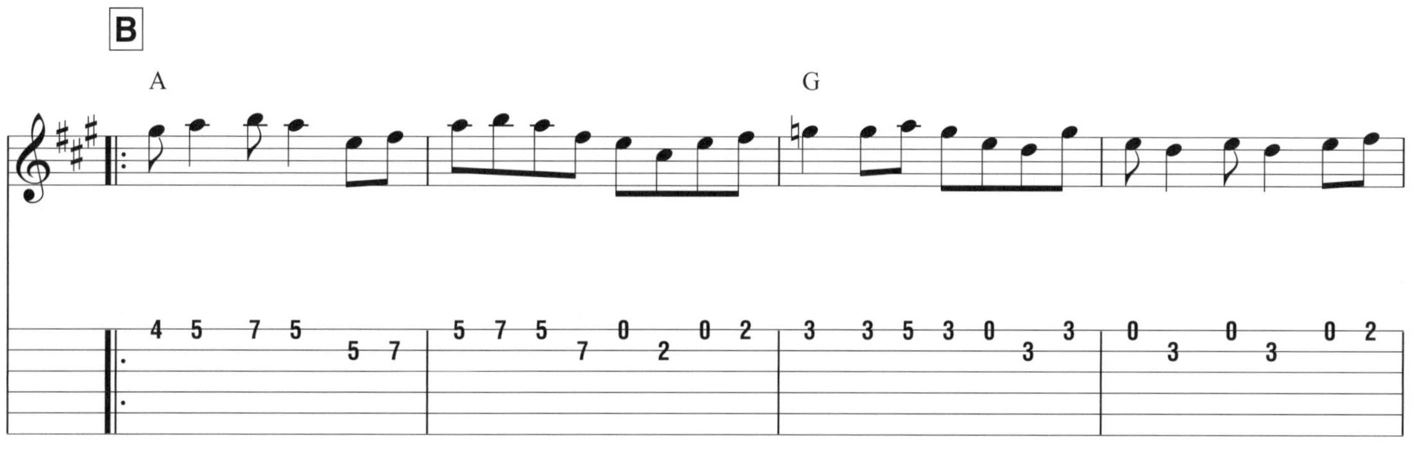
B
A
G

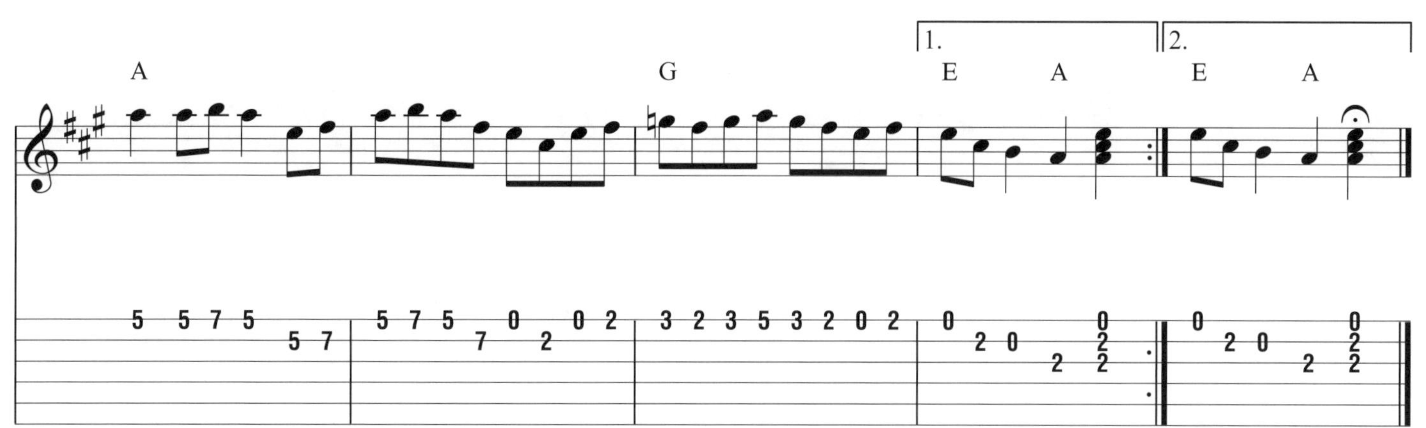
1.
2.
A
G
E
A
E
A

Salty Dog Blues

Words and Music by Wiley A. Morris and Zeke Morris

There are bluesy recordings of "Salty Dog Blues" from as early as the 1920s (by Papa Charlie Jackson, Clara Smith, and others), but the 1945 Morris Brothers' version was the model for Flatt and Scruggs' 1950 recording—which in turn is the arrangement covered by bluegrass bands today. Earl Scruggs played with the Morris Brothers prior to his stint with Bill Monroe and later collaboration with Lester Flatt.

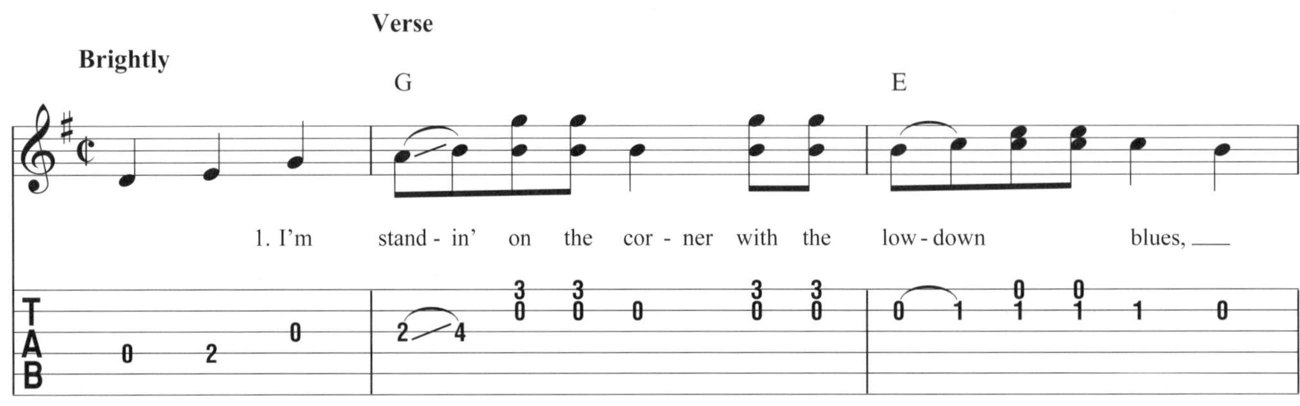

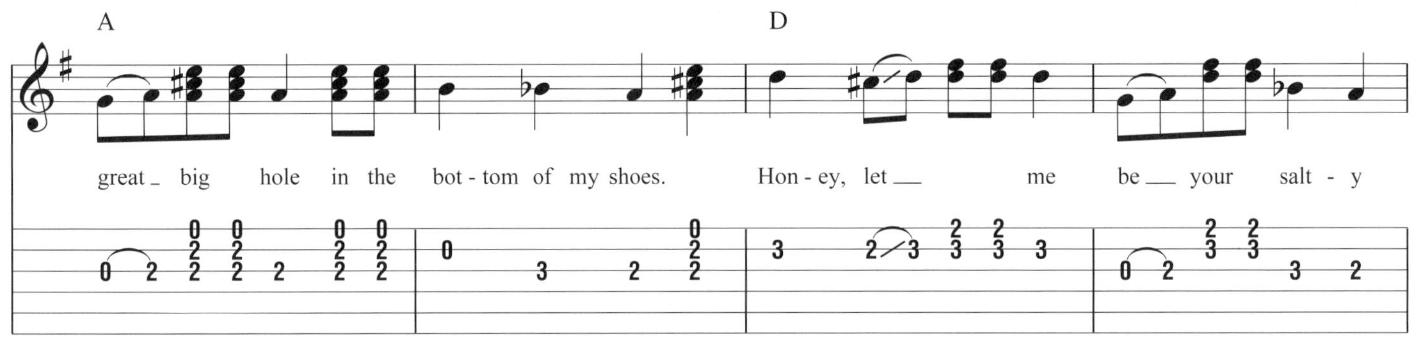

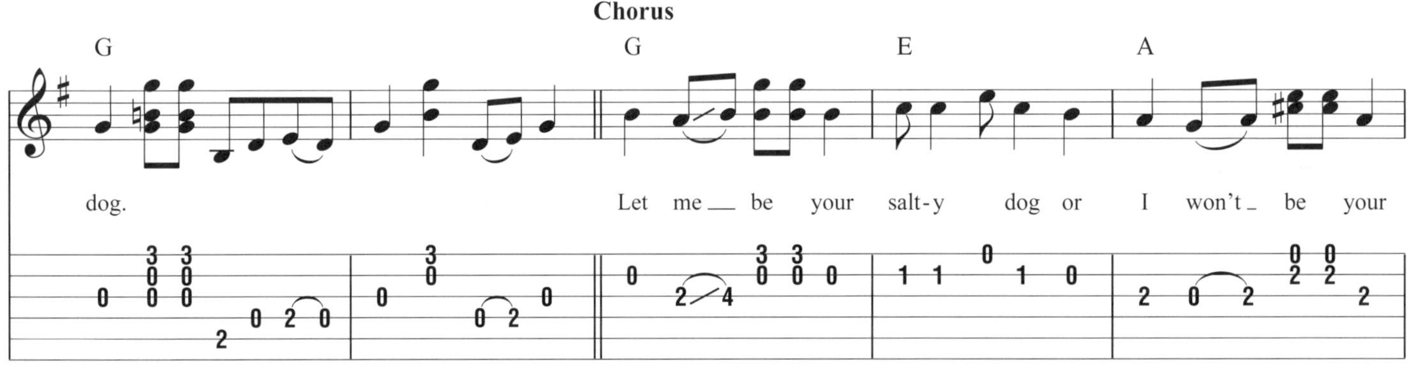

Verse

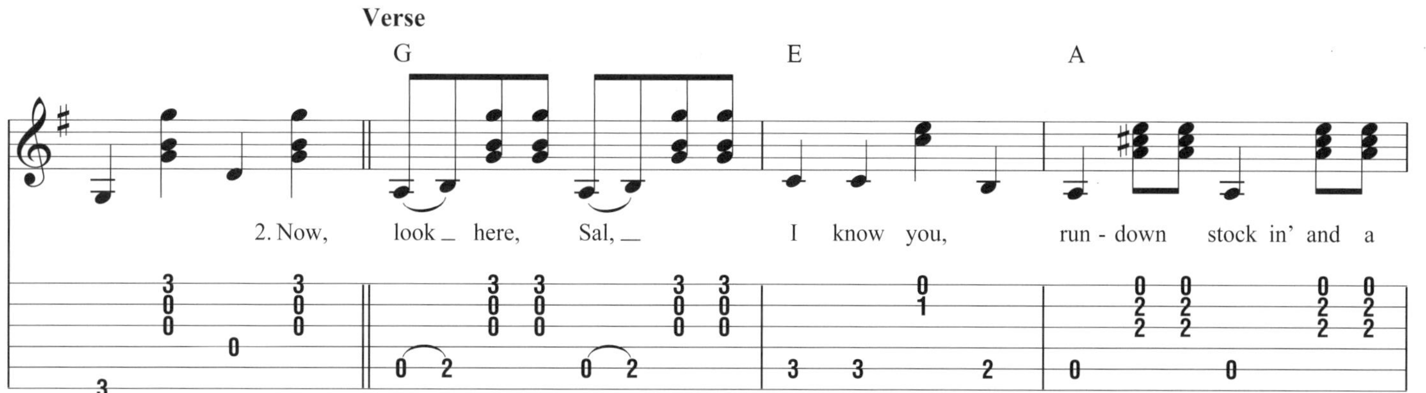

Chorus

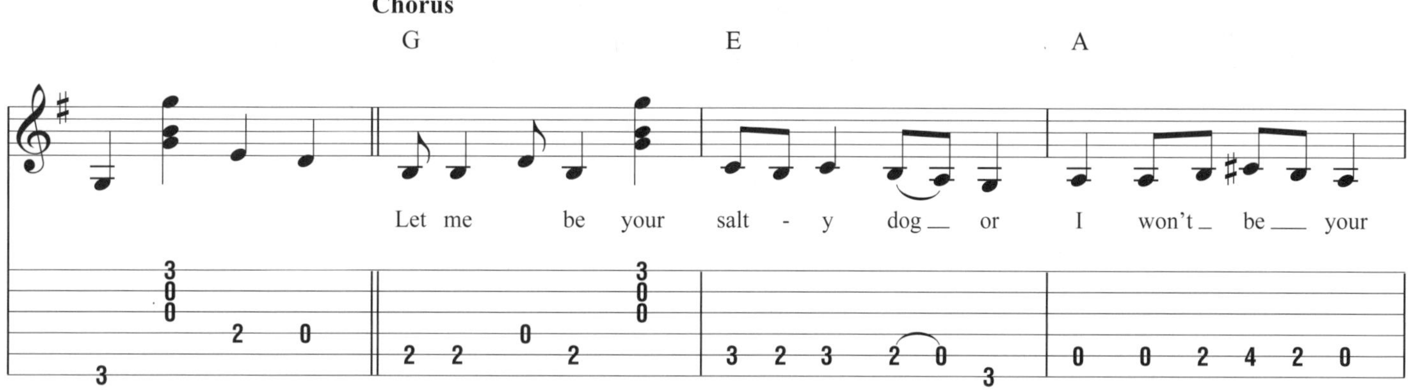

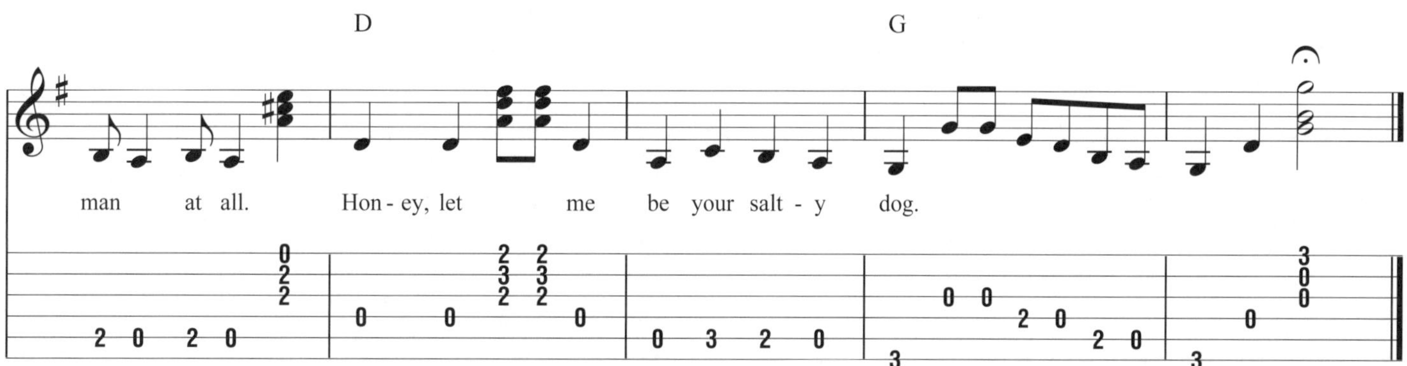

Additional Verses

3. I was down in the wildwood settin' on a log, finger on the trigger and an eye on the hog.
   Honey, let me be your salty dog.

4. I pulled the trigger and the gun said, "Go," shot fell over in Mexico.
   Honey, let me be your salty dog.

Sitting on Top of the World

Words and Music by Walter Jacobs and Lonnie Carter

Walter Vinson of the Mississippi Sheiks wrote this tune, and the Sheiks recorded it in 1930. It has been recorded by countless blues singers and bands, and many eight-bar blues tunes contain a similar melody. It probably entered the bluegrass world when Bill Monroe recorded his version in 1957. Some players add an E minor chord in the chorus over the word "worry."

Key of A

Verse

Brightly

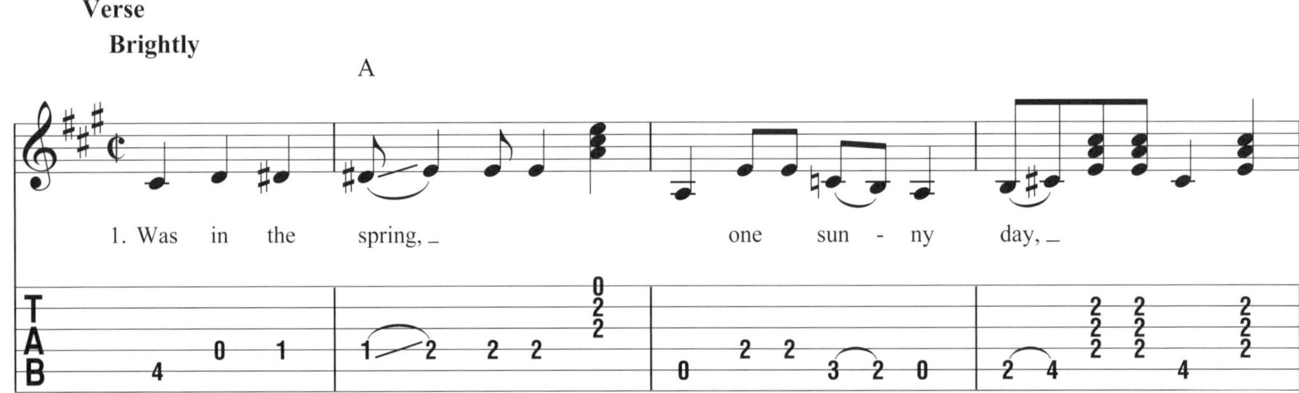

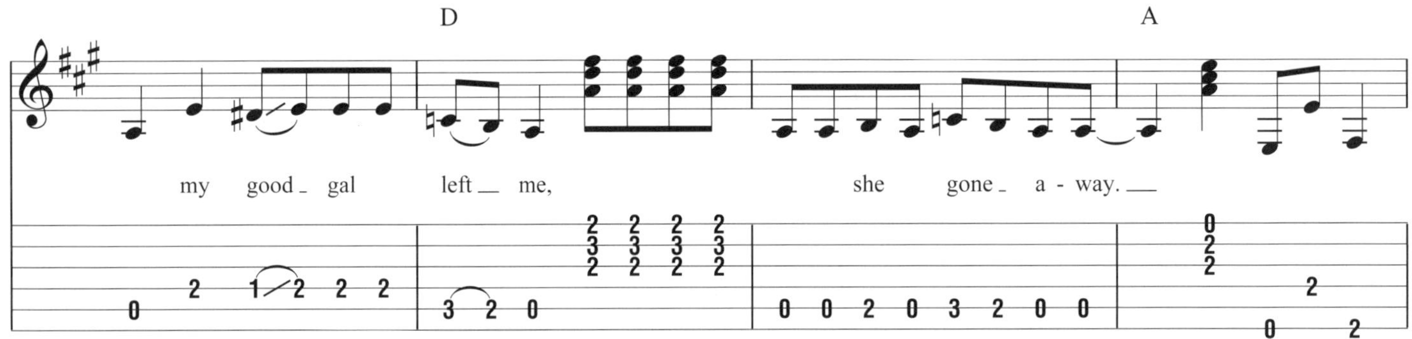

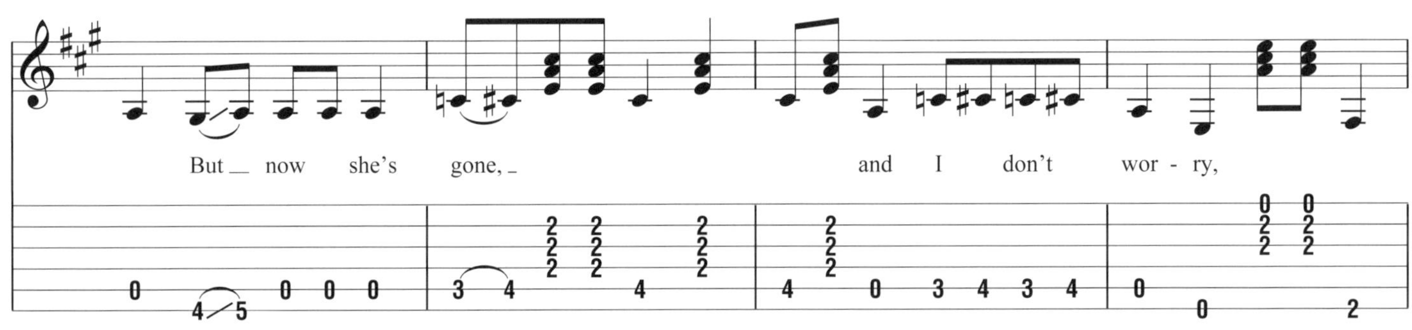

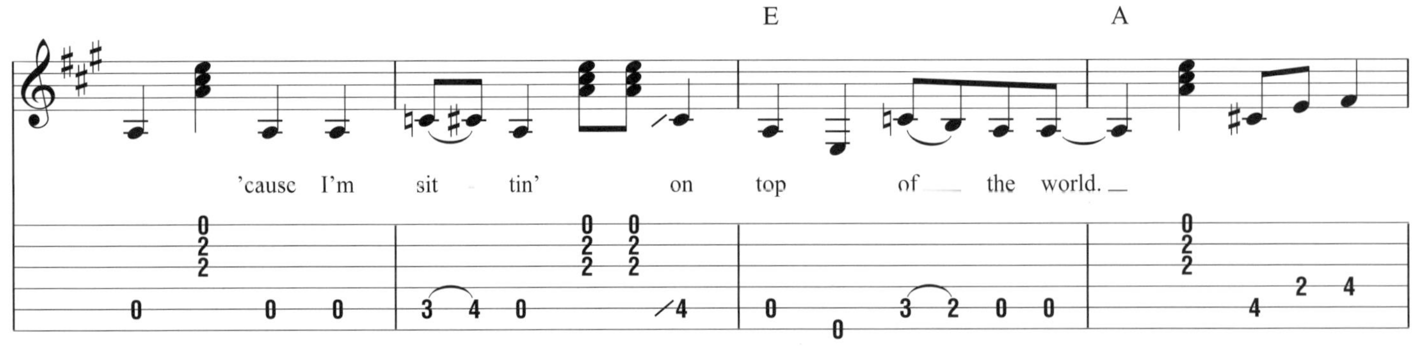

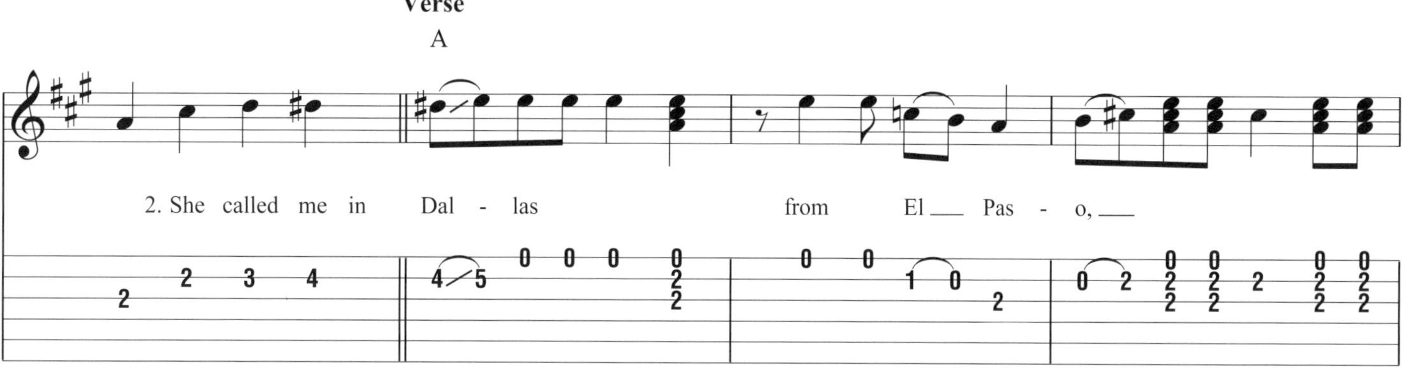

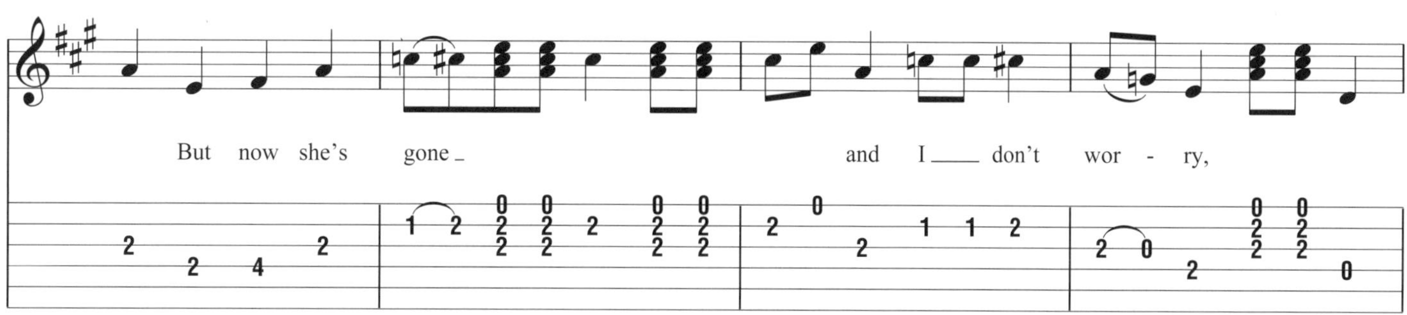

Additional Verses

3. Ashes to ashes, and dust to dust.
   Show me a woman a man can trust.

4. Mississippi River runs deep and wide.
   The one I'm lovin' is on the other side.

5. You don't like my peaches, don't shake my tree.
   Get out of my orchard, let my peaches be.

6. Don't you come here running, holding out your hand.
   I'll get me a woman like you got your man.

Soldier's Joy

Traditional

The tune used in "Soldier's Joy" originated in Scotland, where it has been played for over 200 years. There's sheet music for it dating back to the eighteenth century, making it one of the world's oldest and most popular fiddle tunes. It is usually performed as an instrumental, but when sung, the lyrics indicate that the "joy" in question is morphine…or payday (either of which could make a soldier happy).

1.
2.
G
D
A
D
D
A
D
A
D
A
D
1.
2.
D
B
D
G
D
A
D
G
D
A
D
1.
2.
D

Turkey in the Straw

American Folksong

Like "Soldier's Joy," "Turkey in the Straw" is one of the oldest and most widely used fiddle tunes in existence. It can be traced back to the minstrel shows of the early 1800s, but probably goes back even further. Numerous sets of lyrics have been written for it, though bluegrassers play it as an instrumental. It has been used in movies, cartoons, and video games, and still can be heard playing over the loudspeakers of ice cream trucks.

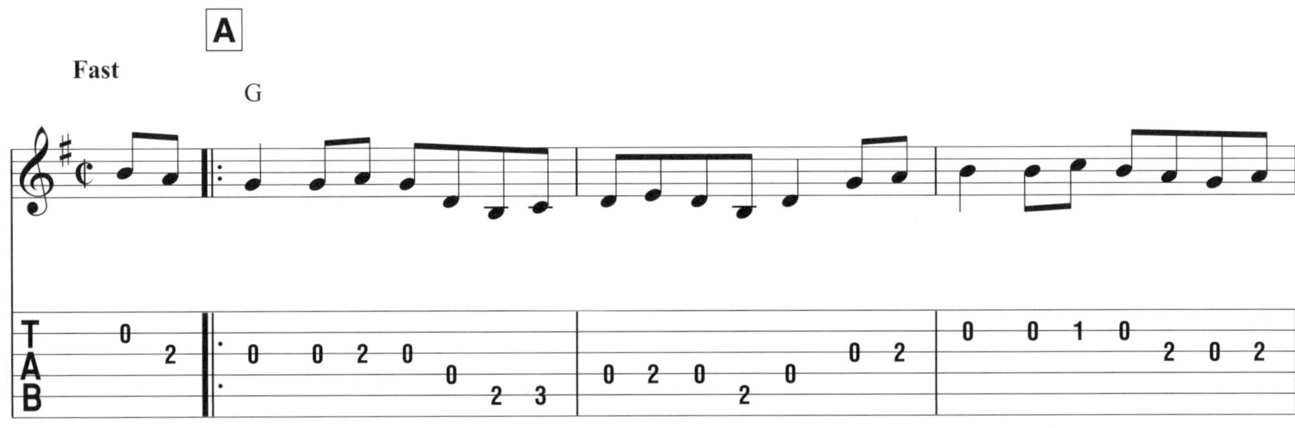

B
G
C
G
D
G
D
G
C
G
D
G
D
G

Wabash Cannonball

Words and Music by A.P. Carter

No one seems to know who Daddy Cleaton was (or Daddy Claxton, as he is called in most versions of the song), and many say the Wabash Cannonball was a mythical train. However, it is known that the lyrics and tune come from a late 1800s song called "The Great Rock Island Route" about an actual train route that stretched across many states. In 1929, the Carter Family recorded a version of the song that had been re-written as "The Wabash Cannon Ball" in 1904. Opry star Roy Acuff's 1936 recording of the tune, which was based on the Carter Family's rendition, became his signature song. The lyrics here belong to the Carter Family, but words vary from one performer to another.

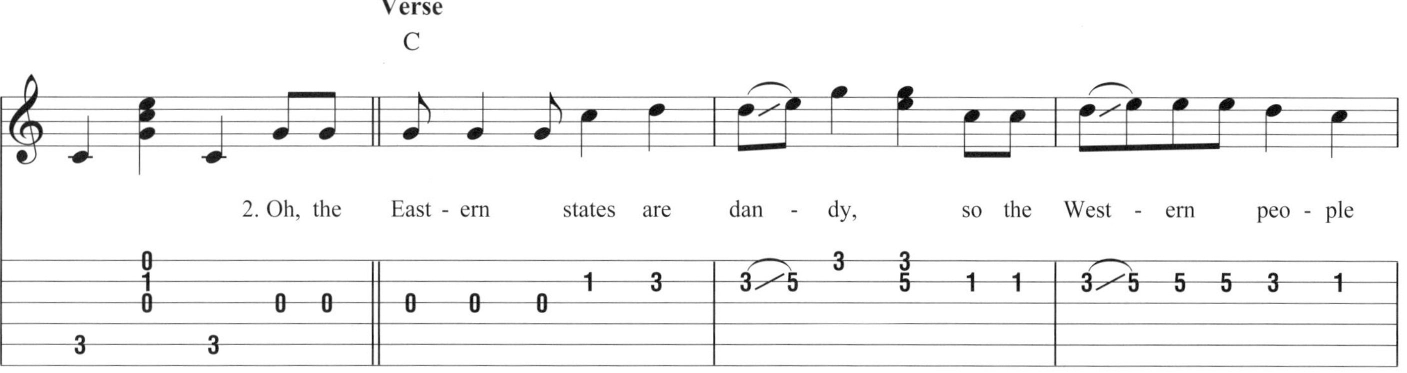

Additional Verses

3. Oh, listen to the jingle, the rumble and the roar
As she glides along the woodland, o'er hills and by the shore.
She climbs the Flow'ry Mountain, hear the merry hobo squall,
She glides along the woodland, the Wabash Cannonball.

4. Oh, here's old Daddy Cleaton, let his name forever be,
And long be remembered in the courts of Tennessee.
For he is a good ol' rounder 'til the curtain around him fall,
He'll be carried back to victory on the Wabash Cannonball.

Way Downtown

Traditional
Arranged by Doc Watson

"Way Downtown" is an old string band standard that borrows verses from many other folk songs. Doc Watson, whose brilliant solo guitar performance inspired bluegrass bands to take up the song, popularized it in the early 1960s. It's safe to say that Doc Watson and Clarence White are responsible for transforming the bluegrass guitarist's role from that of accompanist to accompanist-who-also-solos.

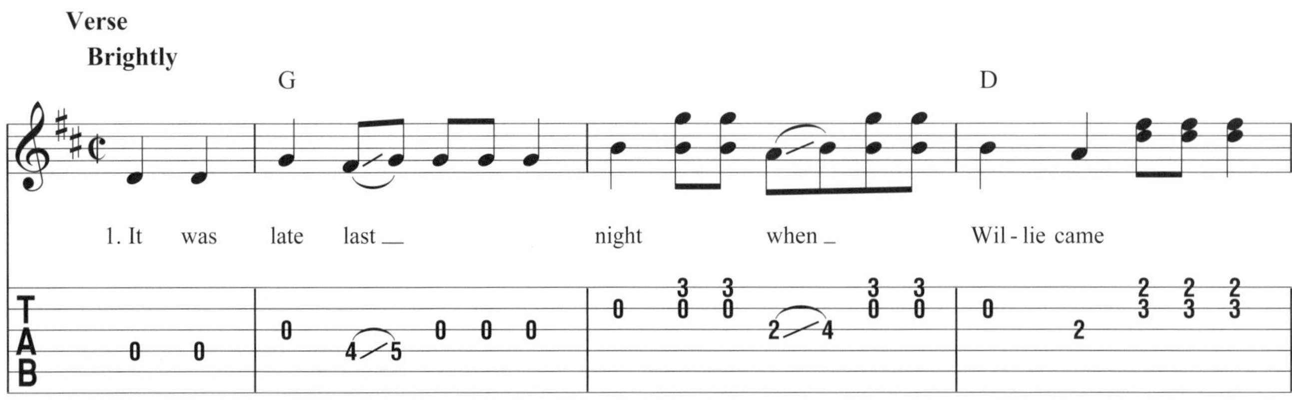

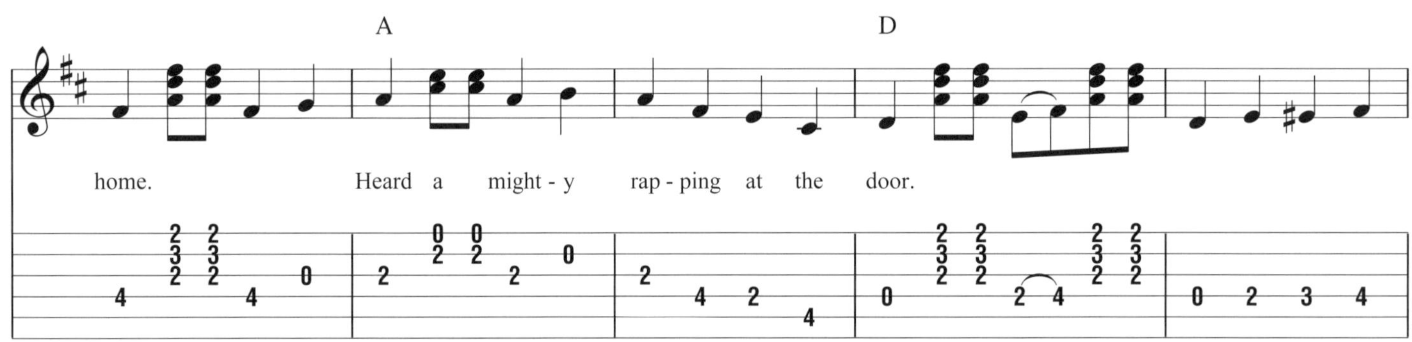

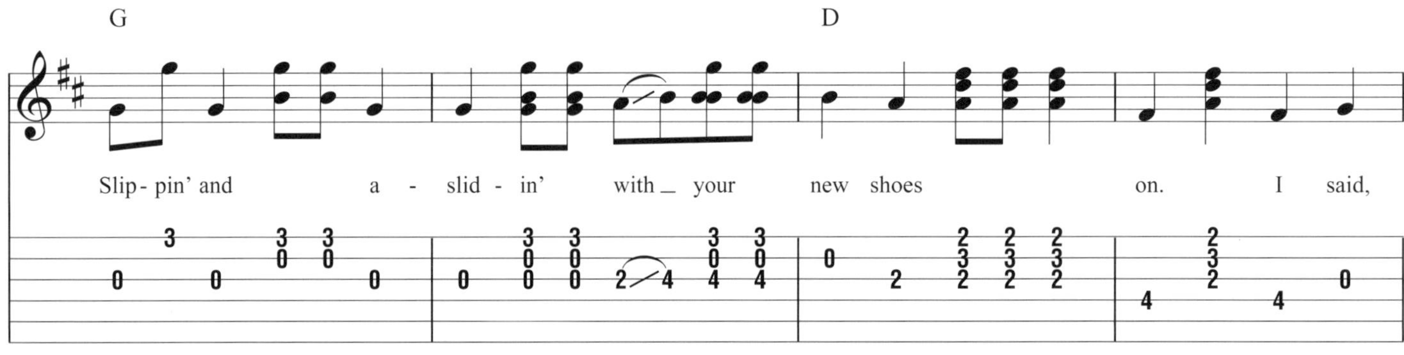

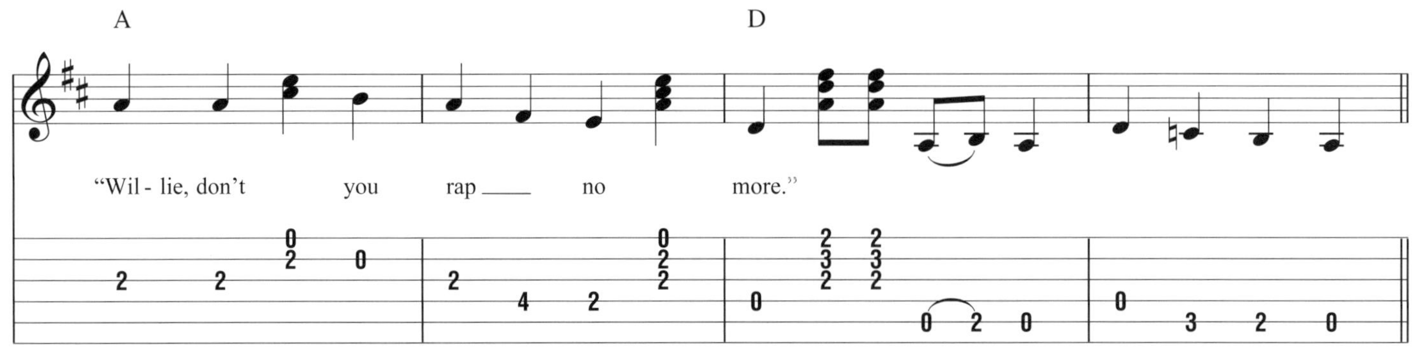

Additional Verses

2. One old shirt is all I have and a dollar is all I crave.
   Ain't brought nothing into this world and I ain't gonna take nothing to my grave.
3. Wish I was down at my old Sally's house, sittin' in her big armchair,
   One arm around my old guitar and the other one around my dear.
4. Where were you last Friday night, while I was locked up in jail?
   You were walking the streets with some other man, wouldn't even go my bail.

Wayfaring Stranger

Southern American Folk Hymn

This gospel favorite goes back to the early 1800s, possibly even further. It was sung at Appalachian revival services and spread west with the pioneers. Folksinger Burl Ives popularized it in the 1940s… followed by Joan Baez in the '60s, Emmylou Harris in the '80s, and Johnny Cash in 2000; and even more recently, Ed Sheeran's cover has been widely viewed on YouTube. Bill Monroe recorded and performed many versions of it, beginning in the 1950s and continuing through to his final years.

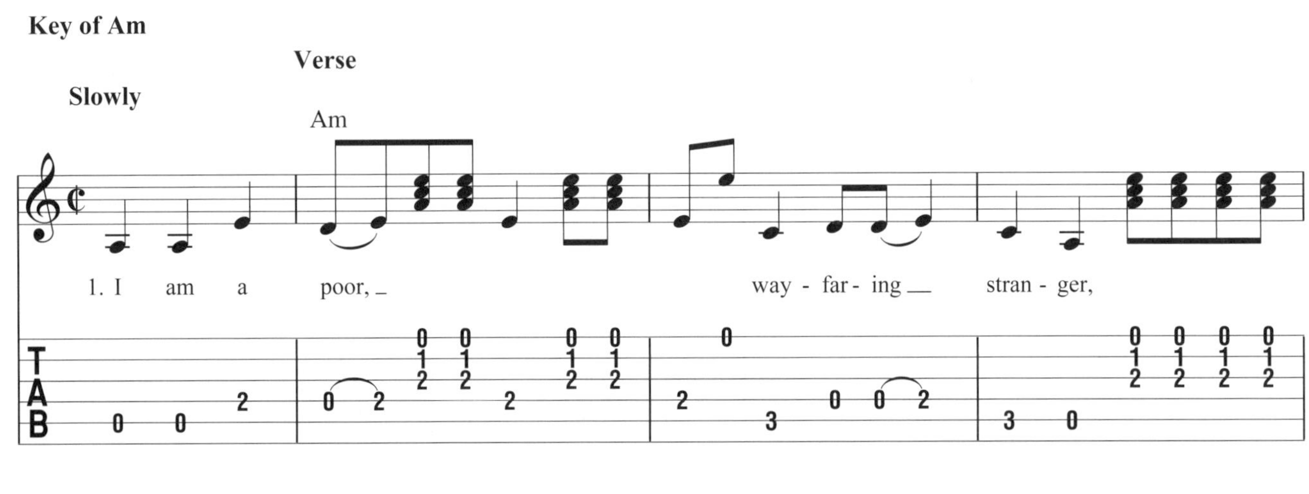

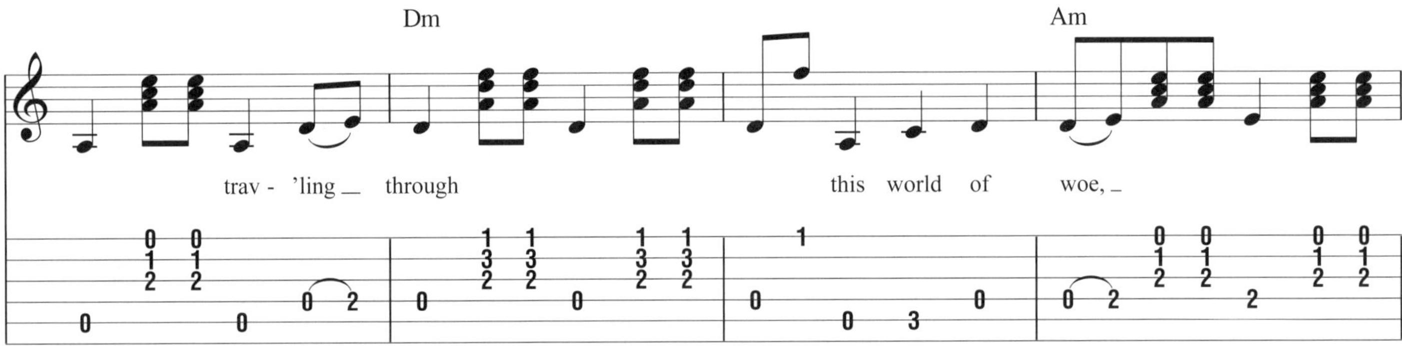

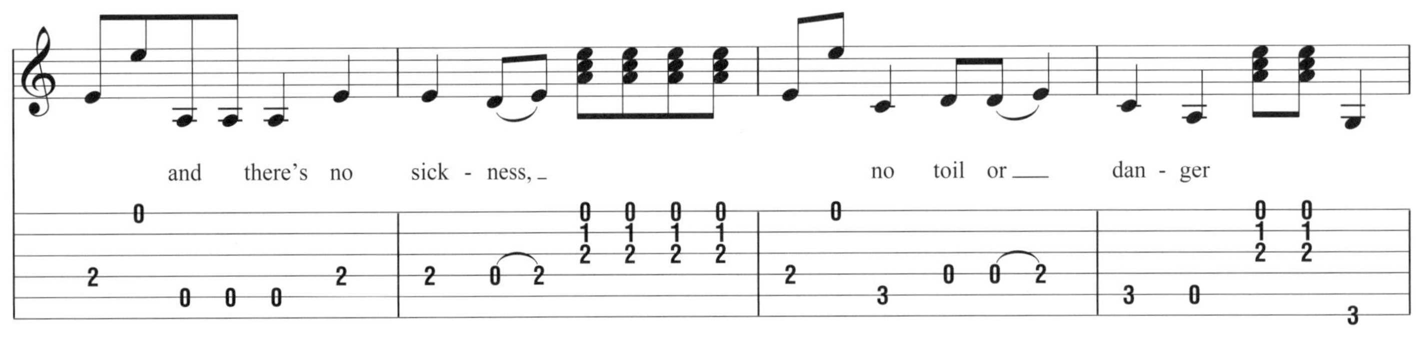

Chorus

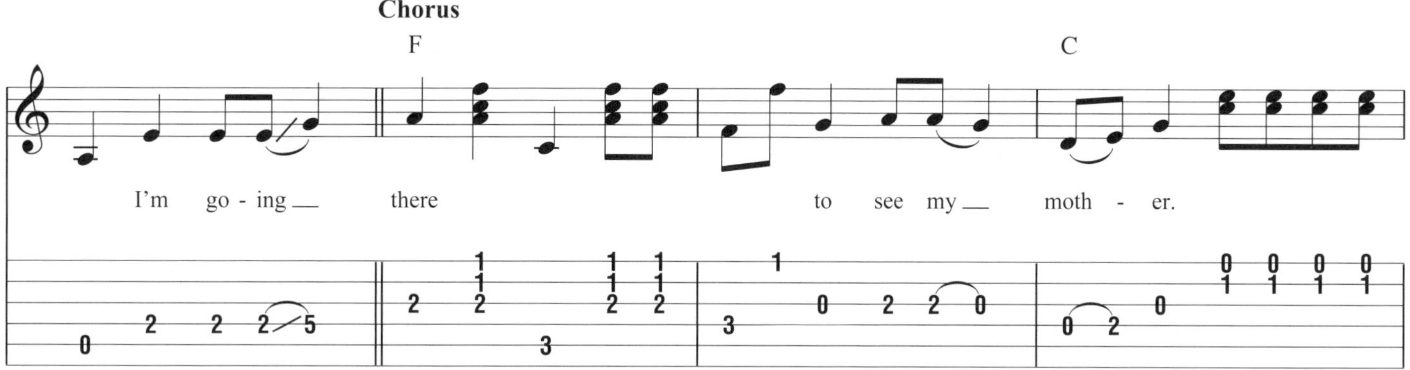

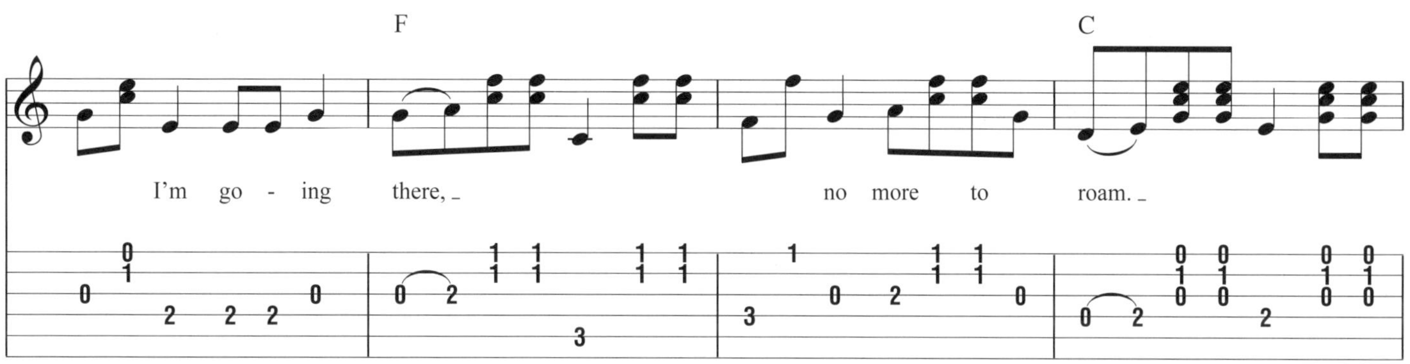

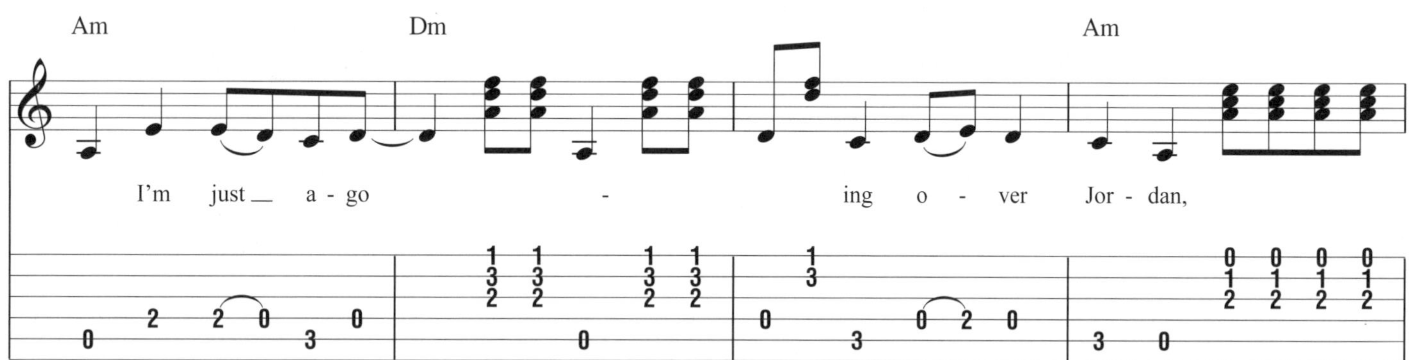

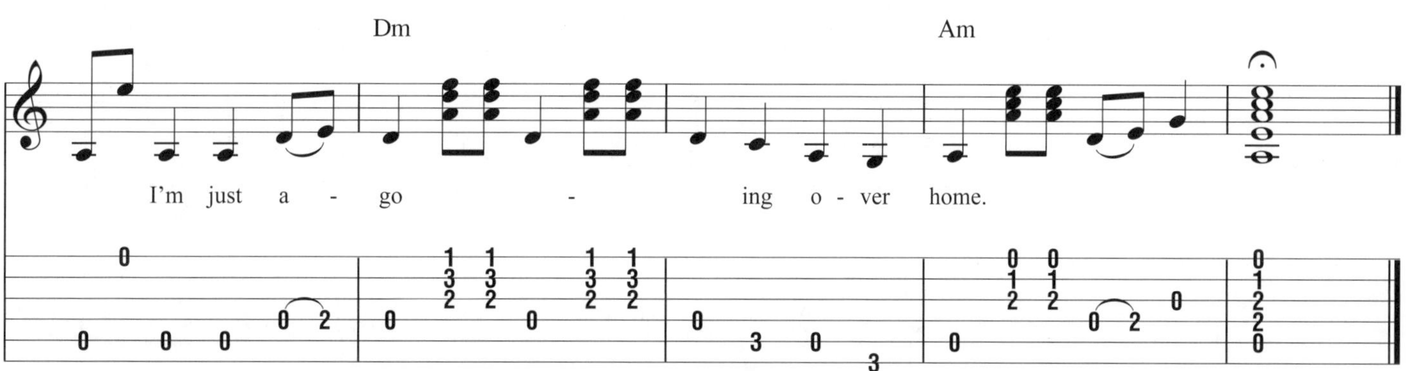

Additional Lyrics

2. I know dark clouds will gather 'round me; I know my way is rough and steep.
   But beautiful fields lie just before me, where souls redeemed their vigil keep.

Chorus I'm going there to meet my mother, she said she'd meet me when I come.
I'm just a-going over Jordan, I'm only going over home.

White Dove

Words and Music by Carter Stanley

In 1949, in the back seat of a car heading home (with his brother Ralph at the wheel), Carter Stanley wrote this beautiful meditation on the loss of his parents. The plaintive waltz has become a favorite among bluegrass performers. The chorus is only slightly different from the verses.

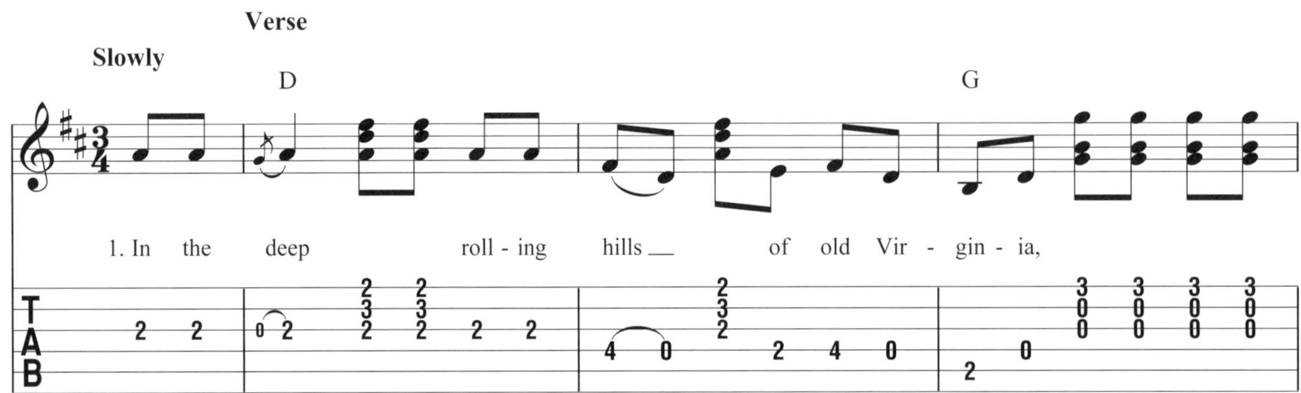

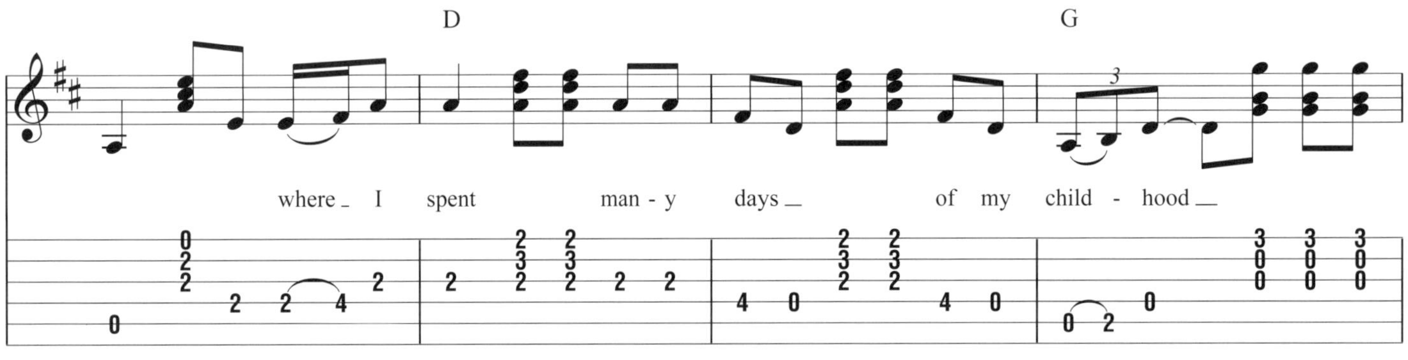

Chorus

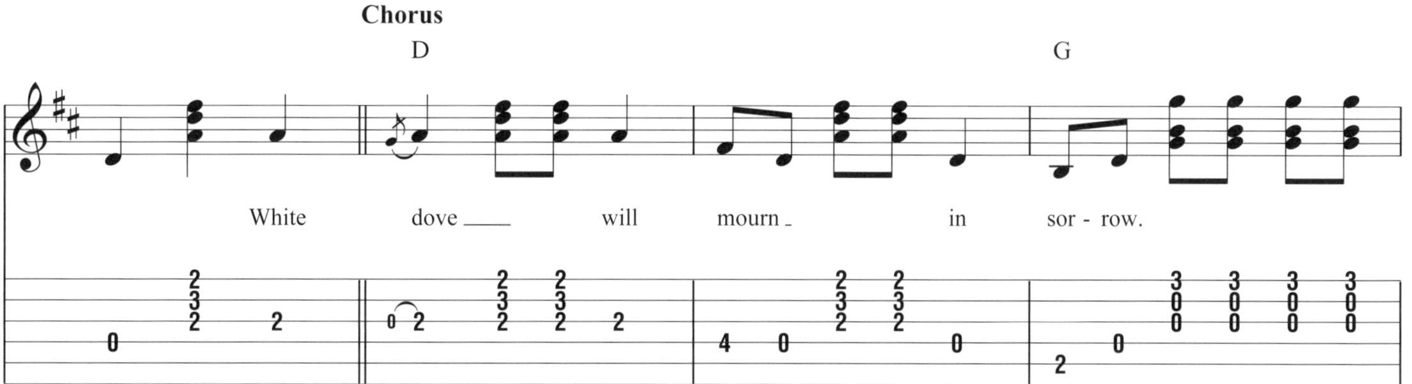

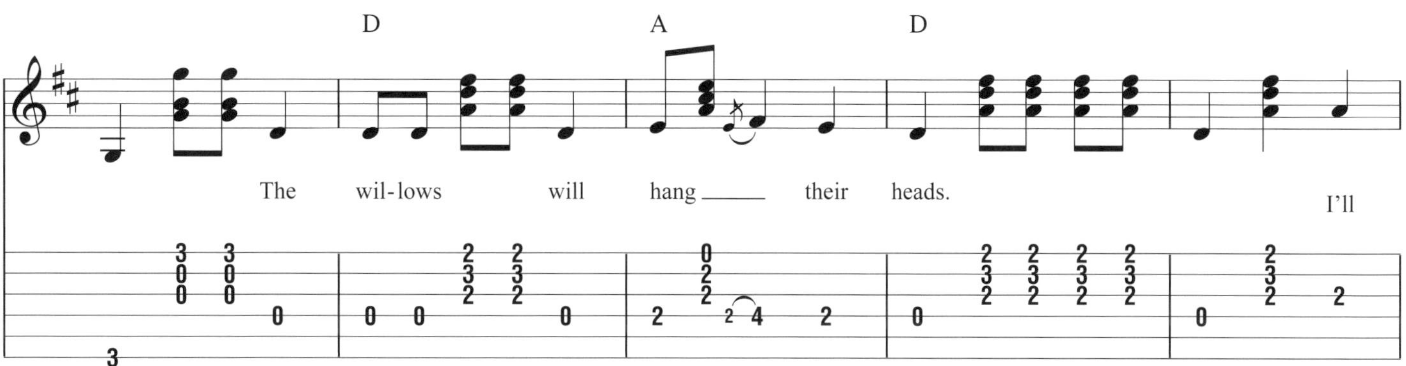

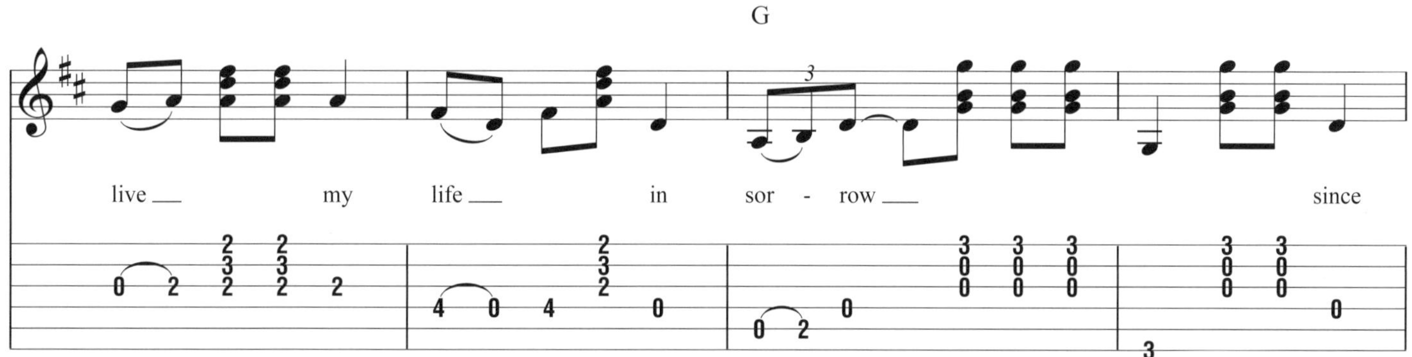

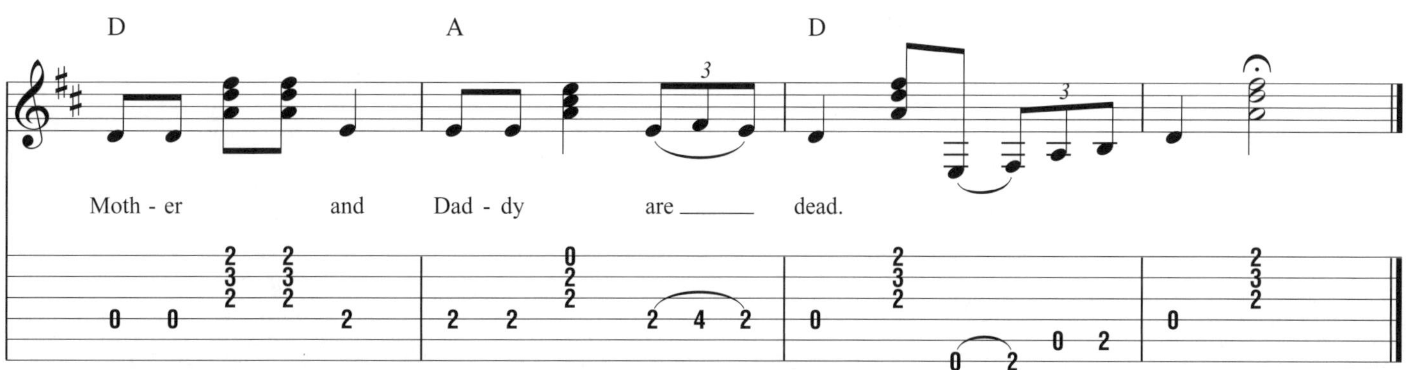

Additional Verses

2. We were all so happy there together in our peaceful little mountain home,
   But the Savior needs angels up in heaven. Now they sing around the great white throne.
3. As the years roll by, I often wonder if we will all be together someday.
   And each night as I wander through the graveyard, darkness finds me as I kneel to pray.

Will the Circle Be Unbroken

Words by Ada R. Habershon
Music by Charles H. Gabriel

In 1935 the Carter Family recorded "Can the Circle Be Unbroken," a revised version of the 1907 hymn "Will the Circle Be Unbroken" in which the singer describes his or her mother's funeral and declares that we'll all be reunited in heaven. The Carter family arrangement has become extremely popular and is often sung as the finale to country music or bluegrass concerts. Numerous singers and bands of all genres have recorded the tune.

Verse

Moderately

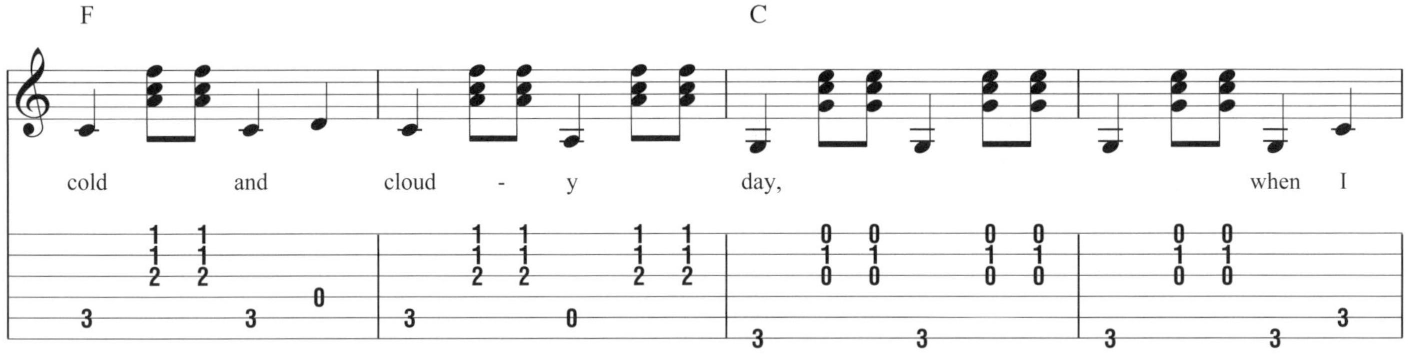

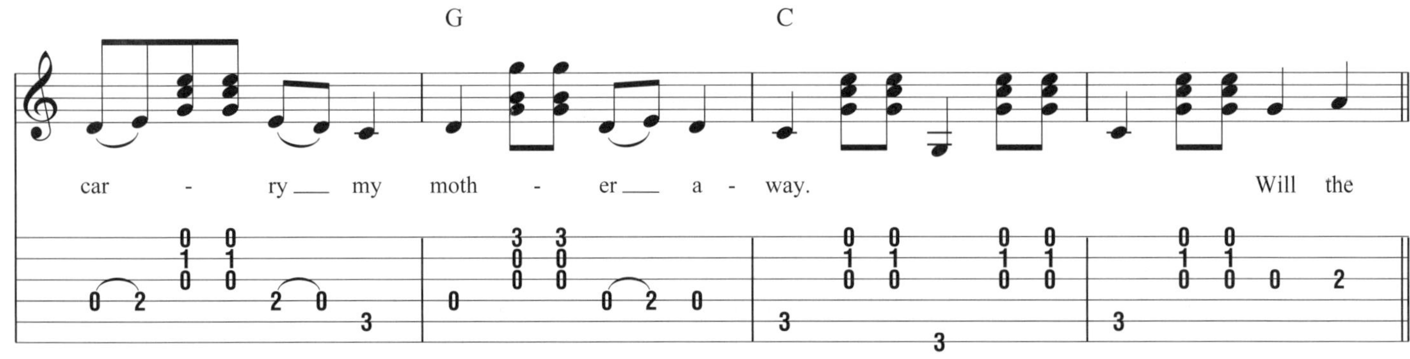

Additional Verses

2. Lord, I told the undertaker, "Undertaker, please drive slow,
For this body you are hauling, Lord, I hate to see her go."

3. I followed close behind her, tried to hold up and be brave.
But I could not hide my sorrow when they laid her in the grave.

4. Went back home, Lord, my home was lonesome, since my mother, she was gone.
All my brothers, sisters cryin', what a home so sad and 'lone.

Wreck of the Old 97

Traditional

This song accurately describes an actual train wreck that took place in 1903. (You can find a photo of the wreckage online.) The identity of its composer is in dispute, but Henry Whitter and G.B. Grayson first recorded it in 1923. Country singer Vernon Dalhart scored the first million-selling country hit with his rendition the following year. The tune has become so popular in the bluegrass and country music community that an alternative country band took the name Old 97's.

Key of G

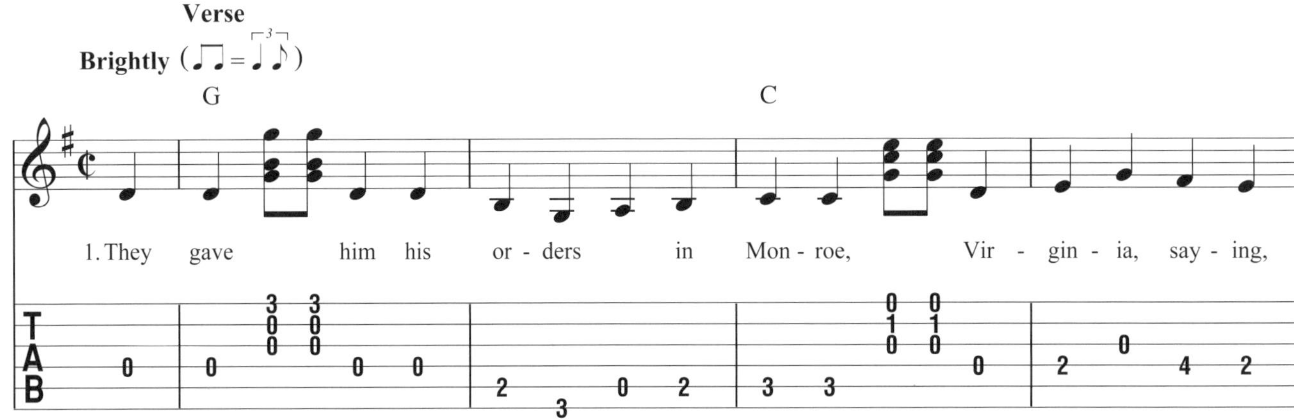

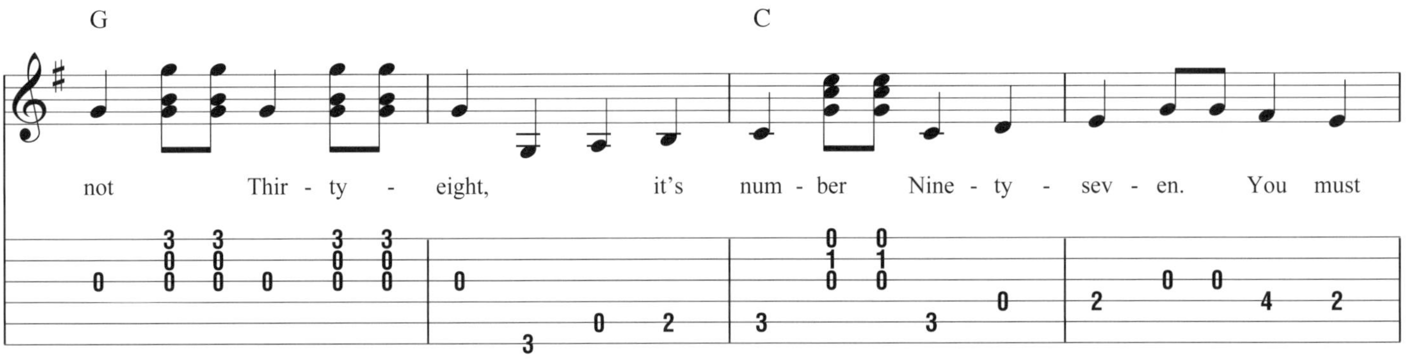

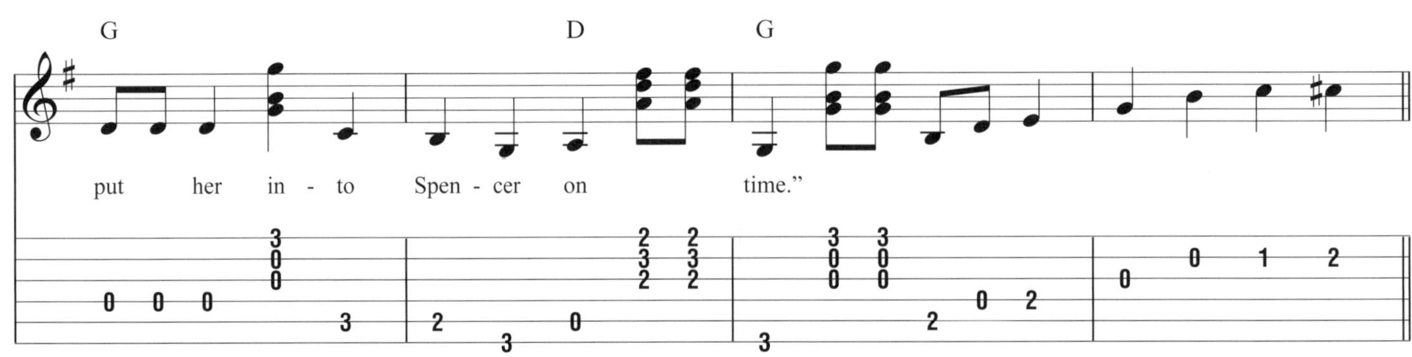

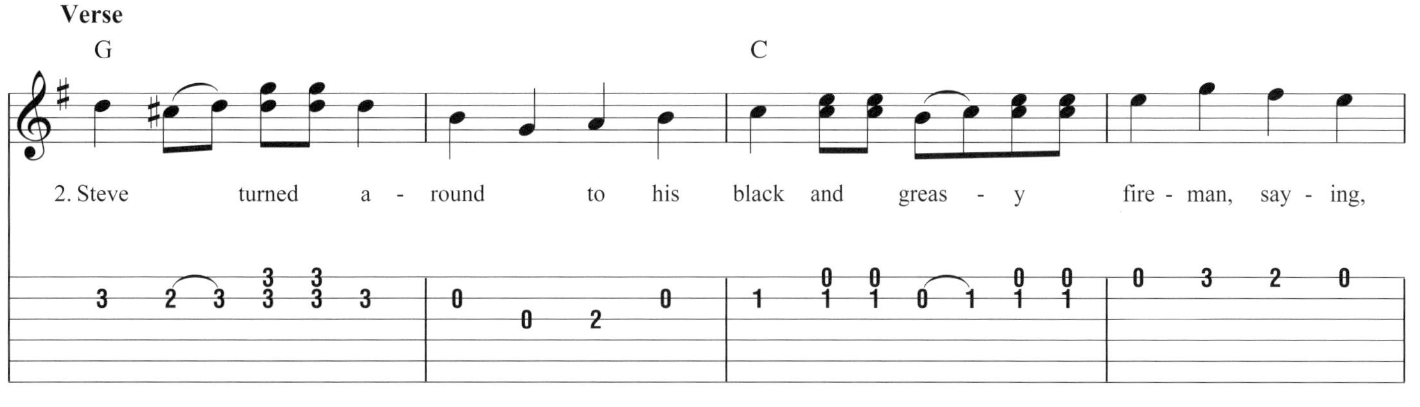

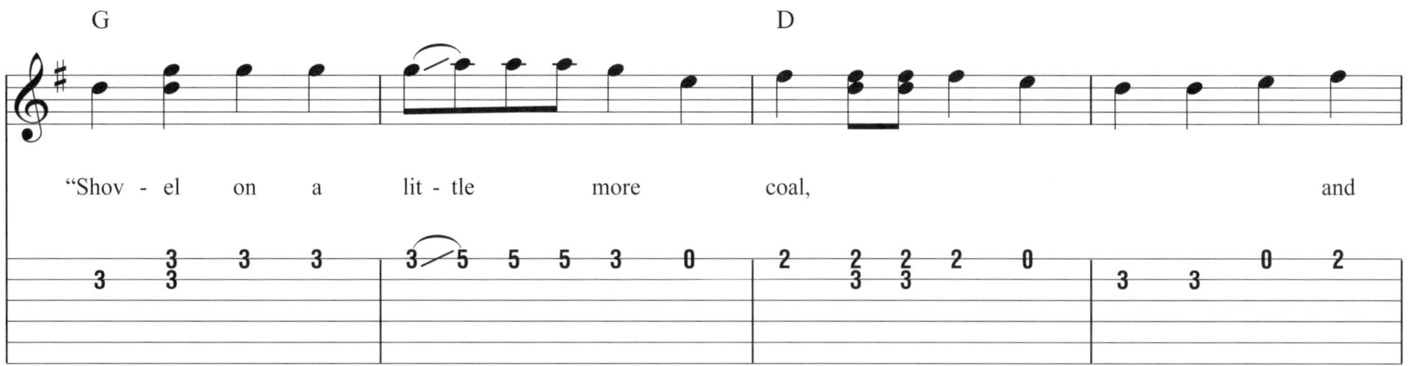

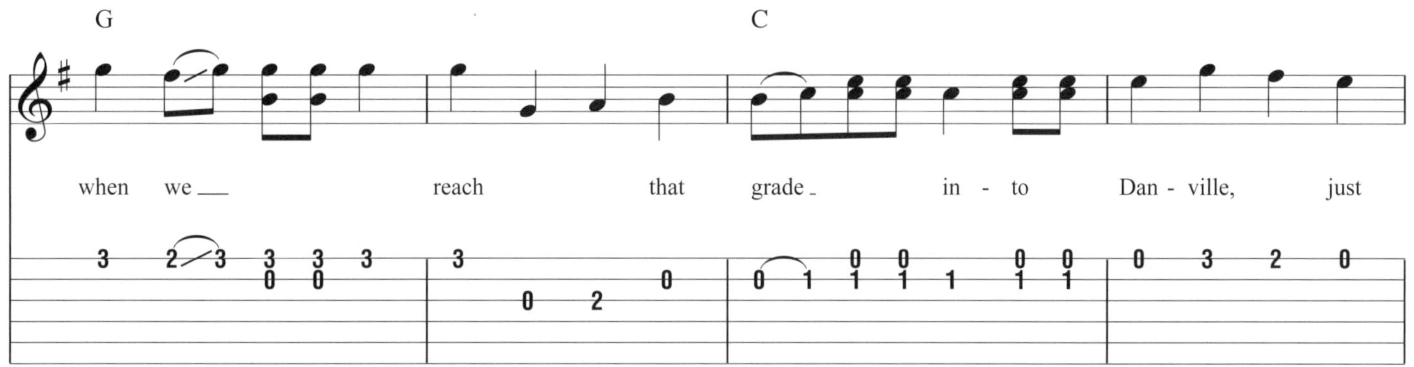

Additional Verses

3. It's a long, hard road from Lynchburg to Danville and it's lined with a three-mile grade.
It was on that road that he lost his airbrakes, you see what a jump he made.

4. They were going down the track, ninety miles an hour, when his whistle broke into a scream.
He was found in the wreck with his hand on the throttle, scalded to death by the steam.

5. Now all you women, please take warning from this day on and learn,
Never speak harsh words to your kind and loving husband, he may leave you and never return.

You Don't Know My Mind

Words and Music by Jimmie Skinner

One of the great tenor singers from the "golden age of bluegrass," Jimmy Martin spent several years playing guitar and singing in Bill Monroe's Bluegrass Boys before leading his own band, the Sunny Mountain Boys. He helped define the "high lonesome sound" of bluegrass vocals and wrote several popular bluegrass standards including "You Don't Know My Mind." The song may well be autobiographical, as Martin was known to be a colorful and cantankerous character.

Additional Verses

3. I've been a hobo and a tramp, my soul has done been stamped.
   Lord, things I know, I learned the hard, hard way.
   I ain't here to judge or plead, but to give my poor heart ease.
   Baby, you don't know my mind today.

4. Honey, you don't know my mind. I'm lonesome all the time.
   Born to lose, a drifter, that's me.
   You say I'm sweet and kind, and I can love you a thousand times,
   But baby, you don't know my mind today.

ABOUT THE AUTHOR

Fred Sokolow is best known as the author of over 150 instructional and transcription books and DVDs for guitar, banjo, Dobro, mandolin, lap steel, and ukulele. Fred has long been a well-known West Coast multi-string performer and recording artist, particularly on the acoustic music scene. The diverse musical genres covered in his books and DVDs, along with several bluegrass, jazz, and rock CDs he has released, demonstrate his mastery of many musical styles. Whether he's playing Delta bottleneck blues, bluegrass or old-time banjo, '30s swing guitar, or screaming rock solos, he does it with authenticity and passion.

Other instruction by Fred, published by Hal Leonard, that can help you progress as a guitar player include:

- *Fretboard Roadmaps for Bluegrass and Folk Guitar* (book and audio)
- *Hal Leonard Bluegrass Guitar Method* (book and audio)
- *Gospel Guitar Songbook* (book and audio)
- *Carter Family Collection* (book and audio)
- *Jimmie Rodgers Collection* (book and audio)
- *Hank Williams Songbook* (book and audio)

Email Fred with any questions about these or his other books at sokolowmusic.com.

GUITAR NOTATION LEGEND

Guitar music can be notated two different ways: on a *musical staff*, and in *tablature*.

THE MUSICAL STAFF shows pitches and rhythms and is divided by bar lines into measures. Pitches are named after the first seven letters of the alphabet.

TABLATURE graphically represents the guitar fingerboard. Each horizontal line represents a string, and each number represents a fret.

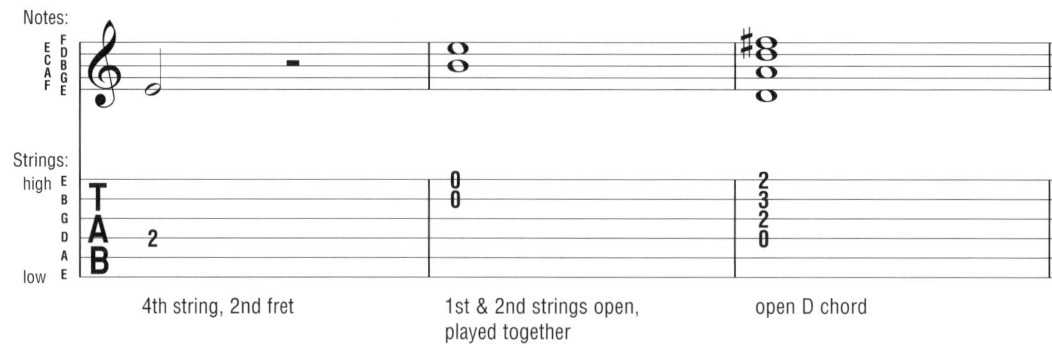

CHORD DIAGRAMS graphically represent the guitar fretboard to show correct chord fingerings.

- The letter above the diagram tells the name of the chord.
- The top, bold horizontal line represents the nut of the guitar. Each thin horizontal line represents a fret. Each vertical line represents a string; the low E string is on the far left and the high E string is on the far right.
- A dot shows where to put your fret-hand finger and the number at the bottom of the diagram tells which finger to use.
- The "O" above the string means play it open, while an "X" means don't play the string.

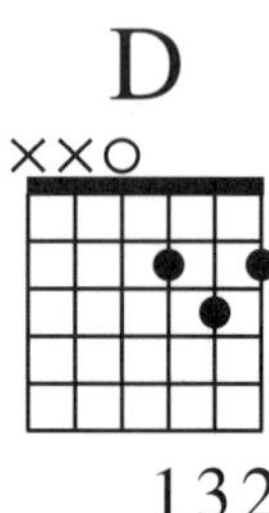

Definitions for Special Guitar Notation

HALF-STEP BEND: Strike the note and bend up 1/2 step.

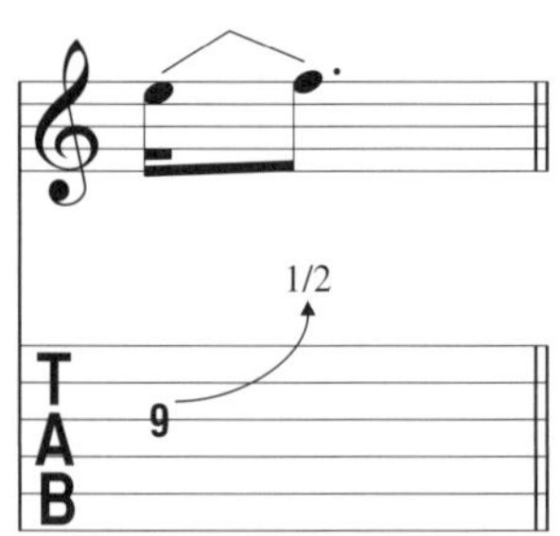

WHOLE-STEP BEND: Strike the note and bend up one step.

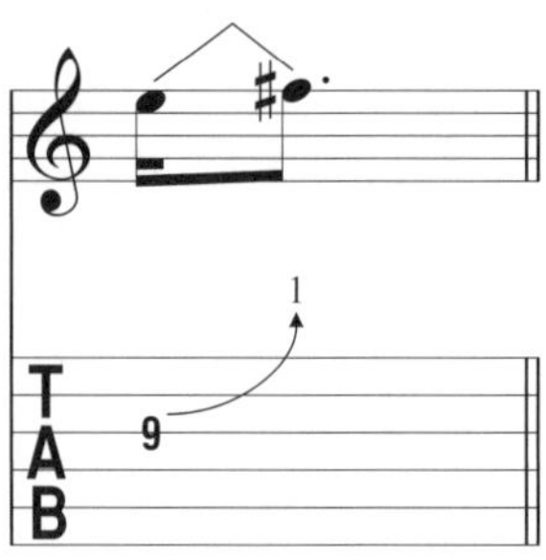

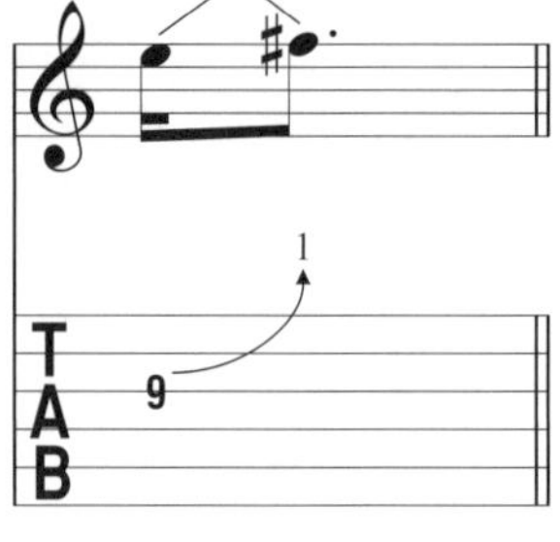

MUFFLED STRINGS: A percussive sound is produced by laying the fret hand across the string(s) without depressing, and striking them with the pick hand.

PALM MUTING: The note is partially muted by the pick hand lightly touching the string(s) just before the bridge.

HAMMER-ON: Strike the first (lower) note with one finger, then sound the higher note (on the same string) with another finger by fretting it without picking.

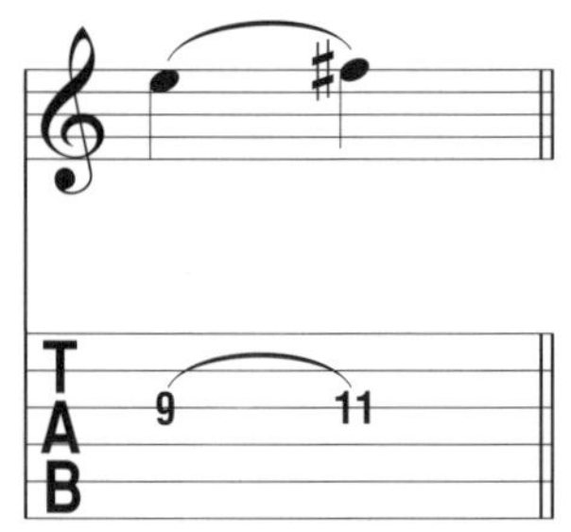

PULL-OFF: Place both fingers on the notes to be sounded. Strike the first note and without picking, pull the finger off to sound the second (lower) note.

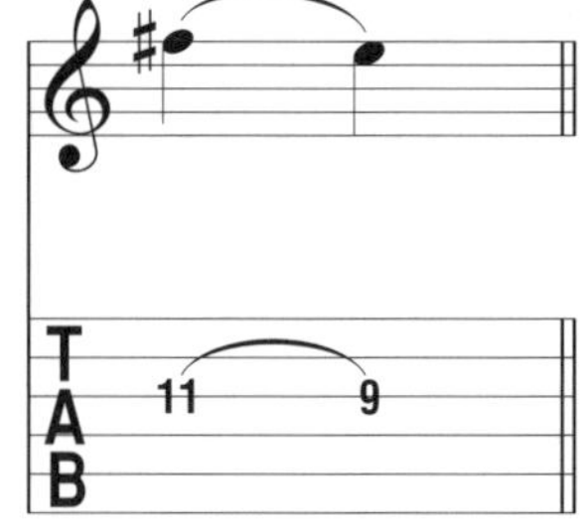

LEGATO SLIDE: Strike the first note and then slide the same fret-hand finger up or down to the second note. The second note is not struck.

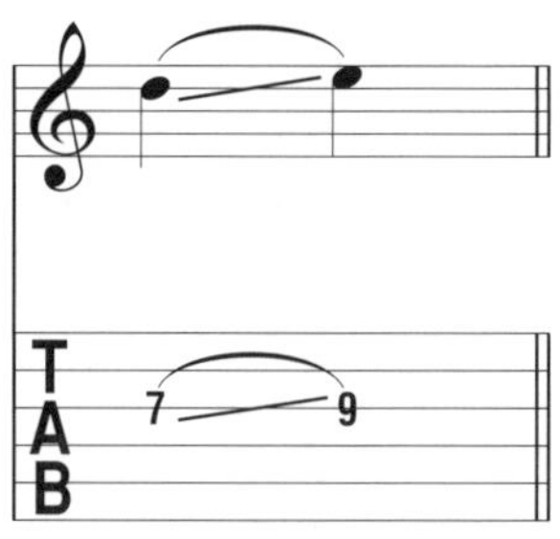

SHIFT SLIDE: Same as legato slide, except the second note is struck.

Additional Musical Definitions

Fill • Label used to identify a brief melodic figure which is to be inserted into the arrangement.

D.S. al Coda • Go back to the sign (𝄋), then play until the measure marked "***To Coda,***" then skip to the section labelled "**Coda.**"

D.C. al Fine • Go back to the beginning of the song and play until the measure marked "***Fine***" (end).

N.C. • No chord. Instrument is silent.

• Repeat measures between signs.

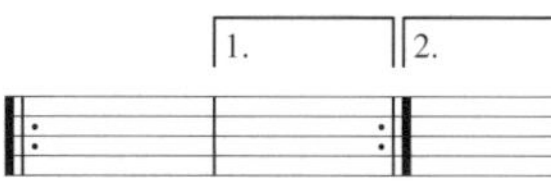

• When a repeated section has different endings, play the first ending only the first time and the second ending only the second time.

FIRST 50

Books in the First 50 series contain easy to intermediate arrangements for must-know songs. Each arrangement is simple and streamlined, yet still captures the essence of the tune.

First 50 Baroque Pieces You Should Play on Guitar
Includes selections by Johann Sebastian Bach, Robert de Visée, Ernst Gottlieb Baron, Santiago de Murcia, Antonio Vivaldi, Sylvius Leopold Weiss, and more.
00322567 .... $14.99

First 50 Bluegrass Solos You Should Play on Guitar
I Am a Man of Constant Sorrow • Long Journey Home • Molly and Tenbrooks • Old Joe Clark • Rocky Top • Salty Dog Blues • and more.
00298574 .... $16.99

First 50 Blues Songs You Should Play on Guitar
All Your Love (I Miss Loving) • Bad to the Bone • Born Under a Bad Sign • Dust My Broom • Hoodoo Man Blues • Little Red Rooster • Love Struck Baby • Pride and Joy • Smoking Gun • Still Got the Blues • The Thrill Is Gone • You Shook Me • and more.
00235790 .... $17.99

First 50 Blues Turnarounds You Should Play on Guitar
You'll learn cool turnarounds in the styles of these jazz legends: John Lee Hooker, Robert Johnson, Joe Pass, Jimmy Rogers, Hubert Sumlin, Stevie Ray Vaughan, T-Bone Walker, Muddy Waters, and more.
00277469 .... $14.99

First 50 Chords You Should Play on Guitar
American Pie • Back in Black • Brown Eyed Girl • Landslide • Let It Be • Riptide • Summer of '69 • Take Me Home, Country Roads • Won't Get Fooled Again • You've Got a Friend • and more.
00300255 Guitar $12.99

First 50 Classical Pieces You Should Play on Guitar
Includes compositions by J.S. Bach, Augustin Barrios, Matteo Carcassi, Domenico Scarlatti, Fernando Sor, Francisco Tárrega, Robert de Visée, Antonio Vivaldi and many more.
00155414 .... $16.99

First 50 Folk Songs You Should Play on Guitar
Amazing Grace • Down by the Riverside • Home on the Range • I've Been Working on the Railroad • Kumbaya • Man of Constant Sorrow • Oh! Susanna • This Little Light of Mine • When the Saints Go Marching In • The Yellow Rose of Texas • and more.
00235868 .... $16.99

First 50 Guitar Duets You Should Play
Chopsticks • Clocks • Eleanor Rigby • Game of Thrones Theme • Hallelujah • Linus and Lucy (from *A Charlie Brown Christmas*) • Memory (from *Cats*) • Over the Rainbow (from *The Wizard of Oz*) • Star Wars (Main Theme) • What a Wonderful World • You Raise Me Up • and more.
00319706 .... $14.99

First 50 Jazz Standards You Should Play on Guitar
All the Things You Are • Body and Soul • Don't Get Around Much Anymore • Fly Me to the Moon (In Other Words) • The Girl from Ipanema (Garota De Ipanema) • I Got Rhythm • Laura • Misty • Night and Day • Satin Summertime • When I Fall in Love • and more.
00198594 Solo Guitar $16.99

First 50 Kids' Songs You Should Play on Guitar
Do-Re-Mi • Hakuna Matata • Let It Go • My Favorite Things • Puff the Magic Dragon • Take Me Out to the Ball Game • Won't You Be My Neighbor? (It's a Beautiful Day in the Neighborhood) • and more.
00300500 .... $17.99

First 50 Licks You Should Play on Guitar
Licks presented include the styles of legendary guitarists like Eric Clapton, Buddy Guy, Jimi Hendrix, B.B. King, Randy Rhoads, Carlos Santana, Stevie Ray Vaughan and many more.
00278875 Book/Online Audio $14.99

First 50 Riffs You Should Play on Guitar
All Right Now • Back in Black • Barracuda • Carry on Wayward Son • Crazy Train • La Grange • Layla • Seven Nation Army • Smoke on the Water • Sunday Bloody Sunday • Sunshine of Your Love • Sweet Home Alabama • Working Man • and more.
00277366 .... $17.99

First 50 Rock Songs You Should Play on Electric Guitar
All Along the Watchtower • Beat It • Brown Eyed Girl • Cocaine • Detroit Rock City • Hallelujah • (I Can't Get No) Satisfaction • Oh, Pretty Woman • Pride and Joy • Seven Nation Army • Should I Stay or Should I Go • Smells like Teen Spirit • Smoke on the Water • When I Come Around • You Really Got Me • and more.
00131159 .... $16.99

First 50 Songs by the Beatles You Should Play on Guitar
All You Need Is Love • Blackbird • Come Together • Eleanor Rigby • Hey Jude • I Want to Hold Your Hand • Let It Be • Ob-La-Di, Ob-La-Da • She Loves You • Twist and Shout • Yellow Submarine • Yesterday • and more.
00295323 .... $24.99

First 50 Songs You Should Fingerpick on Guitar
Annie's Song • Blackbird • The Boxer • Classical Gas • Dust in the Wind • Fire and Rain • Greensleeves • Road Trippin' • Shape of My Heart • Tears in Heaven • Time in a Bottle • Vincent (Starry Starry Night) • and more.
00149269 .... $16.99

First 50 Songs You Should Play on 12-String Guitar
California Dreamin' • Closer to the Heart • Free Fallin' • Give a Little Bit • Hotel California • Leaving on a Jet Plane • Life by the Drop • Over the Hills and Far Away • Solsbury Hill • Space Oddity • Wish You Were Here • You Wear It Well • and more.
00287559 .... $19.99

First 50 Songs You Should Play on Acoustic Guitar
Against the Wind • Boulevard of Broken Dreams • Champagne Supernova • Every Rose Has Its Thorn • Fast Car • Free Fallin' • Layla • Let Her Go • Mean • One • Ring of Fire • Signs • Stairway to Heaven • Trouble • Wagon Wheel • Yellow • Yesterday • and more.
00131209 .... $16.99

First 50 Songs You Should Play on Bass
Blister in the Sun • I Got You (I Feel Good) • Livin' on a Prayer • Low Rider • Money • Monkey Wrench • My Generation • Roxanne • Should I Stay or Should I Go • Uptown Funk • What's Going On • With or Without You • Yellow • and more.
00149189 .... $16.99

First 50 Songs You Should Play on Solo Guitar
Africa • All of Me • Blue Skies • California Dreamin' • Change the World • Crazy • Dream a Little Dream of Me • Every Breath You Take • Hallelujah • Wonderful Tonight • Yesterday • You Raise Me Up • Your Song • and more.
00288843 .... $19.99

First 50 Songs You Should Strum on Guitar
American Pie • Blowin' in the Wind • Daughter • Hey, Soul Sister • Home • I Will Wait • Losing My Religion • Mrs. Robinson • No Woman No Cry • Peaceful Easy Feeling • Rocky Mountain High • Sweet Caroline • Teardrops on My Guitar • Wonderful Tonight • and more.
00148996 .... $16.99

www.halleonard.com

Prices, contents and availability subject to change without notice.

0623
014

Presenting the Best in BLUEGRASS

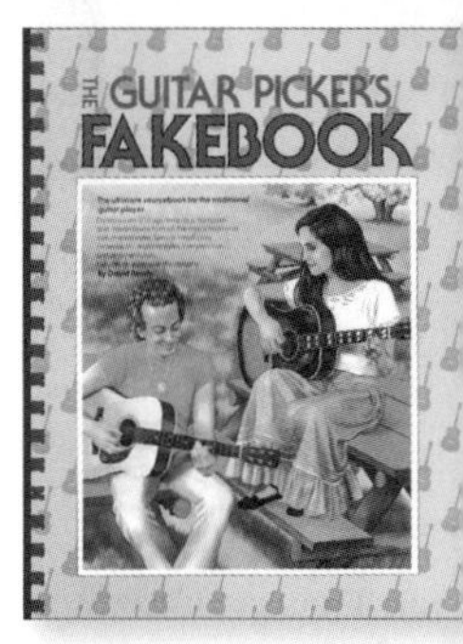

THE REAL BLUEGRASS BOOK

Ballad of Jed Clampett • Bill Cheatham • Down to the River to Pray • Foggy Mountain Top • I'm Goin' Back to Old Kentucky • John Henry • Old Train • Pretty Polly • Rocky Top • Sally Goodin • Wildwood Flower • and more.

00310910 C Instruments.............................$39.99

BLUEGRASS

Guitar Play-Along
Book/CD Pack

8 songs: Duelin' Banjos • Foggy Mountain Breakdown • Gold Rush • I Am a Man of Constant Sorrow • Nine Pound Hammer • Orange Blossom Special • Rocky Top • Wildwood Flower.

00699910 Guitar..$17.99

BLUEGRASS GUITAR

by Happy Traum
Book/CD Pack

This guitar workbook covers every aspect of bluegrass playing, from simple accompaniment to advanced instrumentals.

14004656 Guitar..$27.99

BLUEGRASS GUITAR CLASSICS

22 Carter-style solos: Back Up and Push • The Big Rock Candy Mountain • Cotton Eyed Joe • Cumberland Gap • Down Yonder • Jesse James • John Henry • Little Sadie Long Journey Home • Man of Constant Sorrow • Midnight Special • Mule Skinner Blues • Red Wing • Uncle Joe • The Wabash Cannon Ball • Wildwood Flower • and more.

00699529 Solo Guitar..................................$8.99

BLUEGRASS GUITAR

Arranged and Performed by Wayne Henderson
Transcribed by David Ziegele
Book/CD Pack

10 classic bluegrass tunes: Black Mountain Rag • Fisher's Hornpipe • Leather Britches • Lime Rock • Sally Anne • Take Me Out to the Ball Game • Temperence Reel • Twinkle Little Star • and more.

00700184 Guitar Solo.................................$16.99

BLUEGRASS SONGS FOR EASY GUITAR

25 bluegrass standards: Alabama Jubilee • Arkansas Traveler • Bill Cheatham • Blackberry Blossom • The Fox • Great Speckled Bird • I Am a Pilgrim • New River Train • Red Rocking Chair • Red Wing • Sally Goodin • Soldier's Joy • Turkey in the Straw • and more.

00702394 Easy Guitar with Notes & Tab.......$15.99

www.halleonard.com

Prices, contents, and availability subject to change.

BLUEGRASS STANDARDS

by David Hamburger

16 bluegrass classics expertly arranged: Ballad of Jed Clampett • Blue Yodel No. 4 (California Blues) • Can't You Hear Me Calling • I'll Go Stepping Too • I'm Goin' Back to Old Kentucky • Let Me Love You One More Time • My Rose of Old Kentucky • We'll Meet Again Sweetheart • and more.

00699760 Solo Guitar..................................$7.99

FIRST 50 BLUEGRASS SOLOS YOU SHOULD PLAY ON GUITAR

arr. Fred Sokolow

Songs include: Arkansas Traveler • Cripple Creek • I Am a Man of Constant Sorrow • I'll Fly Away • Long Journey Home • Molly and Tenbrooks • Old Joe Clark • The Red Haired Boy • Rocky Top • Wabash Cannonball • Wayfaring Stranger • You Don't Know My Mind • and more!

00298574 Solo Guitar................................$15.99

FRETBOARD ROADMAPS – BLUEGRASS AND FOLK GUITAR

by Fred Sokolow
Book/CD Pack

This book/CD pack will have you playing lead and rhythm anywhere on the fretboard, in any key. You'll learn chord-based licks, moveable major and blues scales, major pentatonic "sliding scales," first-position major scales, and moveable-position major scales.

00695355 Guitar..$14.99

THE GUITAR PICKER'S FAKEBOOK

by David Brody

Compiled, edited and arranged by David Brody, this is the ultimate sourcebook for the traditional guitar player. It contains over 280 jigs, reels, rags, hornpipes and breakdowns from all the major traditional instrumental styles.

14013518 Melody/Lyrics/Chords.................$32.99

O BROTHER, WHERE ART THOU?

Songs include: Big Rock Candy Mountain (Harry McClintock) • You Are My Sunshine (Norman Blake) • Hard Time Killing Floor Blues (Chris Thomas King) • I Am a Man of Constant Sorrow (The Soggy Bottom Boys/Norman Blake) • Keep on the Sunny Side (The Whites) • I'll Fly Away (Alison Krauss and Gillian Welch) • and more.

00313182 Guitar..$22.99

HOT LICKS FOR BLUEGRASS GUITAR

by Orrin Star

Over 350 authentic bluegrass licks are included in this book, which also discusses how to apply the licks to create your own solos and expand your musical understanding and knowledge of the fingerboard.

14015430 Guitar Licks................................$26.99